C000048520

# Secularization: An Analysis at Three Levels

P.I.E.-Peter Lang

Bruxelles · Bern · Berlin · Frankfurt/M · New York · Oxford · Wien

Karel DOBBELAERE

# Secularization: An Analysis at Three Levels

*To Jim in appreciation of his work done for the first publication of parts of his book*

*19.11-02*

"Gods, Humans and Religions"
No.1

The first part of the manuscript was first published by the International Sociological Association/ISA in *Current Sociology*, Volume 29, number 2, Summer 1981, under the title: "Secularization: A Multi-Dimensional Concept".

No part of this book may be reproduced in any form, by print, photocopy, microfilm or any other means, without prior written permission from the publisher. All rights reserved.

© P.I.E.-Peter Lang S.A.
PRESSES INTERUNIVERSITAIRES EUROPÉENNES
Brussels, 2002
1 avenue Maurice, 1050 Brussels, Belgium
info@peterlang.com; www.peterlang.net

ISSN 1377-8323
ISBN 90-5201-985-1
D/2002/5678/34
Printed in Germany

*CIP available from the British Library, GB and the Library of Congress, USA.*
*ISBN 0-8204-4693-9*

Bibliographic information published by "Die Deutsche Bibliothek"

"Die Deutsche Bibliothek" lists this publication in the "Deutsche Nationalbibliografie"; detailed bibliographic data is avalaible in the Internet at <http://dnb.ddb.de>.

*To Bryan and Jaak, colleagues and friends, for their support and practical help and to Liliane for being more than my colleague and friend*

# Contents

**Series Editor's Presentation** ........................................................ 11
*by Gabriel Fragnière*

**Preface** ................................................................................... 13

### PART I. SECULARIZATION:
### A MULTI-DIMENSIONAL CONCEPT

**Introduction** ............................................................................. 17

**Chapter 1. Theories of Secularization** .................................... 29
   Societal Secularization .......................................................... 29
   Organizational Secularization ................................................ 35
   Individual Secularization ...................................................... 38

**Chapter 2. Societal Secularization** ........................................ 45
   The Historical "Base-Line" ................................................... 45
   The Definition of Religion .................................................... 49
   The Integration of Society .................................................... 52
   Societal Secularization: A Mechanical, Straightforward
   Evolutionary Process? ......................................................... 61
   Theoretical Lines of Analysis ............................................... 82
   Other Approaches to the Process of Societal Secularization ........... 96

**Chapter 3. Organizational Secularization** ............................... 105
   Religious Change and Organizational Secularization .................... 105
   Societal Secularization and Religious Change ........................... 117

**Chapter 4. The Process of Declining Religious
Involvement and Individual Secularization** ................................ 137
   The Comfort Thesis ............................................................. 137
   The Secularization Thesis ..................................................... 140

The "Secularization Thesis" and Some Other Theories ............... 146
The "Secularization Thesis", "Invisible Religion",
and "Alternative Meaning Systems" ............................................ 148
Conclusions ........................................................................................ 153

**Chapter 5. Conclusions** ................................................................ 157

PART II. SECULARIZATION: THE THREE LEVELS
AND THEIR INTERRELATEDNESS

**Presentation** ....................................................................................... 163

**Chapter 1. The Interrelatedness of Societal and Individual
Secularization** ................................................................................... 165
The Secularization Process: A Partial Recapitulation ................... 165
Studying the Effect of Societal Secularization on Individual
Religiosity ...................................................................................... 167
Compartmentalization ....................................................................... 169
The Causal Link between Church Commitment and
Compartmentalization ................................................................... 170

**Chapter 2. Individual Secularization** ........................................... 173

**Chapter 3. Bringing the Actors Back In** ...................................... 181

**Chapter 4. Epilogue** .......................................................................... 189
Societal and Individual Secularization: A Relationship .............. 189
Organizational Secularization and Sacralization .......................... 190
Pluralism: Secularization and Rational Choice Theories ............. 193

**References** ........................................................................................... 197

# Series Editor's Presentation

We are very pleased to be able to publish, as a first volume in this new series devoted to the study of religions in contemporary society, a classical study on the theory of secularization. This book which was first published more than twenty years ago, as a Trend Report for the International Sociological Association, in *Current Sociology*, (Vol. 29, No. 2, Summer 1981) has ceased to be available to the interested readers of today, and might have become definitively lost among forgotten theoretical works of the past.

It is true that twenty years might be considered a very long period in the rapidly changing history of social sciences, and theories which appeared very fashionable at a certain time may no longer be considered up to date two decades later. Much must depend on the questions being raised. Social reality and basic human questioning do not always change according to the abstract principles which, at a given point in time, intellectuals develop as a temporary response to them.

Secularization has been very much discussed during the huge intellectual and scientific revolution that the social sciences faced in the 1960s and 1970s. Sociologists, philosophers, even theologians, fascinated by the apparently unlimited opportunities which were intellectually offered to them, witnessing radical changes in peoples' attitudes and behavior towards moral values and religion – sustained in this by the huge hopes that the *aggiornamento* of Vatican Council II was supposed to bring to the Catholic Church – considered that the observed evolutions portended the existence of an irreversible and universal social change. There was a kind of generally accepted dogma defending the idea that *modernity*, this fantastic progress achieved by Western civilization, was acquired for ever. Secularization was supposed to be its religious manifestation. Many of the theories described by Karel Dobbelaere in his study bear witness of this belief.

We know today that the problems discussed within the framework of the secularization debate are still much in evidence, not only in academic circles, but also and foremost in politics and society at large. This is why we look at a new publication of this early study – in a text seriously revised and completed by the author – not only as an opportunity to reprint a very useful scientific work of the past, but as a chance to contribute actively in a debate which is not closed. There is, today, a renewed urgency in this debate, not only in terms of improved conceptualization, as the author explains in his Preface, but in the global perspective of better understanding the changing civilization that we are facing in this new century. After all, the basic religious questions concerning "ultimate meaning" do not disappear with past intellectual discussions. We are therefore very grateful to Karel Dobbelaere for having revised his classical work, giving us a new vision of what secularization could mean to us today, and pleased to open our new series with this volume.

Gabriel Fragnière
Series Editor

# Preface

The present book builds on my Trend Report, "Secularization: A Multi-Dimensional Concept", which was published in 1981 and which is presented here as Part I. This study was intended to give a structured overview of sociological studies related to the topic of secularization. The major problem emerging from my reading was that the concept of secularization covered and still covers three levels of analysis. Indeed, Fenn (2001) writes about the shape of a secular society; T. Luckmann (1967: 36) refers to the internal secularization of the American Main Churches and B. Wilson (1998: 58-59) calls the New Religious Movements secularized versions of religion; and finally, Stark (1999: 251) claims that secularization also implies the demise of individual piety. In my trend report, I sought to differentiate these three dimensions, by using the terms "laicization" for the societal or macro level, "religious change" for the organizational or meso level, and "religious involvement" for the individual or micro level. The concept of secularization should be used only if one referred to all three levels at the same time. However, this proposal did not produce the expected results.

Chaves (1994 and 1997) reacted positively to the distinction between the three levels, and introduced better names: societal secularization for the macro level, organizational secularization for the meso level, and individual secularization for the micro level. Indeed, the term laicization was not acceptable for two reasons. In English, the term is first and foremost used for designing the process by which ecclesiastics are brought back to the state of layperson. In French, laicization refers to a manifest process of secularization: the polity, in conflict with the churches, emancipates institutions (*e.g.* culture, education, law and medicine) that have long been under the influence of religion by creating state schools, and according autonomy to culture, the constitution, and the law, thus freeing them from religious mores (Champion, 1993: 589-590; and Baubérot, 1998: 175-176). The process of laicization is, according to Champion (1993: 592-602), typical of countries with a Catholic tradition, since the Catholic Church takes the view that its vocation is to impose its moral views on social life. As a consequence, the Church has been coming more and more into conflict with the State since the 18th century. Since secularization is not only the result of a manifest process, but also the consequence of changes that latently secularize organizations[1], we should distinguish both and consider *la laïcisation* as a subcategory of societal and organizational secularization.

Furthermore, the concept of dimensions did not render clearly my purpose to stimulate the sociological analysis of the impact of one level on the other (see *infra*: Introduction, the section "A Methodological Note…" and Part II). For example, does the secularization of society have an impact on the religious involvement of citizens, does it promote individual secularization, and, if so, via which social processes? To what extent does individual secularization have an impact on the process of organizational secularization, and which institutional organizations are most prone to this process? Are such changes the latent consequences of other changes, for example the professionalization of services? Or does the secularization of clients, the micro level, impose changes in organizations? Do conflicts emerge, and who are the supporters of these changes? How does such a conflict evolve and what rationalizations are developed to inspire the movement?

In the first part of this book, I present the initial systematization of secularization studies, first published as the trend report in 1981, in which, to prevent further misunderstandings such as those that I have outlined above, *e.g.* the use of the term laicization, I introduce some minor, mostly conceptual changes. This part is presented under its initial title, which refers to the so-called dimensions of the secularization concept. In the second part, I seek to order the recent developments of secularization theory by stressing the levels of analysis – an issue only latently presented in the first part. The ordering has also been influenced by the distinction the German sociologist, Niklas Luhmann, made between types of differentiation. In that part, I also employ the systematization of secularization theories which by reference to their exemplars was advanced by Olivier Tschannen (1992).

Karel Dobbelaere

---

[1]  E.g. the development of medicine and science imposed their values on Catholic hospitals and schools, secularizing them without the manifest intention to do so (Dobbelaere, 1979a: 46-55)

# PART I

# SECULARIZATION:
# A MULTI-DIMENSIONAL CONCEPT[1]

---

[1]  Reprinted by permission of the International Sociological Association who published this text in 1981 in *Current Sociology*, Vol. 29, No. 2, pp. 1-216, under the title "Secularization: A Multi-Dimensional Concept".

# Introduction

Most sociologists of religion divide the history of their specialty into three periods: a classical period dominated by Durkheim and Weber, an intermediate period of denominational or church sociology inspired by a misreading of Le Bras, and a neo-classical period, which is characterized by a return to the sources of the sociology of religion, and which focuses on "the problem of personal existence in society, [which] is essentially a question of the social form of religion" (Luckmann, 1967: 18).

## Individual Secularization

In the mid-1960s several sociologists of religion were dissatisfied with the narrow "positivistic" methodology of their sub-discipline. Some criticized the decline of the theoretical significance of the sociology of religion, which survived as an applied or ancillary science "at the service of the churches or denominations" (Luckmann, 1967: 20). Others looked for the theoretical frame of reference that was implicitly used in the empirical studies of the intermediate period (*e.g.* Dobbelaere and Lauwers, 1969).

The empirical studies of involvement in denominations were basically studies of normative integration (Landecker, 1951: 340) which measured the accord between the norms of religious communities – in the fields of belief, ritual, and ethics – and the knowledge, attitudes, and conduct of their members. Such studies analyzed individual participation in social structures, but ignored the dynamic relationships between social structures. Similar approaches were found in political sociology and the sociology of trade unionism (*e.g.* Huyse, 1969, and Van Outrive, 1969). In the sociology of religion, such studies analyzed the relevance of the churches for the individual but not their social relevance. We suggested at the time that, in a period of social change, the sociology of religion should shift its attention from participation to secularization (Dobbelaere and Lauwers, 1969: 122-123). But Luckmann (1967: 23) warned against a misunderstanding of secularization "as a process of religious pathology to be measured by the shrinking reach of the churches" which would limit the task of the sociologist of religion to an analysis of "the national and class differences in the process of religious decline – that is, of the shrinking reach of the churches". This suggests that secularization is often used as an equivalent to religious decline measured in terms of individual involvement. Secularization is then equated to a decline in denominational or church participation, which nullifies the proposed shift of our attention. Hence, we should make a clear distinction between levels of secularization, and recognize that a decline in involvement in churches and denominations is to be equated only with individual secularization.

## Return to the Sources

In order to reformulate the concept of secularization, some authors explicitly state their sociological frame of reference (*e.g.* Berger and Luckmann, 1967) others do it implicitly while formulating critical re-marks on the work of others (*e.g.* Martin, 1969). They all converge in their return to the sources of sociology: the work of Durkheim, Marx, Mead, Tönnies, and Weber, to cite the most prominent. This may easily be seen in analyzing an explicitly stated frame of reference.

Berger and Luckmann consider religion to be by far the most impor-tant attempt at cosmization of an externalized objective order: it endows the human nomos with a sacred ontological status. As a form of legiti-mation *in toto,* religion is an example of an all embracing *Weltan-schauung* and probably the most effective of them, most often resulting in a reification of the social order that produces an alienated conscious-ness.

> The fundamental "recipe" of religious legitimation is the transformation of human products into supra- or non-human facticities. The humanly made world is explained in terms that deny its human production. The human no-mos becomes a divine cosmos, or at any rate a reality that derives its mean-ing from beyond the human sphere. Without going to the extreme of simply *equating* religion with alienation (which would entail an epistemological as-sumption inadmissible within a scientific frame of reference), we would contend that the historical part of religion in the world-building and world-maintaining enterprises of man is in large measure attributable to the alien-ating power inherent in religion (Berger, 1967: 89).

The synthesis of the theoretical frame and this citation allow us to see the impact of Weber (externalization, or the subjective meaning-complex of action, and legitimation), Durkheim (objectivation or the objective facticity of social facts), and Marx (reification or *Verding-lichung,* and alienation or *Entfremdung*). But it is also clear that the original use of these concepts is sometimes extended (*e.g.* legitimation is derived from Weber's political analyses and given a broader meaning in the analysis of the social construction of reality) or modified (*e.g.*

Marx equates religion with alienation) (Marx, 1961b: 378-379; and Calvez, 1969: 55-93).

## Societal Secularization

Societal secularization defined in a broader theoretical perspective and not as a process of religious pathology refers to "the shrinking relevance of the values, institutionalised in church religion, for the integration and legitimation of everyday life in modern society". According to Luckmann (1967: 39 and 40), such a definition also raises the question of "what it is that secularization has brought about in the way of a socially objectivated cosmos of meaning". Secularization is described as a latent process as well as a result of deliberate policy.

As a latent process, it is the unintended consequence of actions that promote, in Luhmanian terms, functional differentiation, to wit, the differentiation of sub-systems in society (*e.g.* economy, education, polity and law) on the basis of their specific functions, which are equally important for society. This is a consequence of, among other processes, professionalization. In the medical field, specialization and its professionalization have reduced the place of religion, but this was not because of any sort of manifest attack by that profession on religion. Of course, such societal changes may also be the result of deliberate actions to reduce, in a particular field, the impact of religion. Such was the case in Durkheim's attempt at the *laïcisation* of the French educational system in the early 20th century.

In his analysis of Durkheim's life and work, Lukes underscores his efforts to diffuse the esprit *laïque*. Durkheim had founded at Bordeaux an association of university teachers and students called *La Jeunesse Laïque* and in 1902 was appointed *chargé de cours* in the Science of Education at the Sorbonne to replace the man who implemented the Ferry Laws, the central objective of which was to establish a national system of free, secular education that would secure the moral foundations of the Third Republic. Durkheim's pedagogy lectures to future schoolteachers, his efforts to develop a national system of secular education, and his new republican ideology constituted his contribution to national reintegration. Nizen, Duveau, and others pointed out that the sociology of Durkheim triumphed in the *écoles normales* (teacher training colleges), and his ideas were consequently systematically disseminated throughout the schools of France (Lukes, 1977: 320-360). According to Lukes (*o.c.*: 359-360)[1]:

---

[1] *O.c. (opere citato)* indicates that the reference is to the same book as the preceding reference: *ibid.* indicates that the reference is to the same book and the same page as the preceding reference.

Durkheim believed that the relation of the science of sociology to education was that of theory and practice; and, in this respect, it would become a rational substitute for traditional religion. Teachers should be imbued with the "sociological point of view" and children should be made to think about "the nature of society, the family, the State, the principal legal and moral obligations, the way in which these different social phenomena are formed".

Durkheim also developed a new republican ideology that was both scientifically grounded and pedagogically effective. "What he produced amounted to a distinctive form of liberal and reformist socialism framed in solidarist terms" (Lukes, 1977: 356). In evaluating his success, Lukes (*o.c.*: 358) writes:

> One key element in his success was certainly his aggressive secularism, his desire to establish and inculcate a doctrine that would replace, and not compromise with, religion. Certainly, his view of existing religious beliefs did not allow him to favour any kind of eclectic compromise between the religious and the secular (such as that attempted by his old teacher Boutroux or his rival Bergson), or any attempt to secularize or modernize the teachings of the Church. Like his equally rationalist colleague and close friend, Octave Hamelin, he held that "in a rational morality God could not intervene as the source of obligation".

In the case of Durkheim we can speak of a *manifest policy* of laicizing the educational system. Marx, Lenin, and the Marxist parties also propounded a deliberate policy of laicization of the state. According to Marx, "the state that presupposes religion is not yet a real and genuine state" (Marx, 1961a: 350), and even in his first articles in the *Rheinische Zeitung* he upheld the autonomy of politics (Calvez, 1969: 61-63). This position was later affirmed by Lenin (*e.g.* 1959: 71) and implemented in the USSR by the decree on the Separation of the Church from the State and the School from the Church (January 1918: art. 1 "The Church shall be separated from the State" and art. 9 "The school shall be separated from the Church").

Durkheim, Marx, and Lenin propounded the separation of religion from politics and education, *i.e.* their functional differentiation, and helped to implement this policy. They are examples of actors in a process of manifest societal secularization. Laicization is consequently a manifestly intended action to secularize society, and consequently a subcategory of societal secularization.

Furthermore such processes of laicization also stimulate a counterpolicy. In reaction to the processes of laicization, some churches have set up organizations and proclaimed what they see to be the foundations of society. Pope Pius XI for example, called "secularism or laicism" in politics and education the principal causes of "the disturbed conditions in which we live", and in two encyclicals he encouraged the organization of the "apostolate of the laity or Catholic Action" (McLaughlin, 1957: 6-7, and 16-17). This could be called a manifest policy of anti-laicization.

All in all, societal secularization is a result of manifest and latent processes of secularization and of the reactions they provoke.

## Organizational Secularization

Secularization is a term also used in the sense of the modernization of religion. Lukes, as quoted above, wrote that Durkheim's view of existing religion did not allow him to favor "any attempt to secularize or modernize the teachings of the Church". And Pfautz, to give another example, has defined secularization as "the tendency of sectarian religious movements to become part of and like 'the world'" (1956: 246). This double meaning of "secularization" poses problems.

Yinger discusses Berger's book *The Noise of Solemn Assemblies* (1961) to clarify this problem. Berger uses secularization to mean, on the one hand, "many fields of life's decisions carried out without reference to religion" – what Yinger calls "the usual dictionary meaning of secularization" or what I prefer to call societal secularization – and, on the other hand, the redefinition of religion, "the inevitable adjustment of the church [beliefs and practices] to dramatic changes in the world within which it works" – which, Yinger prefers to call "religious change" (1962: 69-72). Because of this ambiguity in the use of the term, Berger, according to Yinger, must conclude that there is evidence of secularization and non-secularization in the USA. Secularization is occurring through the development of a cultural religion – an "American way of life" with religious overtones. In the churches of the USA, Berger observes the development of a cultural religion, "a religious affirmation of the same values held by the community at large". Secular values ("an intense this-worldliness", "success competitively achieved", "activism", "social adjustment" etc.) replace sacred values (Berger, 1961: 39-50). However, Berger also ascertains that, within the USA, one finds "a strong involvement of our religious beliefs with our political processes and institutions", which he calls symbolic integration – a political, social and psychological religion (*o.c.*: 51-104) and which is a counter indication of secularization (Yinger, 1962: 71).

It seems to me that Berger attempts to indicate a process of de-sacralization in American denominations – a process of "religious change" in Yinger's terms – and that as a result of this process all the churches still maintain their central symbolic position. He makes this point very clear in another book in which he compares Europe and the United States:

At least as far as Europe is concerned, it is possible to say with some confidence ... that church-related religiosity is strongest (and thus, at any rate, socio-structural secularization least) on the margins of modern industrial society, both in terms of marginal classes (such as the remnants of old petty bourgeoisies) and marginal individuals (such as those eliminated from the work process). The situation is different in America, where the churches still occupy a more central symbolic position, but it may be argued that they have succeeded in keeping this position only by becoming highly secularized themselves, so that the European and the American cases represent two variations on the same underlying theme of global secularization (Berger, 1967: 108).

Berger's American case is synonymous with a decline in church orthodoxy, what Luckmann has called the "internal secularization" of the American denominations (1967: 33-37), and, which I call organizational secularization. This adaptation to the secular values of society is only one type of social change; churches may also react by sacralizing aspects of their beliefs, rites, and moral standards, that would be just the opposite of organizational secularization.

## Secularization: A Historical Note

Thus it is clear that the concept of secularization is being used in sociology in different ways. It may refer to decline in church involvement, to the secularization of social sub-systems, or to religious changes. Originally, the Frenchman Longueville, in the negotiations that led to the Peace of Westphalia, introduced the concept in 1648 (Nijk, 1968: 18-19). These negotiators were in need of a term by which the laicization of certain ecclesiastical territories that were being added to Brandenburg as compensation for its territorial losses could at the same time be denied and admitted. Nijk points out that one should not be too surprised by the introduction of the term *séculariser,* as the notion *secularis* had already been in use for centuries not only to distinguish the secular from the sacred, but especially to indicate its subordination and dependence on the latter.

Thus, the concept of secularization has a long history, and Lübbe, Nijk and others make it clear that the concept has always retained the ambiguous and consequently controversial meaning that it had from the start (Nijk, 1968; and Lübbe, 1975). Later, it was introduced into canon law to describe dispensation from religious vows, and it was also linked to the ideas of the Enlightenment. In England, the term "secularism" was related to Holyoake's program of 1846 for an aggressive emancipation policy that would free the secular from "its irrelevant ties to church and religion". Holyoake consequently pleaded for secular education (Nijk, 1968: 24). In twentieth century America, "secularism" refers to "irreligion", "practical atheism", and "the organization of life as if God did not exist" (*o.c.*: 25). According to Marty, "secularism" means "closed to faith" and is to be distinguished from "secularity", which is open to faith but cultivates "a carefully and self-critical (non integral) base of neutrality which withholds judgments until 'after the returns are in'" (Marty, 1964: 145).

It is clear that the stem "secular" is used in opposition to "sacred", and that its derivations suggest a cultural emancipation from religion and church that is more or less open but quite often closed to faith. *Séculariser*, secularism, and secularity are concepts that are used to promote a certain policy, a certain program. Only in the early 20th century does secularization emerge as a scientific or cultural-philosophical category, and as such is mostly traced back to Weber, Tönnies, and Troeltsch (Nijk, 1968: 27-35).

In this Trend Report I do not examine the historical roots and the various uses of the concept in depth. The interested reader is referred to Lübbe (1975) and Nijk (1968) among others. Nor will I consider its use outside sociology, *e.g.* in theology, philosophy and history (Shiner, 1967; and Castelli, 1976). Rather, I limit myself to an analysis of its use in sociological studies.

## Secularization: A Sensitizing Concept

The use of the term "secularization" in scientific discourse to indicate the process of societal secularization is an extension of the original concept. Institutions such as politics and education are withdrawn from the religious sphere; the "sacred" canopy is more and more restricted. Later on, confronted with new empirical material, sociologists extended its meaning. They applied it not only to the societal but also to the individual level. People were said to be secularized when their involvement in the churches declined and when important transformations in the course of life – *e.g.* birth, marriage, and burial – ceased to be sacralized, *i.e.* when fewer and fewer people participated in churchly rites of passage.

As Blumer correctly emphasizes, concepts are used to solve problems (1969: 157). The extension of the use of secularization to religious change is an example of this. Berger tried to solve the apparent contradiction between the empirical facts in the USA and in Europe by suggesting "that the European and the American cases represent two variations on the same underlying theme of global secularization", which Luckmann had called respectively secularization and "internal secularization".

In fact, sociologists have used secularization as a *sensitizing concept,* giving "the user a general sense of reference and guidance in approaching empirical instances", merely suggesting "directions along which to look", and resting on "a general sense of what is relevant" (Blumer, 1954: 7). As Zijderveld (1973: 204) suggests, such concepts belong to "common-sense" knowledge or at least are very close to common-sense concepts that, as we have seen in the case of secularization, have emerged in the everyday world. Once such concepts are introduced in science, they start a new career. As Blumer (1969: 161-162) suggested, "Scientific concepts have a career, changing their meaning from time to time in accordance with the introduction of new experiences and replacing one content with another". But, as Yinger correctly pointed out, the changing meaning of concepts can be very confusing, as is the case with the concept of secularization, which forced Berger to conclude that America was both secularized and not secularized.

To prevent such confusion, I propose to state explicitly the different dimensions of the concept, as I see them, and not to use the term secularization as a "vague stereotype", since such usage does nothing to stimulate our thinking. Rather, it shuts off our probing and blocks our imagination. "It becomes only a device for ordering or arranging empirical instances. As such it is not tested and assayed against the empirical instances and thus forfeits the only means of its improvement as an analytical tool" (Blumer, 1954: 9). In order to improve the concept and work toward a definitive concept (*o.c.*: 7; and Zijderveld, 1973: 204-205), I will consider both the empirical and theoretical studies of secularization along three dimensions in order to refine the analysis, to suggest new problems, and to stimulate new research.

## Secularization: A Multi-Dimensional Concept

Secularization as a sensitizing concept is multi-dimensional. We distinguish a first type: *societal secularization* that refers to a functional differentiation process, *i.e.* sub-systems are developed that perform different functions and are structurally different. Religion becomes one sub-system alongside others and loses its overarching claim. Shiner (1967: 212-214), in his article on six meanings of secularization, calls this type the "disengagement of society from religion", or, following Parsons and Bellah, the process of differentiation. This view goes back to Durkheim (1964: 171-177) and can be related to Weber's analysis of Western society. Indeed, Durkheim's concept of differentiation implies that society gradually takes over all the "secular" functions previously performed by religion, which Shiner (1967: 214-215) calls the "transposition" type of secularization. This transformation of the sacred domain into secular institutions implies a "desacralization of the world" –

Shiner's fifth type of secularization (*o.c.*: 215-216) – which Weber described as the *Entzauberung* (disenchantment) of the world. Mastering the world is now based on technology and calculation, where previously man had recourse to magic (Gerth and Mills, 1958: 139; and Winckelmann, 1980). This is also called the rationalization of the institutional spheres. The link between these different aspects of the process of societal secularization is also documented in Shiner's (1967: 219) view that "Three of the processes discussed above could be embraced significantly by the term – secularization – since they are not contradictory but complementary: desacralization, differentiation and transposition".

Two other types of secularization should, also in Shiner's opinion, be distinguished. Apart from societal secularization as a result of the process of functional differentiation, I want to distinguish *organizational secularization* and *individual secularization*. Individual secularization refers to individual behavior and measures the degree of normative integration in religious bodies. It is an index of the accord between the norms of religious groups – in domains of beliefs, rituals, morals etc. – and the attitudes and conduct of their members. Here Shiner (1967: 209-210) talks about the decline of religion or dechristianization. Organizational secularization, on the other hand, expresses change occurring in the posture of religious organizations – churches, denominations, sects, and New Religious Movements (NRMs) – in matters of beliefs, morals, and rituals, and implies also a study of the decline and emergence of religious groups. This is the type of secularization that Shiner calls "conformity with 'this world'" (*o.c.*: 211-212). ·

## A Methodological Note in Support of the Multi-Dimensionality of the Concept of Secularization

The distinction between the three dimensions promotes, I hope, conceptual clarity and it also has methodological advantages. By distinguishing organizational secularization and individual secularization from one another and from societal secularization, we are in a better position to study the empirical relationships between societal secularization and organizational secularization; between societal secularization and individual secularization; and between individual secularization and organizational secularization.

Statistical data indicating decline in the number of church members and more especially of involved church members, as well as opinion poll data indicating the decline of belief in church doctrines, are often used as indicators of "global secularization". But in the 1950s and 1960s, the USA – the most "modern" of Western societies where functional differentiation and rationalization are most advanced – showed a higher degree of involvement in church religion than in Europe. Thus, what was, according to one dimension societal secularization (differentiation and rationalization), the most "secularized" society was the least "secularized", according to another dimension, *i.e.* individual secularization (church involvement). It is in this context that the notion of "internal secularization" was developed, to make the theory fit, without empirical testing. Here we have, it seems to me, a typical case of circular reasoning. By calling a decline in church practice "secularization", sociologists were then enabled to discover such a decline in highly "secularized" countries, *i.e.* countries that were highly differentiated and rationalized. However, failing to do so in the USA, where statistical data revealed the "non-secularization" of church members in a highly 'secularized' society, sociologists explained this contradictory finding in terms of the so-called "internal" secularization of the churches.

> [The] traditional church religion was pushed to the periphery of "modern" life in Europe while it became more "modern" in America by undergoing a process of internal secularization ... In short, the so-called process of secularization has decisively altered either the social location of church religion or its inner universe of meaning (Luckmann, 1967: 36-37).

By making a distinction between individual secularization and societal secularization – and calling them secularization and differentiation respectively – Martin (1978: 3) advanced a more sophisticated explanation which took into account particular cultural complexes. He used, among other things, pluralism, individualism, and cultural identity to explain high rates of practice in a differentiated structural context. I shall return to this theory at greater length below.

For analytical purposes and in order to study the empirical relationships more effectively, and so prevent their being conceptually contaminated, sociologists of religion should take into account Lazarsfeld's distinction between "expressive" and "predictive" indicators (1959: 49-53). The *expressive* indicators, which describe the "underlying trait" of societal secularization, should be based on aspects of institutional differentiation, the development of institutional values and norms, and the organizational patterns of these institutions. And to prevent contamination, measures of individual secularization and organizational secularization should not be used as indicators of societal secularization. Then, such things as the prediction that societal secularization results in organizational secularization, or in individual secularization, and the suggestion "that the traditional institutions of religion increasingly lack public support" as a result of the churches' loss of moral authority (Wilson, 1976b: 21) could be empirically tested. In addition, such things as the impact of social integration on institutions, which have varying degrees of differentiation, and on various aspects of individual secularization could – if correctly operationalized by distinguishing between expressive and predictive indicators – be studied, not to build a *post-factum* theory (*e.g.* Acquaviva, 1979) but a theory based on hypothetico-deductive procedures.

## Purpose of the Trend Report

The sixth type of secularization that Shiner detected is defined as a general concept of *social change* (1967: 216-217). This definition is based on Becker's (1957: 143) construction of a sacred-secular continuum, which refers to a scale with specified end-points ranging "from estimated maximum reluctance to change old values to estimated maximum readiness to seek new values". Levels of secularization would then be measured in terms of "willingness and/or ability to change", culminating in "change for the sake of change" (*o.c.*: 161). Such a definition of sacred and secular, and the implied meaning of secularization, is also to be found in Durkheim's work on religion. Sacred or consecrated things are "forbidden to touch ... to deny ... or to contest"; "the prohibition of criticism ... proves the presence of something sacred" (Durkheim, 1965: 244). De-sacralization or secularization implies then the possibility of criticism, a willingness to change and to control. Remy (1970) has studied the impact of progressive de-sacralization on the cultural insertion and credibility of the Church. Although such a view of secularization may be applied to religion and the churches, it is not a theory of change specifically related to religion but rather a general theory of social change, applicable to different institutions and organizations (*e.g.* Germani, 1968). Consequently, I do not include a discussion of it in this study.

What I intend to do is to study secularization in its dimensions as a process of *societal secularization*, conceptualized as "a process of functional differentiation, *i.e.* a process of growing independence of societal spheres (such as politics, education, economy, and science), each developing its own rationale, which implies the rejection of the overarching claim of religion". In addition, I shall discuss some studies of the relationship between societal secularization and organizational secularization on the one hand, and between societal secularization and individual secularization on the other. Both topics, organizational secularization and individual secularization, extend beyond the compass of this study, and I discuss them only in so far as they are related to societal secularization.

I begin with an overview of sociological theories of secularization. I seek to summarize their content, building bridges between them even though some of them are not always compatible in their general outlook.

In the next chapter, I discuss certain theoretical difficulties in elaborating a sociological theory of societal secularization and offer some critical remarks. The fourth and fifth chapters deal with the relationship between societal secularization and organizational secularization, on the one hand, and individual secularization, on the other. Some links between societal, organizational and individual secularization are suggested in the final chapter of part I.

One further qualification must be made. The concept of secularization is employed by scholars to explain similar processes occurring in different social settings (Tamaru, 1979). In the first part, I limit myself to an analysis of the use of the concept of secularization in sociological studies in the West. I came to this conclusion at the Tokyo meetings of the Conférence Internationale de Sociologie Religieuse (CISR) on 27-29 December 1978, where secularization as a cross-cultural concept was refuted by a number of scholars but defended by others (Tamaru, 1979; Reid, 1979). This limitation should not detract from the purpose of the trend Report. As Martin correctly stated:

> An analysis of the initial "breakthrough" is usually the crucial part of a theory. The point is that this breakthrough occurred in Christian cultures, whatever the precise relation of Christianity to secularity, and the core of the theory can therefore be stated in relation to those cultures (1978: 2).

# Theories of Secularization

The theories of secularization refer to societal, organizational and individual secularization. Let us start with societal secularization.

## Societal Secularization

Societal secularization is, in Luckmann's terminology, "a process in which autonomous institutional "ideologies" replaced, within their own domain, an overarching and transcendent universe of norms". Church religion, an "institutionally specialized social form of religion" is pushed to the periphery of modern industrial societies, and we notice "the dissolution of the traditional, coherent sacred cosmos" while institutional ideologies, based on a rational orientation in the specialized institutional spheres, are developed (Luckmann, 1967: 101). According to Berger it is:

> [T]he process by which sectors of society and culture are removed from the domination of religious institutions and symbols [...] in modern Western history [...] Secularization manifests itself in the evacuation by the Christian churches of areas previously under their control or influence [...] as in the separation of church and state, or in the expropriation of church lands, or in the emancipation of education from ecclesiastical authority. When we speak of culture and symbols, however, we imply that secularization is more than a social-structural process. It affects the totality of cultural life and of ideation, and may be observed in the decline of religious content in the arts, in philosophy, in literature and, most important of all, in the rise of science as an autonomous, thoroughly secular perspective on the world (1967: 107; see also Weber, 1973: 472 ff).

Berger and Luckmann's concept clearly indicates that the notion of societal secularization implies a comparative historical and evolutionary approach. The institutionally specialized, rational, and secular modern ideologies are compared to an overarching, coherent, transcendent, sacred cosmos. Religion lost its social function of societal legitimation (sacred cosmization), and while religion used to be, as Wilson puts it, "a primary agency of social control and of socialization", and the Church had control over social institutions, in recent times all this has changed (1976b: 3 and 10-11).

This process had already been described by Durkheim (1964: 169-170):

> If there is one truth that history teaches us beyond doubt, it is that religion tends to embrace a smaller and smaller portion of social life. Originally, it pervades everything; everything social is religious; the two words are synonymous. Then, little by little, political, economic, scientific functions free themselves from the religious function, constitute themselves apart and take on a more and more acknowledged temporal character. God, who was at first present in all human relations, progressively withdraws from them; he abandons the world to men and their disputes. At least, if he continues to dominate it, it is from on high and at a distance, and the force which he exercises, becoming more general and more indeterminate, leaves more place to the free play of human forces. The individual really feels himself less acted upon; he becomes more a source of spontaneous activity. In short, not only does not the domain of religion grow at the same time and in the same measure as temporal life, but it contracts more and more. This regression did not begin at some certain moment of history, but we can follow its phases since the origins of social evolution. It is, thus, linked to the fundamental conditions of the development of societies, and it shows that there is a decreasing number of collective beliefs and sentiments which are both collective enough and strong enough to take on a religious character. That is to say, the average intensity of the common conscience progressively becomes enfeebled.

More explicit than Durkheim, Parsons (1966: 21-23) links social evolution to the process of institutional differentiation: institutions are developed that perform different functions, and they become structurally different. Durkheim summed up this social evolution in his magisterial study on religion as follows: "It may be said that nearly all the great social institutions have been born in religion" (1965: 466). The economy, politics, education and other social institutions evolved out of it, and, according to Parsons, differentiation led to an "adaptive upgrading". In the new structures, Parsons holds that what he regards as primary functions are better performed, and that the original structure, religion, undergoes a loss of functions, but, as a consequence of its institutional specialization, it too is able to perform its primary functions better.

The more complex society that is thus created requires a collective consciousness – Parsons calls it a "value pattern" – which, in order to legitimize the substructures' wider variety of functions, is expressed in more general terms. It is in this context that we can situate Bellah's concept of "civil religion" (1967) (cf. *infra* in Chapter 2: Civil religion and the integration of society).

Durkheim also asserted that separately constituted institutions develop an increasingly profane character; an idea we may link to Weber's rationalization process (1947: 117). Action is efficiently organised, because action and the situations in which it takes place are considered to be calculable and controllable. Human behavior is ordered by rationally developed standards and no longer by magical, incalculable powers and forces (Weber, 1973: 317). The roots of societal secularization are, according to Berger:

> [I]n the economic area, specifically, in those sectors of the economy being formed by the capitalistic and industrial processes ... [But] the decisive variable for secularization does not seem to be the institutionalization of particular property relations, nor the specifics of different constitutional systems, but rather the process of rationalization that is the prerequisite for any industrial society of the modern type (1967: pp. 128 and 132).

> A modern industrial society requires the presence of large cadres of scientific and technological personnel, whose training and ongoing social organization presupposes a high degree of rationalization, not only on the level of infrastructure but also on that of consciousness. [...] Furthermore, the secularizing potency of capitalist-industrial rationalization is not only self-perpetuating but self-aggrandizing. [...] As the modern state is increasingly occupied with the political and legal requirements of the gigantic economic machinery of industrial production, it must gear its own structure and ideology to this end. On the level of structure, this means above all the establishment of highly rational bureaucracies; on the level of ideology, it means the maintenance of legitimations that are adequate for such bureaucracies. Thus, inevitably, there develops an affinity, both in structure and in "spirit", between the economic and the political spheres. Secularization then passes from the economic to the political sphere in a near-inexorable process of "diffusion" (*o.c.*: p. 131).

The rationalization process was not limited to the economic and political spheres. I have already referred to science "as an autonomous, thoroughly secular perspective on the world" that "augments the manipulative attitude towards the natural environment and also towards the social environment" (Martin, 1969: 116). Science as a secular potency has diminished the impact of the theological outlook on the world (Wilson, 1969: 63-64; 67 ff) and altered the philosophical perceptions (*o.c.*: 73-74). These changes completely reoriented the educational system, and education has passed from religious control (*o.c.*: 79):

> As knowledge itself became increasingly secular so priests became less appropriate as teachers, and as the content of education shifted from a religious-moral concern (developed at least partially in the interests of the maintenance of social control) to an increasingly instrumental-technical concern (developed in the interests of increased economic productivity), so education emerged into an institutional order in its own right.

And not only were church schools replaced by secular schools, but within secular and religious schools the significance of religious

31

education and rituals greatly diminished (*e.g.* Billiet, 1977: 8-18 and Dobbelaere, 1979a: 49-54).

The growth of a pragmatic *Weltanschauung* also made inroads in the family, *e.g.* on eroticism, effectiveness of sexual performance, and birth control. The use of scientific techniques to control birth – called by some "artificial" and "unnatural" – is clear evidence of the rationalization of procreation.

In most of these rational institutional spheres organizations develop (*e.g.* business organizations and agencies) in which individuals assume positions and perform roles. The rationality of these organizations is determined by an efficient goal-means relationship that is specific for each sphere, unrelated to an overarching meaning-system, so that each person is able to perform his anonymous specialist function. The organization supervises and is concerned exclusively with efficient task-performances: the individual is "replaceable as a person in proportion to the increasing anonymity of specialized roles that are determined by the functionally rational institutions (Luckmann, 1967: 96). What Wilson (1976b: 11) calls a "rational empirical orientation to the world", the opposite of a magical-religious orientation, predominates. Control is technical and bureaucratic, not moral or religious: "It has become impersonal and amoral, a matter for routine techniques and unknown officials" (*o.c.*: 20).

The relationships that develop here and become more and more typical for the different functional spheres are *"gesellschaftlich"* (Tönnies) or "secondary". They are, indeed, positional, contractual, formal, utilitarian, confined to segments of the person, and transferable. The individual is no longer regarded as an end in himself, as in the *Gemeinschaft,* where the dominant relationships were "primary" (Cooley), *i.e.* affective, total, and regulated by habits. "A community really involves face-to-face relationships of known persons. [...] Society, in contrast, involves the interaction of role-performances of unknown role-players" (Wilson, 1976a: 264).

This bureaucratic type of relationship extends into the social world. City life, commerce, welfare, school, entertainment and even the neighborhood are basically *gesellschaftlich.* Whereas the first industrial revolution left certain personal bonds standing – certain sectors of vertical integration, *e.g.* nucleated villages, small firms, a "respectable" working-class, an artisan and a middle class horizontal bond, the second industrial revolution, "of which the typical instance might", according to Martin, "be the advent of electronic media" tends to break all bonds. Over time both have produced conditions of anonymity and depersonalization, the weakening of horizontal bonds (the impact of anomie), and the breaking of vertical bonds (the impact of class).

The institutions congruent with modern industry, with bureaucracy and technical rationality, are large, impersonal, and mechanical in their operation. The intimate bonds of horizontal community, working class or otherwise, are broken up; the ecology of the city encourages fragmentation; the small shop gives away to the supermarket; the family firm enters the international consortium; the small farm is rationalized into larger units run by scientific agriculture; the moderate-sized office is swallowed up in large-scale bureaucracy; the community of school is wrecked by education factories operated by mobile teachers. And overall the urban style associated with these developments englobes a yet larger proportion of the population (Martin, 1978: 83-87).

As the community, the *Gemeinschaft*, ceases to be the basic principle of social organization and develops in a more and more *gesellschaftlich* manner (Weber called it *"Vergesellschaftung"* and Wilson "societalization"), religion loses momentum. As Wilson (1976a: 273) points out, religion offers "redemption" and this personal, total, "indivisible ultimate", unsusceptible to rational procedures or "cost-efficiency criteria", is offered in a "community". He explains the diminishing impact of religion by the decline of community: "My thesis is that secularization is the decline of community: secularization is a concomitant of societalization" (*o.c.*: 265-266).

Wilson explains societal secularization by the decline of community and changes in social control from moral or religious to technical and bureaucratic control. Martin (1978: 88) also links the breaking of the bonds and social control: "the religious symbols of community and the notion of intrinsic morality (which is rooted in religion though not exclusively religious) are both downgraded", and "social control has to shift from intrinsic symbols to an appeal based on interest".

Luckmann (1976: 277) agrees with Wilson and others that "religion is a constitutive element of 'community'" but, the bulk of his argument is linked to the fact that modern societies "no longer need religious legitimations". As a consequence religion became an institution among other institutions, and the church an organization among others. Indeed:

> [T]he more the traces of a sacred cosmos are eliminated from the "secular" norms, the weaker is the plausibility of the global claim of religious norms [... and] the individual [...] tends to restrict the relevance of specifically religious norms to domains that are not yet pre-empted by the jurisdictional claims of "secular" institutions. Thus religion becomes a "private affair". We may conclude by saying that institutional specialization of religion, along with the specialization of other institutional areas, starts the development that transforms religion into an increasingly "subjective" and "private" reality (Luckmann, 1967: 85-86).

Thus, the proper sphere of religion and its organizations is "private life". This segregation of the public and the private sphere is "quite 'functional' for the maintenance of the highly rationalized order of modern economic and political institutions" (Berger, 1967: 133). And since religion is defined as a private matter, the church can "no longer rely on the state to enforce its jurisdictional claims" (Luckmann, 1967: 94). The original jurisdiction claimed by the "official" model of the church was "total"; now it is transformed into "a system of mere rhetoric" (*o.c.*: 96 and 100), manifesting itself as, "public rhetoric and private virtue" (Berger, 1967: 133).

The opposition private-public is described in terms of subjectivism, autonomy, freedom, and communality *versus* objectivity, obligatoriness, control, and *Gesellschaftlichkeit*. The private sphere is consumer-oriented, and the "autonomous" individual is free to follow his own subjective preference. He "may choose from the assortment of 'ultimate' meanings as he sees fit – guided only by the preferences that are determined by his social biography" (Luckmann, 1967: 99), in the same way that he chooses friends, a marriage partner, neighbors, goods and services, holidays, a car, hobbies, and the like. In order to construct his personal identity and his system of "ultimate" significance, "a variety of models is socially available – but none is 'official' [...] None is routinely internalized *au sérieux*. Instead, a certain level of subjective reflection and choice determines the formation of individual religiosity" (*ibid.*).

Thus the "autonomous" consumer selects certain religious themes from the available *assortment* of "ultimate" meanings and builds them into a somewhat precarious private system of "ultimate" significance. Individual religion is no longer a replica or approximation of an "official" model (*o.c.*: 102). And, according to research on church religion "even in the case of church-oriented individuals it is likely that effective priorities of everyday life, the subjective system of "ultimate" significance and the rhetoric of the traditional "official" model are incongruent" (*o.c.*: 100). And Berger (1967: 133-134) states:

> The world-building potency of religion is thus restricted to the construction of subworlds: of fragmented universes of meaning, the plausibility structure of which may in some cases be no larger than the nuclear family. Since the modern family is notoriously fragile as an institution (a trait it shares with all other formations of the private sphere), this means that religion resting on this kind of plausibility structure is of necessity a tenuous construction ... This tenuousness can (indeed must) be mitigated by seeking more broadly based plausibility structures. Typically, these are the churches and other wider religious groupings. By the very nature of their social character as voluntary associations "located" primarily in the private sphere, however, such churches can only augment the strength and durability of the required plausibility structures to a limited extent.

The polarization of the sacred (religion) and the secular (society) brought about by societal secularization, is the result of the changes described: traditional *versus* complex, pragmatic, and modern societies; magical and religious *versus* rational and empirical orientations; an overarching sacred cosmos *versus* institutionally specialized ideologies; incalculable magical powers and forces *versus* calculable and controllable actions and situations; traditional values *versus* secular law; moral habits *versus* legal routines; a religious ethic *versus* instrumental technical control; community *versus* Gesellschaft; total personal relationships *versus* specialized anonymous roles; face-to-face relationships with known people *versus* social interaction between unknown role players; affective *versus* contractual, formal, and utilitarian relationships; horizontal and vertical bonds *versus* anomie and social class; small workshops and offices *versus* large factories and bureaucracies; the church as a total and official organization *versus* churches as voluntary associations. Polarization "brings about a demonopolization of religious traditions and this, ipso-facto, leads to a pluralistic situation" (*o.c.*: 134), and "the religious tradition, which previously could be authoritatively imposed, now has to be *marketed*" (*o.c.*: 137). This situation further de-objectivizes the sacred cosmos and makes it less plausible, even at the level where it has to compete with non-religious rivals. And here the argument moves in the direction of religious change resulting from social changes, but sociologists also scrutinize the capacity of organizational secularization to secularize the world.

## Organizational Secularization

The social changes that stimulated societal secularization were brought about by rational processes that extended from the economic into the social world, leaving no sphere untouched: even the religious sphere had to rationalize. The pluralistic market situation forced the religious institutions to market their commodities, the religious traditions. And in order to achieve "results", the socio-religious structures were bureaucratized, which stimulated the professionalization of religious personnel and ecumenicity (Berger, 1963, and 1967: 137-148). But the above explanation has to be expanded. As Berger stated, "a historical phenomenon of such scope will not be amenable to any monocausal explanations". In *The Sacred Canopy,* he explores "the extent to which the Western religious tradition may have carried the seeds of secularization within itself", and closely follows Weber's studies, particularly *The Protestant Ethic and the Spirit of Capitalism,* to analyze the peculiar role Protestantism played in the establishment of the modern world (Berger, 1967: 110-111; Weber, 1958; and Eisenstadt, 1968).

But he also looks for the roots of this development in the religion of ancient Israel.

According to Berger, Israel's double exodus – from Mesopotamia and from Egypt – constituted a break with an entire universe: "At the heart of the religion of ancient Israel lies the vehement repudiation of both the Egyptian and the Mesopotamian versions of cosmic order, a repudiation that was, of course, extended to the pre-Israelite indigenous culture of Syria-Palestine" (1967: 115), which was "cosmological" in the sense that it failed to make a differentiation between the human and the natural spheres of empirical reality, and, more importantly, which posited continuity between the empirical and the supra-empirical (*o.c.*: 113). The Old Testament, to the contrary, "posits a God who stands *outside* the cosmos, which is his creation but which he confronts and does not permeate" (*o.c.*: 115). The radical transcendentalization of God is reflected in the creation story of Genesis: "We find here expressed very clearly the fundamental Biblical polarization between the transcendent God and man, with a thoroughly "demythologized" universe between them" (*o.c.*: 117). Besides the transcendentalization motif, Berger also points towards historization and the rationalization of ethics.

> It may be said that the transcendentalization of God and the concomitant "disenchantment of the world" opened up a "space" for history as the arena of both divine and human actions. The former are performed by a God standing entirely outside the world. The latter presuppose a considerable individuation in the conception of man. Man appears as the historical actor before the face of God (*o.c.*: 118).

And the motif of ethical rationalization, closely related to both other motifs, was "carried" by priestly and prophetic groups in the priestly ethic and the prophetic ethic (*o.c.*: 120-121).

Christianity as it finally became dominant in Europe "represents a retrogressive step in terms of the secularizing motifs of Old Testament religion", according to Berger (*o.c.*: 121-124). Although the transcendent character of God was strongly asserted, the notion of incarnation, the Trinitarian doctrine, the angels and saints, and the glorification of Mary as mediator and co-redeemer, "remythologized" the world. Because its pervasive sacramental system provided "escape hatches", Catholicism also arrested the process of ethical rationalization demanded by Old Testament prophecy and rabbinical Judaism, and confined the ascetic life to the monastic system. "But whereas it can be plausibly argued that Christianity, specifically in its victorious Catholic form, reversed or at least arrested the secularizing motifs of transcendentalization and ethical rationalization, this cannot be said of the motif of historization" (*o.c.*: 122-123). And one of the Church's central characteristics – its institutional specialization – further promoted the

36

process of secularization. As a result, the rest of society was defined as "the world", as a profane realm. With the disintegration of Christendom,

> "[T]he world" could all the more rapidly be secularized in that it had already been defined as a realm outside the jurisdiction of the sacred properly speaking. The logical development of this may be seen in the Lutheran doctrine of the two kingdoms, in which the autonomy of the secular "world" is actually given a *theological* legitimation (*o.c.*: 123-124; see also Troeltsch, 1931; and Weber, 1958).

The Protestant Reformation may be understood as a powerful re-emergence of precisely those secularizing forces that had been "contained" by Catholicism, and it went decisively beyond the Old Testament. "At the risk of some simplification, it can be said that Protestantism divested itself as much as possible from the three most ancient and most powerful concomitants of the sacred – mystery, miracle, and magic" (Berger, 1967: 111). Weber called it the "disenchantment of the world" (*die Entzauberung der Welt*) (1958: 105; Roof, 1978a; and Winckelmann, 1980).

The disenchantment of the world or the elimination of magic from the world implies the repudiation of all "magical" means to salvation: the sacramental apparatus is reduced to a minimum and the sacraments "are not a means to the attainment of grace, but only the subjective *extra subsidia* of faith". The absolutely decisive difference between Calvinism and Catholicism was Calvinism's "complete elimination of salvation through the Church and the sacraments" (Weber, 1958: 104-105). What also disappeared was

> [T]he immense network of intercession that unites the Catholic in this world with saints and, indeed, with all departed souls (Berger, 1967: 111).

> The genuine puritan even rejected all signs of religious ceremony at the grave and buried his nearest and dearest without song or ritual in order that no superstition, no trust in the effects of magical and sacramental forces on salvation, should creep in (Weber, 1958: 105).

We may, it seems to me, conclude this exposition by stating that culturally speaking a process of rationalization developed in the Judeo-Christian religious tradition that allows Berger (1967: 125) to suggest that the roots of the process of societal secularization are religious.

> Religious developments originating in the Biblical tradition may be seen as causal factors in the formation of the modern secularized world. Once formed, however, this world precisely precludes the continuing efficacy of religion as a formative force. We could contend that here lies the great historical irony in the relation between religion and secularization, an irony that can be graphically put by saying that, historically speaking, Christianity has been its own gravedigger (*o.c.*: 127).

The capitalistic spirit that emerged in modern times is connected to the fundamental religious ideas of ascetic Protestantism. As Weber (1958: 180) stated, "one of the fundamental elements of the spirit of capitalism, and not only of that but of all modern culture: rational conduct on the basis of the idea of the calling, was born – that is what this discussion has sought to demonstrate – from the spirit of Christian asceticism". And he concludes his monograph by specifying that the externalized spirit of modern capitalism became objectified and confronted man as a facticity outside of himself.

> The Puritan wanted to work in a calling; we are forced to do so. For when asceticism was carried out of monastic cells into everyday life, and began to dominate worldly morality, it did its part in building the tremendous cosmos of the modern economic order. This order is now bound to the technical and economic conditions of machine production which today determine the lives of all the individuals who are born into this mechanism, not only those directly concerned with economic acquisition, with irresistible force (Berger, 1967: 181).

Weber calls this objectified economic order an "iron cage" from which the spirit escaped. "To-day the spirit of religious asceticism – whether finally, who knows? – has escaped the cage. But victorious capitalism, since it rests on mechanical foundations, needs its support no longer" (Weber, 1958: 181-182).

The rationalization process in the economic order brought about large factories and huge bureaucracies resting on mechanical foundations, in which the individual is reduced to being a role-player. Such institutional arrangements had their impact on other social institutions such as politics, education, and the family. In fact, social life became dominated by *gesellschaftliche* relationships: most vertical and horizontal social bonds were broken. Man lost his communal relationships, and religion, which has a communal base, lost its impact on society. It was reduced to precarious subworlds: the family, the private sphere, and religious groupings. What impact does this exert on the religious behavior of the individual?

## Individual Secularization

In the analysis of the "dechristianization" of the 19th century, references are generally made to the dechristianization of the working class. Although the use of this term is criticized by several authors, as we shall see below, dechristianization is generally used to indicate a drop in church practice and beliefs. In a well known article, McLeod (1980: 191-214) tried to point out the different causes that were at work in Western Europe and that varied in different regions. Several of his arguments can be subsumed under the notion of societal secularization.

Some refer to a latent process of societal secularization, especially the breaking of social and communal bonds. He mentions "the development of agrarian capitalism and of the rural proletariat, and the growing estrangement between the various sections of the rural population" (*o.c.*: 198). He describes depersonalization and uprooting of city life attributable to industrialization, immigration, poverty, and class antagonism. Industrial conflicts between workers and owners destroyed harmonious relations in the parishes and chapels (*o.c.*: 203-204). Other arguments can better be regarded as a manifest process of societal secularization, *i.e.* laicization. The churches were mostly linked to the middle and upper classes through financial dependence and its paternalist social ideology, and the lower classes were attracted to the opposition. Socialism was gaining a hold over the working class at the end of the 19th century, and in most European countries, the socialist leaders and activists were atheists. The secularist policy of the socialist parties alienated the workers from the churches. But in the early 19th century, the involvement of the Catholic Church in the old order and the alienation of the working class from local political and Christian traditions had already stimulated the working class in some countries to abandon the church and to move to the left politically. Radical liberalism and socialism manifestly estranged the workers from the churches. Indeed, the workers were already latently alienated from them.

The link between societal secularization attributable to a latent or manifest secularist policy and the individual abandonment of church practice encouraged sociologists to use decline of church involvement as an indicator of secularization and caused them to be puzzled about the presence of a high degree of church practice in the highly differentiated, bureaucratized, rational, and *gesellschaftlich* society of the USA. An example of this is Luckmann's (1967: 29-35) conclusion that "The most 'modern' of the countries under discussion, the United States, shows the highest degree of involvement in church religion". As already stated above, he explains it by the notion of the "internal secularization" of the American churches:

> Today the secular ideas of the American Dream pervade church religion. The cultural, social and psychological functions which the churches perform for American society as a whole as well as for its social groups, classes, and individuals would be considered "secular" rather than "religious" in the view the churches traditionally held of themselves (*o.c.*: 36).

In the Eastern European world, studies of secularization are limited to church practice and the beliefs of the people. A manifest policy of laicization has secularized these societies. On the basis of sociological studies, the intention is to evaluate the success of direct and indirect atheistic policies in "overcoming religion".

This laicization policy was based on Marxist thought. For Marx (1961b: 378) the basic criticism of religion is that "*man made religion,* it is not religion that made man". Religion is the outward sign of real misery and a protest against it. Religion is the sigh of a creature oppressed by misfortune, but it is also "the opium of the people". Religion is the form of alienation *par excellence* (Calvez, 1969: 55). Hence it is in the real interest of the people to abolish religion "as an *illusory* happiness of the people". This implies that a situation that needs illusions should be changed. "The critique of religion is also, in embryo, *the critique of the vale of tears* of which religion is the halo" (Marx, 1961b: 379). Marx's criticism goes well beyond Bauer's. In *Zur Judenfrage* he writes: "the emancipation of the state from religion is not the emancipation of the real man from religion" (1961a: 361). The privatization of religion is not enough; the emancipation of man presupposes a real critique of religion and alienation, which implies a critique of the real world (1961b: 379). Consequently, a Marxist will build a social world that is not based on oppression, and his task of denouncing religion as an illusion is subordinated to this. "The *true* happiness of the people requires that religion, being an *illusory* bliss to the people, be abolished. To renounce the illusions of our situation is *a demand to renounce a situation that needs illusions*" (Marx, 1961b: 379). And in the *Manifest der Kommunistischer Partei* he and Engels also express the relationship between religion and oppression. For the proletariat, religion, laws and morals are, "as so many bourgeois prejudices, behind which just as many bourgeois interests are hidden" (1959: 472).

Lenin, too, believed that "the deepest roots of religion lay in the social oppression of the masses" (Timofeyev, 1974: 4) and, in the USSR, he began building a society that would not need religion. Such a society would abolish "private ownership of the means of production" and its "advancement becomes a scientifically controlled process. This makes it possible to prevent the negative consequences which often result from the spread of the latest methods of intensifying production in the capitalist countries" (*o.c.:* 4 and 6-7). But, although "the Bolsheviks believed that with the abolition of economic exploitation of man by man, religion would gradually wither away" they realized "that the forces of reaction would remain at work in Soviet society during the early years of socialist construction". As a consequence "they thought it necessary to adopt measures to hasten the dying out of religion"(Lane, 1978: 27). Hence they withdrew all social support from religion and disseminated vigorous scientific-educational and anti-religious propaganda. The main provisions of the 1918 decree on religion reflect this policy. It establishes the "freedom of conscience for individuals with a heavy emphasis on the rights of atheists rather than believers" and also decreed that religion is "an entirely private matter" the practice of which should not "interfere with the rights of other people or citizen's other obligations". At the same time they separated the church from the state and from the schools (*o.c.*: 27). Later legislation confirmed "this policy of directly restricting and controlling the activities of religious organizations and their members". In addition, a militant atheist campaign was supported by atheist propaganda and education (*o.c.*: 28-29).

Most studies of religion in the USSR now focus, it seems to me, on individual behavior: membership figures, socio-demographic distribution and social composition of churches and sects, and the nature of the religious commitment of their members (cf. *e.g.* Lane, 1978) This seems to be a consequence of the fact that, in the Soviet Union, an understanding of religious phenomena "is still sought to further the eradication of religion from the social life of a socialist society" (*o.c.*: 15).

The same can be said of the sociology of religion of most other communist states (*e.g.* Klohr, 1966 and 1967). Let us take Bulgaria as a last and typical example. Ochavkov has published in 1962 the results of a major study on religion and in 1968 one on town and village life (1966a, 1966b, and 1978). According to Marxist-Leninist theory, a hypothesis was formulated that religion in Bulgaria was doomed to disappear as a result of the change from a capitalist to a socialist society. Such a change implied "the socialist ownership of the means of production" and consequently the disappearance of the "classes of exploiters", which liquidates the "basic social root" of religion. "However, this does not lead to the immediate and automatic disappearance of religion – due mainly to the fact that religion, just as every other main area of social life, possesses a certain relative independence" (Ochavkov, 1978: 299-300). The new economic base has also changed other components of the new society, that have helped to overcome religion: education and communication have raised the level of "scientific and other types of knowledge", and politics has had its effects on "the political consciousness which is of a scientific nature". Politics also privatized religion, providing "a possibility for the functioning of religion, to the extent to which it still constitutes a need for part of the members of our society" (*o.c.*: 300-302).

The Marxist-Leninist hypothesis is then checked, using as dependent variables membership in and commitment to religious bodies, and as independent variables time series, sex, level of education, reading habits, attendance at cultural meetings, and technical level of the labor force. Ochavkov stresses, as a result of this analysis, the "very strong influence of socialist education". According to him, religion lingers on under the influence of religious parents and, particularly, of religious grandparents.

However, in view of the fact that, by virtue of the implacable demographic laws, the time will come when the pensioners of today [of which 64.14% are religious] will be no more, when the younger generation of today will become pensioners, and when their place will have been taken by members of our society who will have at least secondary education [of which now 7.49% are religious], it could easily be assumed that the Bulgarian people will enter the stage of communism as an almost irreligious people (*o.c.*: 317).

Ochavkov's explanation proves to be simplistic when data from Poland and the other eastern socialist states are considered. Swiecicki's data (1977: 412) corroborate the association between the level of education and church commitment but his comparative study reveals that there are great differences in the decline of religious commitment among these states, Poland having the highest proportion of believers. He suggests that variables other than those based on the schemes of historical materialism may account for the differences between the religious commitment of the inhabitants of different eastern socialist states: such variables might include the type of religion that was predominant prior to the advent of communism and its relationship to the state, and, especially, the freedom of the churches (which is highest in Poland) to organize catechisms and to publish religious materials. "Familial and pastoral transmission of religious beliefs and values without a specialized catechetical education produces a factual situation that is characterized by a popular faith inserted in the *Weltanschauung* but separated from the well-thought out beliefs of the clergy" (*o.c.*: 420).

We shall come back to the hypotheses that explain differential church commitment in the Eastern European socialist countries. All that matters at this point is that some links can be traced between laicization and individual secularization. In the West, the decline of church commitment and societal secularization can be explained by the same processes, *i.e.* societal changes that broke the social and communal bonds and political opposition between the churches and the new a-religious or anti-religious Left. As a result, a decline of church commitment is also used as an indicator of societal secularization (Wilson, 1969: 21-39). In Eastern Europe the individual is considered to be the last bastion of religion in a laicized society where the deepest root of religion – "social oppression" and "economic exploitation" – are abolished, and religion is attacked as an illusion by "scientific" atheistic propaganda. Private religion, which still "survives", but which, according to the schemes of historical materialism, is doomed to disappear, withers away very differentially, depending on, among other things, the pre-revolutionary relation of church and state and the present freedom granted to organized religion.

So much, then, for the very general and broad outline of the theories of secularization as a process of societal secularization, and the links between societal secularization, organizational secularization, and individual secularization. In the following chapters these theories will be critically analyzed in more detail.

# CHAPTER 2

# Societal Secularization

The notion of secularization as a process of societal secularization implies a comparative historical perspective, an historical "base-line", and the evaluation of the process depends not only on the base-line selected but also on how religion is defined. These, then, are the first two points to be taken up in this section. As mentioned above societal secularization is basically a consequence of a functional differentiation process that results in a process of specialization of sub-systems. This poses the problem of the integration of society and the role that religion plays in it, which I shall take up as the third problem.

Up to now, the presentation of societal secularization might give the reader the impression that it was a straightforward evolutionary and mechanical process. These two problems are next in line, and I will end this chapter by suggesting that two major lines of analysis can be discerned in the theoretical approaches to secularization, each with its own basic concepts, and that these are responsible for one-sidedness in the evaluation of the process.

## The Historical "Base-Line"

As mentioned en passant, the notion of societal secularization implies a comparative historical perspective. Indeed the process of societal secularization, being a process of social change, implies "a base-line as well as an end-point" (Glasner, 1977: 67-76).

Sorokin provides a very good example of this approach, since he is quite explicit. The base-line is "the religiously animated Medieval Christian culture and society" and, according to him, the process of secularization had begun

> [A]lready at the end of the twelfth century A.D. After the fourteenth century this process, with temporary interruptions, progressively grew, expanded over an ever-increasing sector of Western cultural, social, and personal life, and during the last five centuries radically transformed the pre-eminently religious Medieval sociocultural world into a basically different secular Western human universe (Sorokin, 1966: 9-10),

To make his point he uses different indicators:

(1) An increasing demotion of Christian dogmas, beliefs, rituals and moral imperatives from the status of the God-given "revelations", unconditional moral commandments, and the sacred values to the status of secular, man-made, questionable rules of conduct, fallible human beliefs, and relative values.

(2) A decline of inspirational power of Christianity in animating, shaping, and determining the content as well as the style of the Western fine arts.

(3) In the field of morality the decline of Christian religion, of its ethical ideals, values, and precepts and of their power in controlling the behaviour of the Western population has similarly manifested itself in many basic changes in Western morality and law, of the ethical and legal behaviour of Western population during the last five centuries.

(4) *The decline of the Christian Church as a social institution* [... means that] the medieval unity of the Christian Church has been increasingly broken, split, and fragmented into numerous denominations and sects fighting one another ideologically, politically, economically, and, once in a while, militarily and bloodily. [...] It means also an increased "alienation" and "estrangement" of a considerable part of the Western population from the institutionalized Christian "Churches" and "sects" and a transfer of their allegiance to the secular substitutes of Christian religion, beginning with the atheistic, agnostic, sceptical and "humanistic" opponents of all religions and ending with the religiously indifferent political, occupational, economic and social organizations and their secular ideologies and *Weltanschauungen*. [...] In many European countries the defection from Christianity manifested itself in an increase of persons not affiliated with Christian or any other religion, in decline of attendance of religious services by formally affiliated members, and in an enormous decline of beliefs in the main dogmas of Christianity ... (*o.c.*: 10-24).

A first reaction to this line of reasoning is clearly expressed by Martin, who calls it "Catholic utopianism".

Secularist history tends to accept Catholic laments about the period when men were truly religious. In this instance the backward-looking utopia of medievalism becomes the basis for writing about secularization. [...] The more sophisticated versions of this fairy story select certain features of Catholicism which happen to be empirically coexistent from the eleventh to the thirteenth century and use these as a definition of religion. Broadly, the selective elements are the temporal power of the Church, extreme asceticism, realism in philosophy, and ecclesiastical dominance in the sphere of artistic patronage and learning. Clearly, if these are defined as religion it is difficult to cope with any religious change in immediately succeeding centuries except in terms of secularization" (Martin, 1969: 30-31 and 36).

Parsons (1967: 36-37) also opposes Sorokin's views on the basis of his selection of religious elements. "Sorokin clearly regards Protestantism, compared with medieval Catholicism, as primarily a step in the general decline of religiousness". This is based on a "degree of religiousness" identified with a

[T]ranscendental orientation in the sense of *other-worldliness*. [...] The religious person will tend to renounce the world and engage so far as possible in ascetic or devotional practices or mystical contemplation and purely spontaneous acts of love, reducing his involvement in "practical" affairs which involve institutionalized obligations to a minimum.

And he refers to another element relative to the degree of religiousness, identified by Weber as the *inner-worldly* orientation: "an orientation to mastery over the world in the name of religious values". Pursuing this line of analysis, Parsons reverses Sorokin's secularization sequence and suggests that the "denominational phase", most conspicuously in the United States,

[C]ould not prevail were the secular part of the system regarded as radically evil [...] for such a religious constitution to function, on the institutional level the society must present not a less but a more favorable field for the Christian life than did the society of earlier periods of Western history; its moral standards must in fact be higher. [... And Parsons suggests] that in a whole variety of respects modern society is more in accord with Christian values than its forebears have been – this is, let it be noted, a *relative* difference; the millennium definitively has not arrived (*o.c.*: 65).

Referring to still another element used by Sorokin, Le Bras and Delumeau warn us to be cautious of the idea of a Christian France before 1789: "*Pour être déchristianisé*[es], *il faut bien que* [les populations] *aient été un jour christianisé*[es]!" (Le Bras, 1963: 447). Delumeau forcefully demonstrates that the great moment of Christianization of Europe was not the Middle Ages but the "modern" period, beginning with the two Reforms. In Catholic and Protestant countries, the two Reforms fought "superstition" and "idolatry", for they wanted to sever the people, especially the rural population, from paganism. But these types of Christianization practiced a pedagogy of fear and depended on the State (Delumeau, 1975: 9-14). As Le Bras (1963: 448-449) states, prior to 1789 Catholicism was the religion of the French people by virtue of the monarchic constitution. It is impossible to detect "personal" religion, which alone could bear witness to "Christianization". An historical comparison is meaningless in view of the different situation: compulsion *versus* individual freedom. And Vergote (1976: 361) adds that the most indisputable effect of secularizing scientism is not the diminution of religious belief, but the secularization of superstitions. In fact, fortune-telling with a scientific appearance, having recourse even to the computer, has taken over from the titular saints and benedictions that exorcized bad luck. This allows us to estimate the impact that irrational motifs and archaic needs could have on religious practice in a society that was officially Christian.

47

Wilson (1976b: 8-11) would certainly agree with Le Bras and Delumeau, but he argues that it was not "an age of faith, but of faiths". He does not seek "to make any fine distinctions – and they are distinctions notoriously difficult to draw – between magic and religion". Referring to the Middle Ages and primitive societies, he only states the existence of "man's long pre-modern history of belief in spirits, gods, demons, spells, and witches". And he concludes "that perhaps [this] is all that need be asserted to make the point about the process of secularization", which enables him to oppose the modern "rational empirical orientation" to the religious magical orientation of pre-modern times.

But here again scholars disagree. Mary Douglas (1973: 36-37) for example, would object to this opposition between primitive and modern man:

> Secularization is often treated as a modern trend [...]. But we shall see that it is an age-old cosmological type [...]. The contrast of secular with religious has nothing whatever to do with the contrast of modern with traditional or primitive. The idea that primitive man is by nature deeply religious is nonsense. The truth is that all the varieties of scepticism, materialism and spiritual fervour are found in the range of tribal societies. They vary as much from one another on these lines as any chosen segments of London life. The illusion that all primitives are pious, credulous and subject to the teaching of priests or magicians has probably done even more to impede our understanding of our own civilization than it has confused the interpretations of archaeologists dealing with the dead past.

And Vergote could refer to "scientific" superstition, which contradicts the "rational empirical" orientation of modern man.

With regard to the positions of Sorokin *versus* Parsons, of Martin, Le Bras and Delumeau *versus* theorists like Sorokin, and of Wilson *versus* Douglas, some conclusions should be drawn. First of all, if one takes one institutionalized religion as model, then all transformations are a form of religious change of which some changes may be organizational secularization. The same can be said about taking one type of religious orientation as paradigmatic. Here again, changes in religious orientation are rather religious changes and should be studied as such. If not, value judgments creep in: some call the "base-line" orientation sacred and the "end-point" secular, *e.g.* Sorokin calling the Middle Ages "ideational" and modern times "sensate" (1962: 320-321 and 537-658), others reverse it, *e.g.* Parsons.

If the scholar takes the degree of religiousness of the people as a yardstick, then he has to compare people in different situations and with different religions: modern *versus* traditional and primitive societies. But even if he restricts himself to the Christian world, then the problem is still quite complex, as the comments of Le Bras, Delumeau and

Vergote indicate. One other problem is that the scholars who jump from the individual to the societal level commit an ecological fallacy. As I said at the outset, we cannot equate a decline of personal involvement in religion – in churches, denominations, sects or cults – with societal secularization.

The level of comparison for the evaluation of the societal secularization must be the societal level. I quite agree with Wilson (1976b: 9-10) that if we take the age of Innocent III as "the base-line", it is because we see it as

> [T]he apotheosis of Church control over society [...]. The Church controlled [...] formal processes of political, juridical, commercial, and social inter-course – the institutional operation of society [...]. Even for that age, "the age of faith" is perhaps a misnomer; we should refer only to the age of religiously prescribed social order.

Speaking of the 12th Century and referring to Innocent III, Knowles (1968: 285-286) thinks it is justified to call this period "the triumph of the papacy".

## The Definition of Religion

The study of societal secularization not only implies a base-line, but we also need a definition of religion. And the type of definition used largely determines the "diagnoses of secularization as a major socio-cultural tendency in modern societies" (Robertson, 1978: 265). It is impossible to discuss here all the problems involved in such a definition and to refer to all the material published on this subject. I seek only to indicate some implications for the study of secularization and explain certain options (Dobbelaere, 1974; Robertson, 1978: 302-304).

In the sociology of religion discussions of types of definitions have always concentrated on the alternative of *substantive versus functional* definitions (Berger, 1967: 175-178 and Berger, 1974). Robertson (1970: 36-43) also rightly distinguishes between *nominal* and *real* definitions, and *inclusive* and *exclusive* (exclusive implying restrictive or narrow) definitions.

Yinger (1970: 7) offers us a good example of a functional definition of religion: a system of beliefs and practices by means of which a group of people struggles with the ultimate problems of human life. Such a functional definition is also inclusive. For Yinger (*o.c.*: 11-12), it includes communism, nationalism, and science as a way of life, along with theistic systems of belief. For Greeley (1974: 61 and 120), following Geertz's functional definition of religion (1968: 4), it also includes evolutionism, Marxism and scientism.

49

Acceptance of such a definition poses several problems. First of all, religion is *defined* as being functional for the group. Thus Yinger (1970: 6) writes: "If religion is defined by what are thought to be its functions, then one should not be surprised to find it functional, that is, having only supportive consequences". Second, how is it possible to talk about *functional alternatives* if everything that fulfils the function is, by definition, religion? And third, if man is by definition a *religious* man, each and every "solution" to his ultimate problems is religious. What then are the consequences for studies of secularization?

Greeley's refutation of the individual secularization thesis is self-fulfilling: his "unsecular man" is unsecular by definition; the "persistence of religion" is a definitional artefact. And so he may conclude "there is in the human condition a built-in strain toward evolving an ultimate meaning system and making it sacred" (Greeley, 1974: 241). Of course, man needs a meaning system, but must that meaning system be religious? Is it scientific to answer the question of the function of religion for society and man today with a functional definition? Such definitions do not help us very much, so we must turn to the alternative – a *substantive* definition.

Such a definition offers us the possibility of looking for "functional alternatives" to religion, or what Robertson calls "surrogate" religiosity. I agree with him that

> one of the interesting and significant characteristics of modern societies would be lost to the sociological perspective if the various "isms" of which we have spoken [Communism, nationalism, Fascism, secularism, humanism, psycho-analysis 'as a way of life', and so on] were regarded as fundamentally religious for sociological purposes; since their adherents have in many, if not all, cases chosen to renounce contact with the supernatural or spiritual, and the explicit, official values of such groups also obviously deny their reality (Robertson, 1970: 39).

Since the utility of an all-inclusive definition of religion in a study of secularization is obviously questionable, (see also Glasner, 1977: 11) a substantive and *exclusive* definition is needed (Robertson, 1971: 303).

An additional argument for a substantive definition is that scholars working with a functional definition implicitly or explicitly introduce substantive elements in their definition to prevent "a circularity of reasoning" (Yinger, 1970: 6) or to be able to do their "sociological" research (Luckmann, 1967: 56; Dobbelaere and Lauwers, 1978: 540 and 538; and Robertson, 1970: 42). Finally, some theorists, such as Parsons and Bellah

> [C]ling to a purely functional and nominal definition when speaking in very abstract terms of systems of action. But, when confronted with concrete cases, they veer, inconsistently, towards a commonsense definition based on

conventional, everyday usage. This inconsistency and the intellectual strains arising from it are undoubtedly associated with the acceptability to these theorists of such notions as "the religion of Americanism", "secular religion" and "civic religion". These notions *do not* conform to the spirit of conventional definitions – which emphasize beliefs about a transcendent or superempirical reality; rather, they overarch and "contain" religious beliefs and values as normally understood (Robertson, 1970: 41).

This implicit use of a conventional (substantive) definition also emerges with another functional and nominal *but* exclusive definition given by Luhmann (1977: 9-10). He suggests defining religion not only by the problems that it solves but also by the way in which it solves them. Religion is then defined positively, by the problems it solves, and negatively by the differences from its functional alternatives in the way it solves them. But, first of all, Luhmann (*o.c.*: 46) considers the problems of immanence and transcendence to be typically religious, since for these problems no functional alternatives are available. This is an indication that I.uhmann implicitly operates with a conventional definition of religion based on the type of problems. Secondly, he does not specify the *typical* way in which religion solves problems; or whether religion is defined by the combination of problems that the religious sub-system solves (*o.c.*: 84), which is a different combination from that dealt with by the other sub-systems. As a sub-system, religion is considered to be a given: it is self-governing and self-substituting (*o.c.*: 48-49). Religion is dealt with as an autonomous sub-system that reacts to its environment, adapting itself by taking up newly developing religious modes, and eliminating the non-religious functions that it performed in the past. Luhmann's central system-hypothesis is "*dass das Religionssystem sich als eine selbstsubstitutive Ordnung ausdifferenziert hat*" (*o.c.*: 48). Such a self-substituting system orients itself toward the social system, the other sub-systems, and itself. As a result, he comes back to traditional religion and its functional relationships. Spiritual communication to the total system is the primary function, which is performed by the church through rituals (*die Funktionsorientierung*). Its relations to the other social sub-systems are called ancillary functions (*die Leistungsorientierung*), and reflexion on the religious system itself is the third type of function (*die Theologie*) (*o.c.*: 56-59). All three different functions have to be performed separately but combined together (*o.c.*: 62; cf. also *infra*: Other approaches to the process of societal secularization).

I seek to work with an explicit rather than an implicit substantive definition. And since we have always defended the view that a sociological definition must be formulated in relation to the empirical phenomena under study if it is to grasp their diversity and uniqueness (Dobbelaere and Lauwers, 1973: 549 and Dobbelaere, 1974: 16-23), I end up with the same conclusions as Robertson, opting for a substantive, exclusive and *real* definition of religion. For the purposes of studying secularization, the definition of religion might read: a unified system of beliefs and practices relative to a supra-empirical, transcendent reality that unites all those who adhere to it into a single moral community (Dobbelaere, 1974: 19). Of course, such a definition does not in any way exclude a functional analysis of religion.

## The Integration of Society

As a sacred canopy, religion integrated society in the age of Innocent III, and societal secularization implies that religion became an institution among other institutions without overarching claims. A question that emerges is this: does modern differentiated society need cultural integration, and what role does religion still play in it? It would not be difficult to list several sociologists who differ in their answers to the first part of the question. Parsons, for example, stresses value and normative integration; Luhmann rejects it (1977: 243-244). This discussion would lead us too far. I will limit myself here to a derivative question: to what extent does religion still integrate, and provide legitimation for modern societies? Again, I shall restrict my analysis to two typical answers given in the sociology of religion. Of course, they are to a certain extent linked to the answers given to the first question.

### *Modern Society does not Need Religion for its Integration*

I have already referred to Wilson who states that in modern society, the basic locus of operation is no longer the local community but the societal system, which is organizationally integrated on the basis of impersonal roles. Consequently, the traditional, moral and religious culture is no longer the basis for legitimated control. In a societal system control is impersonal, technical, legal and bureaucratic: not local, human and moral as it was; it is increasingly mechanical, technical, computerized and electronicized (Wilson, 1976b: 20 and 102). "As our society has become less dependent on moral regulations, and as our relations to each other have become more role-regulated and less personally involved, so the functions of religion have declined"(*o.c.*: 20). Fenn (1972: 19) not only argues that religion is unnecessary: "differentiation in modern societies makes it impossible... for religion to provide the basis for cultural integration". As far as legitimacy is concerned, duly established priorities, effectiveness and propriety – not religious or moral values – become the primary sources. In discussing Bellah's contention "that religion is the most general mechanism for integrating meaning and motivation in action systems", Fenn concludes:

While it is possible to agree with Bellah that all societies have the problem of structuring the motivations of individuals, it has been argued here that the process of automation in modern societies will increasingly diminish the severity of this problem so far as recruitment for civic and productive roles is concerned. Modern societies, that is, will be able to afford higher levels of motivational *non*commitment and may even seek to raise the level of *non*commitment in order to "cool out" overmobilized segments of the population (1972: 28-29).

In other words, the increases in productive capacity of modern societies tend to make less difficult the tasks of providing "legitimacy" for the social order and of motivating enough individuals to work. A religious basis to the normative order becomes less necessary.

In a later article Fenn (1974: 151), comes back to this problem and accepts that "differentiation is a necessary, if not sufficient, cause of problems of legitimation" and he develops "a theoretical framework which can be used for developing and testing propositions concerning religious legitimation" (*o.c.*: 144). The influence of a differentiated religious system – viz. a system of religious roles, statuses, and organizations "separate from roles, statuses, and organizations in political, educational, occupational, ethnic or legal systems" (*o.c.*: 152) – on the process of legitimation is, according to Fenn, mediated by three intervening variables which should be studied on national, regional, local and personal levels (*o.c.*: 145 and 149-157). The *autonomy* of the religious structures – *e.g.* on the local level, the ability to withstand pressures from clients, and, on the national level, the freedom from governmental sanction – influences the effectiveness of religion in the process of legitimation. Autonomy at the macro social level may be inversely related to autonomy at the local level. The level at which autonomy is achieved may in turn affect the level at which religion exercises effective cultural sanctions. Whether these sanctions are negative or positive depends on another variable: *cultural integration – i.e.* the degree to which the religious cultural system is integrated with non-religious cultural elements. The less integration, the more likely, according to Fenn, it is that religious symbols will be a source of negative sanctions. The effectiveness of the sanctions depends on the degree to which religious structures are *interdependently* related to other structures in modern societies. Structural interdependence refers to the degree to which religious affiliation is interrelated with ethnic, occupational, political or other sources of social location. To the extent that religious roles, for instance, occupy a different category from occupational roles, the less likely it is that religious sanctions will be effective in the process of legitimation outside the religious subsystem.

Summarizing his argument, Fenn (*o.c.*: 157) concludes:

The process of differentiation has the somewhat paradoxical impact of proliferating religious roles and organizations while at the same time making the effect of religion on the society more contingent and indirect. Religious influence is more indirect in highly differentiated societies because it is mediated through a complex set of roles and organizations. And such influence is more contingent because it depends on the operation of other variables in the religious system. The effectiveness of religious legitimation is dependent on the degree to which religious institutions are both independent of secular authorities and yet interdependent with them. Religious institutions which depend on secular sanctions at either the macro social or the micro social level cannot exert independent influence, and even highly autonomous religious institutions cannot be effective if they are segmented from (rather than interdependent with) other role-systems, organizations, or collectives in the society. Similarly, whether religious institutions exert negative as well as positive sanctions depends on the degree to which the religious and secular aspects of the culture are relatively well integrated with each other. Integrated cultural systems, however, do not provide prima facie evidence of religious legitimation in the present; the evidence for such legitimation depends on the degree of interdependence between religions and secular institutions and symbolic systems

Fenn's first answer to the question "Does religion integrate and provide legitimation for modern societies?" is that a modern society does not need it, and what is more, "[i]n modern societies the process of differentiation has reached the point at which a normative order based on religious beliefs and values is no longer possible" (1972: 16). In his second article (Fenn, 1974), however, he agrees that, depending on three intervening variables – autonomy of the religious structures, cultural integration of the religious systems, and structural interdependence between religious structures and other structures – a differentiated religious system might still legitimate the social system and its substructures. Bellah, contrary to Fenn, is quite positive in answering the same question. He argues that religion is "the most general mechanism for integrating meaning and motivation in action systems" (1970: 12). But Bellah limits himself to the societal level and discusses an undifferentiated system, *i.e.* civic or civil religion (1967).

## *"Civil Religion" and the Integration of Society*

Since Bellah's paper appeared, books and articles have been published on the subject, and in a bibliographic essay, Hammond describes civil religion as "any set of beliefs and rituals, related to the past, present and/or future of a people ("nation") which are understood in some transcendental fashion" (1976: 171). American civil religion is akin to Rousseau's outline of "the simple dogmas of the civil religion: the existence of God, the life to come, the reward of virtue and the punishment of vice, and the exclusion of religious intolerance" (Bellah, 1967:

5). In the inaugural addresses of the presidents of the United States and in the Declaration of Independence, reference is made to God, the Creator, the Supreme Judge, divine Providence, the Almighty Being, that God's work must be truly our own etc. "Though much is selectively derived from Christianity, this religion is clearly not itself Christianity": Christ is never mentioned in the presidential inaugural addresses or in the Declaration of Independence.

> The God of the civil religion is not only rather "Unitarian", he is also on the austere side, much more related to order, law, and right than to salvation and love. Even though he is somewhat deist in cast, he is by no means simply a watchmaker God. He is actively interested and involved in history, with a special concern for America (*o.c.*: 7).

"From the Pilgrims on, America has been conceived by some as 'God's New Israel' [...] God's 'almost chosen people'" (Hammond, 1976: 171). In other words America is equated with Israel; it is the Promised Land. And "With the Civil War, a new theme of death, sacrifice, and rebirth enters the civil religion. It is symbolized in the life and death of Lincoln" (Bellah, 1967: 10). This symbolism then found both physical and ritualistic expression, *e.g.* in national cemeteries and Memorial Day. Concluding his article Bellah (*o.c.*: 18) writes:

> Behind the civil religion at every point lie Biblical archetypes: Exodus, Chosen People, Promised Land, New Jerusalem, Sacrificial Death and Rebirth. But it is also genuinely American and genuinely new. It has its own prophets and its own martyrs, its own sacred events and sacred places, its own solemn rituals and symbols. It is concerned that America be a society as perfectly in accord with the will of God as men can make it, and a light to all the nations.

According to Martin (1978: 70), it is the:

> [E]xplicit separation of church from state that enables a pluralistic religion-in-general to buttress the higher level legitimations of American society. Indeed, since religion has been set free to move downstream with the ebb and flow of sub-cultural change it is more likely to provide generalized legitimations of a more apparently modern kind. Such legitimations must, of course, not only be general but vague. They must be above specific denominations and specific institutional arrangements, whether these be religious or secular.

In fact, as Bellah mentions, American civil religion, "borrowed selectively from the religious traditions in such a way that the average American saw no conflict between the two", and as a result it never was anticlerical or militantly secular.

> Such an achievement is by no means to be taken for granted [...] One needs only to think of France to see how differently things can go. The French Revolution was anticlerical to the core and attempted to set up an anti-

Christian civil religion. Throughout modern French history, the chasm between traditional Catholic symbols and the symbolism of 1789 has been immense (Bellah, 1967: 13).

Martin (1978: 71) explains this by referring to the different socio-cultural complex, categorized as "organic monopoly" (in Catholic countries) as against "individualistic pluralism" (in Protestant countries) (cf. *infra*: p.63): "The Latin pattern contains enormous pressures toward the separation of church and state, of Christianity and civil religion, simply on account of the immense split over religion per se".

## *Discussion*

In a later publication, Fenn directly confronts his views with Bellah's. According to Fenn (1978: 42), Bellah understands civil religion as the religious system of American society, which "guarantees the reality of that society regardless of the extent to which these symbols are taken seriously by any number of individuals". Bellah, in other words, conceives of America as a cultural whole. This is a *mythic* perspective, which is also typical of, for example, Durkheim and Shils; it regards "society as the really 'real'", as the "given". On the contrary, the *discursive* type of reasoning, of which the works of Weber, Simmel, and Bell are prototypes, finds no substantive reality beyond the level of the individual, "values are like the gods; multiple, often conflicting, and momentary, now present but soon hidden or gone" (Fenn, 1978: 7). Fenn opts for the latter posture, and as a result his views on civil religion are different from those of Bellah.

Both seem to agree that in the 1960s the citizens of the States were caught in a "double-bind", between loyalties to the American nation and the desire to protest illegitimate uses of political authority. *"The same symbols [e.g. the flag] functioned to express both solidarity with the nation and support for the official exercise of political power"* (Fenn, 1978: 44). Bellah's way out of this dilemma is to affirm the "seriousness and authenticity of civil religion", and "to interpret current events as a 'breaking' of a covenant which is itself above history and whose validity cannot be tested empirically" (Fenn, 1978: 43 and 50; and Bellah, 1975). Fenn (*o.c.*: 43) sees yet another way out: we can "reduce the use of religious symbols at the national level to inauthentic rhetoric", and consider "it as a potentially deceptive form of communication". If there are groups which take this standpoint, then they challenge civil religion and at the same time America as "a cultural whole from which this speech derives and to which it legitimately refers" (*o.c.*: 50). They claim "that such speech is inauthentic: *i.e.*, that it claims to represent a whole but actually expresses the private and partial interests of the speaker" (*o.c.*: 51). Social historians, sociologists, and political analysts have referred to religious themes in presidential addresses as "idiosyncratic", "an elitist version of American nationalism that is more easily located in Presidential speeches than in the ideas and values of the average citizen", and to the use of religious symbols by national politicians as "difference in personal style or the canny political manipulation of religious images for political gain" (*o.c.*: 46 and 51-52). When social scientists enter a debunking comment on political discourse that refers to civil religion, they suggest that those politicians are speaking for an elite, a region, or merely for themselves, but not for a collectivity such as the nation.

> In the process of secularization, therefore, doubt about religious symbols is stimulated by doubt concerning the whole which underlies or is represented by certain religious symbols. *The "civil religion" is more likely to be seen as a cultural fiction to the extent that the nation itself seems to be merely an arena for the conflicting and co-operative activities of the classes, ethnic groups, large corporations, and various organizations which pursue their ideals and their immaterial interests under rules enunciated and enforced by the state.* The awareness of a social whole then lends credence to religious symbols that express that underlying unity, and they in turn lend authority to those who use the religious symbols. Conversely, religious symbols, when used authoritatively, may also supply a sense of unity and wholeness to a particular society. A civil religion is precisely such an authoritative metaphor for the nation's underlying values and commitments. It is a metaphor because it speaks of a social system in terms that are appropriate only to the individual, terms of sacrifice and fidelity, birth and death. Whenever it is said that an organization or society "wills", "decides", "acts", "intends", "believes", or "hopes", such a metaphor is in progress. For instance, [...] while there are constitutional guarantees against giving the metaphor the force of state action, the Supreme Court has on occasion legitimated its decisions by reference to the "Christian" or "religious" convictions of the American people [...]. Such official use of religious symbols, however, encourages opposition and resistance (*o.c.*: 52).

Fenn notes how state action of this sort has been opposed by religious sects with deviant viewpoints or by individuals and groups engaged in a non-religious defense of their basic rights. Most of these contests are fought out in the courts (*o.c.*: 54-63). It is clear that Fenn questions whether America is "really real" as a "nation", and considers it as a composite of interrelated and conflicting groups, collectivities, and individuals. Civil religion then is not authentic; it is the rhetoric of persons or groups concealing their partial interests.

In a later article, Fenn again poses the question of the extent to which American civil religion does speak for American society. This time he attacks the problem on the basis of a distinction between cohesion or solidarity and integration. Cohesion refers to a type of integration based on collective values and beliefs – Durkheim's mechanical solidarity, *i.e.*

the integration of "primitive societies" based on a collective conscience (Fenn, 1979: 437 and 428-430). And he argues "that a civil religion that provides for societal cohesion at the expense of minority cultures is superfluous to societal integration" (*o.c.*: 435). I would then argue that a civil religion, based on main-line Protestantism certainly does not integrate members of cults, sects, and creedal, confessional, and ethnic churches and denominations. What type of integration, then, is to be expected in a modern society?

According to Fenn, high levels of non-solidarity integration are likely to be achieved through the courts and educational institutions of American society, despite the survival of communities or groups whose symbols provide a powerful source of solidarity feeling and shared moral obligation among their own members (*o.c.*: 437). In order to integrate secular societies, courts and educational institutions divest the sacred discourse of these groups of its cherished meanings. The secular language that is used there is "integrative, precisely because it creates a pragmatic and temporary consensus on usage, on the meaning of words, on the legitimacy of motives, and on the speaker's self-declared intentions" (*o.c.*: 432). We may then conclude that the *cohesion* provided by American civil religion is particular to certain groups of American society and that the societal integration of secular states can only be achieved without such a "religion".

## *Empirical Studies*

Bellah's hermeneutics of the American "sacred texts" (Bellah, 1976: 153), are supplemented by empirical research with an analysis of the civil religious consciousness of the American people and elementary school children today, and of the support given to the civil religion theme by specific denominations. According to Bellah such studies do not prove that civil religion never or ever existed, but do make apparent the fact that the American nation no longer has the same civil religion that its founding fathers had. According to him, each nation has and needs a civil religion, but the content may vary (*o.c.*: 154; Robertson, 1978: 160). He is also very critical of the possibility of operationalizing civil religion and suggests that Wimberley in his early studies elicited "public theology" instead of getting "at the core of civil religious faith" (*o.c.*: 155). Wimberley (1979) examined empirically the validity of the indicators used in his empirical studies, and they proved to factor together with statements drawn from the "sacred scriptures". So he was confident that he was studying American civil religion.

The first empirical studies that Wimberley (1976 and Wimberley *et al.*, 1976) conducted were concerned with the question of whether and to what extent there existed a "separate civil religious dimension" apart from conventional religion. In his study, in North Carolina a civil religious dimension emerged distinct from several church dimensions (belief, experience, knowledge, private and public religious practice etc.). This study then supports Bellah's contention that civil religion "exists alongside of and rather clearly differentiated from the churches", but it "is not readily distinguished from church religion in the general population as it is among the religiously active" (Wimberley, 1976: 349-350; Wimberley *et al.*). Pursuing with Christenson his research on civil religion, he then asked, "Who is civil religious?" It is the religiously conservative, the least educated, the poor, the unemployed, the retired, the rural and elderly people, who are predominantly civil religious. But, while civil religion shows variation with these variables, "the dominant finding is that a fair amount of civil religious consensus is found across most social segments". Although the study "suggests that civil religion may receive broad support", one can question its "effectiveness" as an ideology in America, as those in potential power positions – those having graduate degrees beyond college, the professsionals, the officials, and the ministers – have the lowest scores (Christenson and Wimberley, 1978). It seems then that civil religion rests rather on the masses than on the elite. Furthermore, according to a study by Smidt (1980: 38) in Illinois, civil religious beliefs begin to be acquired during childhood. "As early as the fourth grade, a large proportion of children express civil religious orientations".

According to the same study, "children who were more civil religious tended to be more trusting of political authority, more willing to obey laws which were perceived to be morally wrong and more supportive of the American way of life" (*ibid.*). In 1972, Wimberley found that the more civil religious people had a greater preference for Nixon than McGovern, suggesting that "a vote against an incumbent president might be perceived as contradictory to the voter's civil religious commitments" (Bourg, 1976: 144-145).

## Conclusions

That civil religion should be the religion of the masses more than of the elite raises some questions. Is civil religion not an inauthentic "faith" supported and used in the interest of its proponents? Do the schools, especially the elementary schools, achieve "non-solidarity integration" regarding the nation, as Fenn suggested they seem to do with respect to communities and groups? And what is the impact of traditional religion, as civil religion seems to be linked to conventional religiosity? According to a study by Mueller and Sites (1977: 231-244), civil religion was supported on the 200th anniversary of the founding of the American republic, 4 July 1976, in the sermons of Presbyterian and

Lutheran churches in a metropolitan area in the Lower Great Lakes section of the United States. Their last sentence reads: "The covenant may indeed be broken [referring to Bellah], but these clergymen are doing their best to mend it". The question of course is whether they explicitly preach or indirectly and latently support a civil religion.

If we move to a more theoretical-sociological level, then the idea of civil religion appears to be a particular formulation of the relationship between the individual and society (Robertson, 1978: 161-162). This general problem has been formulated in terms of civil religion in two types of countries: where society is considered primary, and the individual secondary, *e.g.* in France; and where the individual is primary and society secondary, *e.g.* in the USA. Such formulations did not emerge in societies where society and individual are accorded parity (*e.g.* Germany) or are relatively fused (*e.g.* England) (*o.c.*: 167). In France this was done particularly by Rousseau, Saint-Simon (*le Nouveau Christianisme*), Comte (*la Religion Positiviste*), and Durkheim; in the USA by Bellah and Parsons. According to Robertson, civil religion is formulated with greatest intensity in cases where society has precedence "when the efficacy of the societal entity is at risk"; in the other case, where the individual level takes primacy, "advocacy of civil religion is likely when there is difficulty in aggregating sub-societal, particularly individualistic wants and demands 'up to' the level of the society as a whole" (*o.c.*: 171-172). This shows how a more general question is specified in particular countries according to their cultural setting. But, if we consider the type of civil religions mentioned, then the question should be raised of the extent to which we can really speak of a "religion".

To call the American value pattern that operates on the political level a civil *religion* is based on two arguments: the integrative function of this "value pattern" (Bellah, Parsons etc.), and the references to elements borrowed from conventional religions: Deism, references to sacrifice, themes such as "the chosen people", and national rituals having "religious" overtones.

> In the United States religious and political symbols have been closely intertwined over the past three hundred years despite the institutional separation of Church and State. That is perhaps the underlying truth to various arguments that America enjoys a "civil religion" or that its dominant values and ideals have the weight of religious concerns (Fenn, 1978: 49).

Borrowing from religion occurs in several fields – *e.g.* actors speak about the "sacred" stage; certain roads and places closely connected to human sacrifices in war situations are called "sacred" and reverence is asked from the public; the family acquires religious connotations when people refer to the "sacred" bonds of blood. But, by virtue of such borrowing, such phenomena do not become "religious". Of course, such borrowing linked to a functional definition of religion promotes definitional misuses from the standpoint of those working with a substantive definition.

According to my definition, civil religion is not a "religion". It is not a unified system of beliefs and practices relative to a transcendent reality (*supra*: the definition of religion). It is rather a political ideology that borrows religious concepts and symbols from the religious traditions of America. That the (mis-)use of the term religion can lead very far is proved by an article of Cole and Hammond (1974), who studied the relationship between religious pluralism, societal complexity, and legal development. According to their analysis, a universalistic legal system facilitates societal complexity, and this association increases with an increase of religious pluralism (*o.c.*: 184-186). It is this legal order that they call "civil religion" or "political religion" (*o.c.*: 180-181). I can agree with the statement "that a generalized legal system facilitates the interaction of religiously diverse people" (*o.c.*: 178), and that the legal order supplies meaning (*o.c.*: 181). But again, do we have to call all systems of meaning "religious"?

## Societal Secularization: A Mechanical, Straightforward Evolutionary Process?

In the first chapter, I tried to set out the broad process of societal secularization as it has been most frequently presented. I now turn to some complicating factors, and I will indicate ways in which the general line of development may have been modified according to the socio-cultural complex within which the process has unfolded. The "universality" of this process might be described in a set of propositions about what tends to occur, all other things being equal. But, as Martin (1978: 3) has pointed out, "things are not equal – ever – and [...] they are most conspicuously not equal with respect to the particular cultural (and general linguistic) complex within which they operate".

Not only is the particular cultural complex important in the unfolding of the societal secularization process, so also are the evaluations of this process by individuals. We must, therefore, divest our thinking about societal secularization of its mechanical character. Two aspects of secularization will be discussed in this section: (1) the impact of the cultural complex, and (2) the impact of people, groups, and quasi-groups. Finally, I will show that secularization as a process is not irreversible.

## The Cultural Context

Most authors indicate national and regional variations in degrees of differentiation, as well as variations among social institutions (*e.g.*, Wilson, 1969: 75-95). They sometimes refer to it implicitly by stating that "political, religious and economic institutions became increasingly specialized" (Luckmann, 1967: 95), thereby suggesting a differential evolution. Berger (1967: 128-130) quite explicitly speaks about "cultural lags" when comparing institutional spheres and nations, and Martin tries to explain these differences systematically. Martin's analysis (1978: 17-27) of the impact of the socio-cultural complex focuses primarily on degrees of religious pluralism, but also on the size of religious minorities, their territorial dispersion, and the nature of their exclusion from traditional elites, or, indeed, from liberal and Marxist elites. His study is not limited to the effect of the social location of a religion, it also incorporates the inherent character of different religions: pluralistic and democratic *versus* organic, *e.g.* Protestant denominations *versus* the Catholic Church. Finally, his categorization of countries takes into account whether the "frame" of the society is set up through conflict against external or against internal oppressors. Thus Poland's structure emerged through conflict against external threats and domination, whereas France's emerged through conflict between *intégristes* and republican secularists. Without going into detail, the main line of his argument may be indicated by reference to his categories and by suggesting the effects of some of the typical social constellations that he depicts in the unfolding of societal secularization, especially in social institutions.

Martin's main categories are *total monopoly*, *e.g.* Catholic and Orthodox countries; *duopoly*, which only arises when the Protestant church is the major partner and is also labeled the "60:40 pattern" or the "mixed pattern", *e.g.* Holland; and *Protestant pluralism*, the Anglo-American and Scandinavian patterns, differing, however, in degrees of pluralism. Where the Catholic Church is in the majority, the monopoly may be broken but only by small groups. In a more detailed analysis he also discusses *exceptions to the Catholic pattern* under external pressures, *e.g.* Ireland, or internal pressure, *e.g.* Flanders, Belgium. He also shows how the vicious spiral of the Catholic monopoly can in the end partially unwind, as in Chile and Brazil, where "the Church" sees its survival as dependent upon its dissociation from conservative authority. He also discusses *statist regimes of the right*, *i.e.* Catholic monopolies of the right, *e.g.* Spain, and *statist societies of the left*, *i.e.* secular monopolies of the left, *e.g.* Russia (1978: 27-58). To indicate the impact of the socio-cultural complex on societal secularization, I begin with the principal opposed types (total monopoly and Protestant pluralism in the

USA). The discussion of particular social institutions will bring both the mixed type and the exceptions to the Catholic pattern into the picture. Finally, I consider the monopolies to the left and the right.

## Total Monopoly

The socio-logic of Catholic societies, as Martin puts it, may, at the risk of losing many of its nuances, be rendered in a few propositions. Where society had split into intermittently warring halves, Catholicism is straightforwardly identified with the antecedent system of authority, with which it was rigidly linked, and there develops a union of the Church with the political right.

> Since revolution had to break a single system which it identified as one throughout all its corrupt parts, and since revolution included a strong component of individualism which is opposed to organicism per se, the symbiosis of Catholicism with the right wing fraction of society was inevitable. [...] In Catholic societies there arises a social split, with Catholics and legitimists on one side and other groups, either newly ascendant or previously persecuted, or both, on the other (Martin, 1978: 38).

Religious groups, *e.g.* Protestants and Jews, might even ally themselves with irreligion, and associations that in Protestant societies were mildly religious in nature, such as the Freemasons, became secularists under the impact of the same split.

The existence of rival societies within a single social whole, says Martin, creates violence of expression and clarity of difference. The symbols of Catholicism become objects of assault, *e.g.* the priesthood and the religious orders, and there is also a clear split between militant faith and militant unbelief, in contrast with what occurs in Protestant societies.

> Moreover the very notion of an "intellectual" belongs to this specifically Catholic pattern and suggests people given to the elaboration of large scale social and philosophical systems parallel to and in rivalry with Catholicism. Such systems may even reflect Catholicism in inverted form [*e.g.* Saint-Simonianism and Comteanism] (*o.c.*: 39).

The split is also endlessly reproductive of itself. It is found on the local level: *curé* against schoolmaster, even father against mother; it is transferred from generation to generation through rival school systems; and it heavily reinforces other fissures such as class and regional conflicts. Reactive organicism, in contrast to Protestant pluralism, even carries forward all the multiple functions of religion into a context where they would be in partial dissolution, *e.g.* Catholic political parties, trade unions etc. (*o.c.*: 36-41). It is clear that Martin here describes a manifest process of societal secularization, *i.e.* laicization.

### Protestant Pluralism

The opposite type is a pluralistic culture, and the most pluralistic culture of Protestant societies is the USA. Its pluralism, as in Britain and Scandinavia, is not primarily based on religious enclaves, "but on religious alternatives differentially associated with different status levels and different politics". In America more than in the other Protestant societies there is "universalization of dissent". There are no churches but denominations and a great number of sects and cults, and this "permits religion to take on as many images as there are social faces" (*o.c.*: 30). As a result, religion *as such* cannot be identified with any social or class enemy. "The model of religion implies infinite variation [...]. Experimental religion allows all kinds of religious experiment." (*o.c.*: 30-31).

> By the same token the universality of experimental religion implies a pragmatic, experimental model of political activity. [...] Insofar as social alienation exists it can organize behind the mask of religion and when a stratum becomes self-conscious it will politicize within a religious format [... *e.g.*] the Black Muslims. Most political movements take religious colouring, though without religion acting as a functional alternative to politics as it sometimes does in European contexts. [...] Even the politics of spontaneity itself finds a mystical religious clothing in meditation, ecstasy and the like, to protest against the domination of the Protestant Ethic and the hard-had Puritan character structure. In this way major shifts become possible by individual contagion and incorporation, not structural oppositions and overturning (*o.c.*: 31).

American religion has never seriously been a bone of political contention as such; pluralism and participation are high; the intelligentsia is less inclined to participation than are its status equivalents, but is not particularly anti-religious; clerical status is usually not high but anticlerical sentiment is low; churches play a large role in the interstices of society, englobing those institutions for care and welfare which are elsewhere under the aegis of the state; fundamentalist religion retains its grip on the major periphery, *i.e.* the South, and although associated with the Right, also fosters populist tendencies; finally, Social Democracy is absent (*o.c.*: 28, 35 and 59). Comparing this situation to those of Great Britain and Scandinavia, Martin makes it clear that "different degrees of pluralism" make for different socio-cultural contexts for religion, especially, it seems to me, if compared to the Catholic situation described above. American Protestantism unhinged the centre, made politics and religion federal, separated and dissociated religion from social authority and high culture, and allowed religion to adapt to every status group through every variety of pullulating sectarianism.

The result is that nobody feels ill at ease with his religion, that faith is distributed along the political spectrum, that the church is never *the* axis of dispute. *But* unity has to be preserved through a school system which keeps religious plurality out and by a national myth which represents a common denominator of all faiths: one nation under God, not under Catholicism or Anglicanism or Presbyterianism (*o.c.*: 36).

This is what Bellah called "civil religion", a pervasive religion that legitimates the overall social order.

[It] also illustrates a basic Protestant tendency, which is the cumulative character of legitimation whatever the logical contradictions of the component parts. In America enlightenment and evangelicalism colluded whereas in France enlightenment and Catholicism collided. But then, of course, the American banner was unfurled against foreign rule not against internal reaction (*o.c.*: 29).

The emergence of a civil religion is certainly not to be explained by a different formal relationship between church and state, for the continuity of the church-state relationship in England and Scandinavia neither prevented the established church from becoming "a *generalized* symbol of a religious presence in the state", nor impaired its contribution to societal legitimation. The latter is, however, rather exiguous and based on a "generalized historical nostalgia" (*o.c.*: 70-71).

### *Catholic Organic Monopoly* versus *Protestant Individualistic Pluralism*

Other differences between the USA, the prototype of Protestant pluralism, and Catholic societies, considered as examples of organic monopoly, are to be found in the sphere of politics, associations for work and labor, and the network of voluntary associations.

"In the United States religion is the matrix and dominant frame of political utopia and it provides the mirrors in which each emerging group envisages its new social self" (*o.c.*: 62). There is no sequence from religion to politics as there is in Catholic societies. Thus, in America,

The Baptists provide the framework of emergent black awareness, first passively and then actively; the Civil Rights Movement took up this activity and translated it into pressure group politics, but without emptying the churches or eliminating their role. [...] Moreover there is a level of cultural sensitivity about morals, and manners which is always likely to be grounded in a religious frame of reference. [... E.g.] The symbolic crusades against alcohol [...], and the antipornographic campaign [...]. And just as cultural defence has a religious face so too utopia acquires religious expression [... E.g.] the Oneida Community [...] or the Jesus communes... (*o.c.*: 62-63).

In Catholic societies, on the other hand,

Certain kinds of millenarian expectation and communal experimentation certainly occur but in the end these are mostly subsumed under the banner of militant secular politics and ideological dogma. [See for example Dobbelaere and Billiet, 1976: 243-246]. Each emergent group eventually picks up the secularist masks constructed by the metropolitan intelligentsia and moulded for use by secular oligarchies leading the non-catholic labour unions (*o.c.*: 63).

The difference is that in the first category "The range of religious masks on offer allowed each new social face to find a religious persona"; in the opposite category "an all-englobing single religion cannot provide enough varying masks for the newly emerging social faces to wear" (*o.c.*: 62 and 63).

A further difference in the political field and also in the sphere of work and labor is that in the USA no party nor union can claim to represent religion, since religion as such is not an issue and religious people are found at most points of the political spectrum. The same holds for Great Britain and Scandinavia, although members of a particular religion may tend to favor a particular party, and unions draw their leaders differentially from particular denominations (*o.c.*: 73). In contemporary Catholic countries, we may observe a delayed differentiation: relative withdrawal of the Church from involvement in parties claiming to be Christian. The Church also wishes to dissociate from governmental corruption, *e.g. Democrazia Christiana*, and such controversial issues as divorce, education etc. come to be considered matters of the Church's internal discipline or arenas of compromise (*o.c.*: 75). In Catholic countries today, the Church itself has quite often set in motion a process of differentiation from specific political parties and unions.

As far as the network of voluntary associations is concerned, the American churches constitute the major context of association, and this, according to Martin, "by virtue of their subcultural adaptability and ethnic role" (*o.c.*: 75). In Catholic countries, a visible confessional system is built up, which results in pillarization: the rival pillars being Catholic and secularist. And, according to Martin, "there is [also] a tendency for these to have political functions" (*o.c.*: 76).

The discussion of the subcultural adaptability and the ethnic role of America's denominations introduces the problem of cultural differentiation. Martin considers several categories of religio-cultural identity, and, searching for what governs the degree of vigor and pertinacity exhibited by religion in relation to sub-culture (*o.c*: 77-81), he advances a sociological conclusion. The key element, he contends, in the unity of religion and sub-cultural identity is the relationship of centre to periphery.

This relationship runs along a continuum from metropolitan dominance to genuine bi-polarity. Wherever an alternative pole of consciousness exists, whether massive or marginal, religion is likely to be incorporated as part of its system of defence and may perhaps be the sole source of that defence. The chances of a successful resistance are increased wherever there is historical and geographical peculiarity, a distinctive language and mythology. Where the Centre is perceived as according inadequate respect [to the periphery] and where this is supplemented by a real or plausible economic exploitation then there is a further strengthening of resistance. If an enclave of the majority or of a different minority intrudes within the periphery then consciousness of local kind may be further accentuated. Indeed if such an intrusive enclave should be relatively secular or of a different faith and disposed to monopolize certain urban occupations, the rest of the locality and social structure will embrace religion with redoubled fervour. The political tone of the religio-cultural resistance will in part depend on the perceived political tone of the dominating or oppressive alien centre, as well as on the occupational structure of the region concerned. The achievement of political autonomy or cultural recognition may eventually slacken the tide of local awareness, including its religious component, more especially where social and geographical mobility and shared media weaken the sense of difference and of deprivation. The important underlying point with respect to religion and secularization is that religious practice will in part reflect the constellation of factors just referred to. It is these factors which accentuate the union of religion and culture or grant free passage to the process of differentiation (*o.c.*: 82).

## Duopoly or the Mixed Pattern

Having discussed "Protestant individualistic pluralism" on the one hand, and "Catholic organic monopoly" on the other, and having introduced the impact of ethnicity, I turn briefly to Martin's "mixed pattern or duopoly".

The "mixed" cultures exemplify what Martin calls a "beneficent spiral" as opposed to the "vicious circle". In this case, the spirals of internal hostility and of mutually antagonistic and self-reinforcing definitions that occur in Catholic cultures do not begin, or at any rate are mitigated. This beneficent spiral may be attributed to the appearance of the Catholic Church on the centre-left, and it then assists in stabilizing the political sphere and in removing the issue of religion *as such* from the arena of confrontation. In fact, it breaks up the image of a unified politico-religious conservatism. This political stance derives from a situation of partial exclusion that is suffered by the religious community as such (*o.c.*: 50-51). Another element that promotes the beneficent spiral is the inherently "federal" structure of these "60-40" countries. According to the empirical cases Martin presents, "centralization creates a vigorous disunity in which religion as such is an issue and federalism creates a moderate unity in which religion as such is not an issue" (*o.c.*:

50). Finally, the issue of education also suggests another element helpful to the beneficent spiral: changing alliances.

> The basic tendency of "mixed" cultures is towards a liberalized élite centre and to sub-cultural integrations both posed against it and in intermittent alliance with it. A large Catholic sub-culture lies to the centre left with a particular regional redoubt, while an orthodox Protestant sub-culture lies to the right, maybe also with some territorial concentration (*o.c.*: 52).

The best examples are Germany, Switzerland, and especially Holland (*o.c.*: 168-208). Religious parties and unions are typical of the "mixed pattern": each confessional nexus gathers around it a complete voluntary associational system, and most particularly, an educational system. Even the mass-media are pillarized. Pillarization begins in the minority culture, but the need for it is obviated if religious groups live in large, near-homogeneous areas, constituting something close to regional segregation (*o.c.*: 201).

### Catholic Exceptions

Pillarization is typical not only of the "mixed" pattern, but also of the category of Catholic exceptions, *e.g.* Belgium and Austria (*o.c.*: 42-43, and 126-128). Belgium is an exception to "monopolistic organicism" because, on the one hand, Catholic and liberal forces initially had to fight a common "foreign" enemy and to structure the country once it emerged, and on the other hand, there were sub-cultural differences including the fact that Flanders was, until recently, economically depressed in comparison with Wallonia. The relative economic deprivation expressed itself in religious and linguistic terms. Flanders was forced back on a sharper identification with Catholicism since Wallonia was French-speaking and French was associated with secularism. The crucial issue between "Catholics" and "secularists" was education, and the first "school war" (1879) resulted in the formation of a complete Catholic school system, from kindergarten to university. This school system is the cornerstone of pillarized Belgium (Billiet, 1973; Billiet, 1977; Billiet and Dobbelaere, 1976, Dobbelaere, 1979b; and Voyé, 1979).

Martin's (1978: 189) evaluation of the pillar system is correct:

> The stability of such a system when contrasted with the centralization, polarization and instability of France is very clear. Neither generation gap nor female emancipation have disrupted this stability. There is not even the dichotomy presented by the Walloons and the Flemish in Belgian society. As in America the political parties, especially the religious one, have taken up conflict *internally*. And like those who reject the caste system in India, the Liberals and Socialists by virtue of their rejection of pillarization only build yet another pillar. Because socio-economic and religious matters criss-cross

they confuse the issues and assist stability and this is further assisted by an element also traditional in England: civility and the tradition of public order-liness.

## Secular Monopolies

Finally, we turn to monopolies of the left and right (*o.c.*: 209-243 and 244-277). Patterns of secular monopoly are found in the statist societies of the left where the church tries to resist differentiation, "which the state pushes forward with 'unnatural' speed". The basic impulse of such societies is to ideological monopoly. Here the state endeavours to replace religion by politics, and the churches are at the mercy of secularist elites. They control formal education in the service of the regime, and use the power of appointment and subvention to make the churches

> Agents of control and also simultaneously deprive [them] of all autonomous efficacy. [...] The only checks on power are those deriving from the paradox that total control breeds heterodox movements which escape the net of over-sight and control. [...] Any church associated with a dissident national sub-culture will bear the brunt of administrative pressure, as for example, Ca-tholicism in Lithuania. Thus the Church becomes a modern guardian of cul-tural integrity as well as of individual psychic space (*o.c.*: 47-48).

A factor that also comes into the picture but that does not weaken the basic impulses of statist societies of the left is the historic unity and identity of the state. If the state, as in Poland and Romania,

> [E]xperiences a pressure against its historic unity and identity it will lean on the church to help resist that pressure even though state and church are ideo-logically opposed. [...] A society which *per contra* experiences *disunity* on account of religion will seek to control and weaken it (*e.g.* Yugoslavia, Al-bania) and so too will a society whose religion has been historically cut off from its national myth (*e.g.* Czech Lands) (*o.c.*: 48).

## Monopolies of the Right

In the statist societies of the right we encounter again the "Catholic pattern", but with the special characteristics found where a pressured Catholic right has succeeded in taking over the reins of power for a time. The pattern found in the statist societies of the left is repeated inversely in the Catholic monopolies of the right, but here the Church itself partly initiates the movements towards differentiation from the pressure of authority, because the state desires to use the Church in so instrumental a manner, *e.g.* in education, that aspirations to autonomy are awakened. Furthermore, some

> Segments of the Church perceive that there is a cost for its own specific mission in being identified with authority and in representing cultural styles

alien to emerging social groups. [...] In addition the international shifts of the Catholic Church as a whole add new social and intellectual catalysts dissolving the unity of political right and the Church. The old split between Church and left now reproduces itself as a generation split within the Church itself. However, the Church remains in a quandary since liberalism is historically associated with anti-clericalism, and – more important – offers freedoms which totalitarian movements of the left attempt to utilize for their own purpose. Thus the Church has to edge its way out of the embrace of the right without eventually finding itself suppressed by the left (*o.c.*: 45-47).

## Conclusions

If I understand Martin correctly, the basic explanatory variable that promotes or curbs the societal secularization process is "monopolistic organicism" *versus* "individualistic pluralism".

In a monopolistic situation, religion *as such* is directly linked to the process of change and quite explicitly so in the political sphere. The organic character of Catholicism, then, gives rise to anti-clerical and even anti-religious expression, *e.g. laïcisme* in France. Here, there develops a process of manifest secularization of society, the process of laicization. A split develops over religion *per se* – legitimists and Catholics on one side and revolutionaries and laicists on the other – and engenders quasi-organic alternatives that reinforce the vicious circle. This "social schizophrenia is transferred to whatever other social fissures appear" – classes and regions – and is endlessly reproductive on regional and local levels, in families, and especially in the educational system. The "internal" violence of these competing "organicisms" can be checked only where the nation must unite against "external" domination or where a bipolar balance of forces rooted in another bipolarity is acute enough to threaten the system as a whole (*e.g.* Belgium).

In a system of complete pluralism, this vicious circle does not occur because religion is not an issue, since its organizational expressions adapt to status and ethnic differences. Cumulative legitimation allows a vague and general civil "religion" to emerge, and the institutional differentiation is quite different from the organicist case. In pluralist countries, no party or union can claim to represent religion, but in Catholic countries such parties and unions do exist, although the Church itself has quite often had to stimulate the process of differentiation. In both types, a network of voluntary associations emerges: in a pluralistic country such as the United States, these result from the sub-cultural and ethnic adaptability of religion; in Catholic countries, they try to insulate their members against anti-religious tendencies.

The monopolistic type is realized in its extreme form in the statist societies of the right, where we find the "Catholic pattern", and in the statist societies of the left, which represent the "inverted" pattern. The basic drive of the elites in these societies is to achieve an "ideological monopoly".

The "mixed pattern" or duopoly is an example of federalism. Federalism promotes a beneficent spiral as the "minority" church stabilizes the political sphere by appearing on the centre-left. Martin (1978: 57) also calls this type "segmented pluralism". Here "rival churches exist in territorial concentrations" and they give rise to "heavy sub-cultural integration" as well as to "confessional parties and unions, more especially in the subdominant Catholic sector". Pillarization is to a certain extent less developed in cases of ecological homogeneity. In between "complete pluralism", *i.e.* the USA, and "segmented pluralism" are countries typified as manifesting "qualified pluralism", *e.g.* Great Britain and the Scandinavian countries. Here "there is a partial association of a particular religious body with the élite and with social authority and this largely constricts active alternative religion to a sector of the upper working and lower middle class (*ibid.*).

It is clear from Martin's work that societal secularization is not a straightforward evolutionary process: it proceeds with ups and downs. He suggests that the underlying propositions are not always confirmed, depending on the particular socio-cultural complex within which they operate. For example, when discussing the organic church and the anti-organismic groups that fight it – *e.g.* secularist elites – or describing the conflicts between the Catholics and legitimists and the *laïcistes* and revolutionaries, he suggests that people in different social positions have different evaluations of both religion and the social situation in which it operates. Societal secularization must allow, of course, for adaptations on the part of those who have more or less grasped its development and the best manner of either channeling or nullifying it (Martin, 1978: 2). His book, more than others, suggests that individuals affect this process, although other sociologists have also considered, to some extent, the roles of groups and quasi-groups. In the next section I will bring people back into the process. In doing so, I want to counteract an impression that it is a mechanical process, something that *must happen,* which is often given by the literature on societal secularization cited in the previous section.

## *The Impact of People, Groups and Quasi-groups*

Berger suggests that the motif of ethical rationalization of Biblical religion was "carried" by both priestly and prophetic groups (1967: 120). Wilson (1969: 40-47) indicates the relationship between emerging new strata and denominationalism, *e.g.* townsmen and traders supported Calvinism, and within Methodism there arose the more respectable strata of the working classes in England. Luckmann (1967: 62-64) points out that the development of institutionally specialized religion was dependent upon the growth of bodies of experts. But, in discussing the emerging, institutionally non-specialized social form of religion, he stipulates the dominant themes in the sacred cosmos of modern industrial societies – individual autonomy, self-realization, self-expression, the mobility ethos, sexuality and familism – without mentioning the social categories that embody them (*o.c.*: 109-113). There is a reference, however, to the young and urban segments of the population who reject some themes available in the modern sacred cosmos, themes that can be traced to certain values of formerly dominant political and economic ideologies (*o.c.*: 108).

In spite of these hints concerning social categories and groups, the general focus of criticism that was developed by my colleagues and me while we were analyzing studies of secularization may be reiterated: too little attention has been paid to the question of just which people in just which social positions become the "sacralizers" or the "secularizers" in given situations (Dobbelaere, Billiet and Creyf, 1978: 97-98). More empirical work is needed to answer questions such as these: In what social situation does a social definition – such as the definition of religion itself or the definition of religious commitment – become problematic? What social categories, groups or quasi-groups are likely to challenge it, to change it, or to reinterpret it? What categories of people seek to sustain definitions that have already been formulated, and that are part of a received tradition? How does conflict about such issues as religious commitment and religious functions arise? This last question has been put by Lauwers (1974: 120):

> By what mechanisms do those who occupy different social positions attempt to put into effect their definitions of religion? Where and how well do they succeed? What other groups or quasi-groups are marginalized by this process, and how does this take place? How are conflicts between people in different social positions concerning the realization of their conception of religion resolved? What are the results of this realisation for the organisational patterns in which it takes place, as well as for other related social structures?

Martin takes up these questions in his book, *A General Theory of Secularization* and shows how secularist elites use education, mass communication, legal and administrative measures, discrimination against religious people, appointments and subsidies, to promote ideological orthodoxy in statist regimes of the left and to privatize religion (1978: 209-243), in other words how in such regimes laicization was achieved. He also analyses the particular power relationship between church and state in Poland and how "each side utilizes the existence of the other to maintain discipline in its own ranks" (*o.c.*: 210). The relative power of the state is clearly dependent upon, first, the historical links between religion and nationalism; second, the type of denomination – resistance to secularization varies by denomination (*o.c.*: 235-236); third, the fact that total control breeds heterodox movements especially with respect to less visible forms of individualistic religion, *e.g.* Baptism in Russia (*o.c.*: 23) and Pentecostalism in Bulgaria (*o.c.*: 224); fourth, the importance of a religious intelligentsia and lay organizations, *e.g.* in Poland (*o.c.*: 211 and 223). Analyzing Catholic monopolies of the right, he discusses among other elements the impacts of lay organizations, *e.g.* Opus Dei in Spain; the actions of many Catholics, especially amongst workers, students and members of the liberal professions who felt the need of a degree of independence from the State; and the generational conflict which occurs most markedly within the priesthood (*o.c.*: 244-264).

The centre-periphery relationship is discussed with respect to different types – especially the mixed type – and in his analysis of the impact of regional differences. The latter situation implies the study of party formation, changes in expressive politics "from the classic issues of Puritan control, like prohibition, to the post-industrial issues of self-expression" (*o.c.*: 67), and the impact of the expressive professions, especially in the mass media, which promote homogenization (*o.c.*: 61-69, and 86-87). "One of the major effects of [...] the communications media [...] is homogenization, so that recalcitrant peripheries converge on the norms of the centre. If then the centre, as in America, is favorable to religion then again the spiral of erosion is limited, but if not it is that much the more extended" (*o.c.*: 86). For the mixed cultures, Martin analyses the changing alliances, *e.g.* in the Netherlands between liberals, Catholics, and orthodox Calvinists; the emergence of pillarization; the historical alliance between bourgeoisie and aristocracy and its impact on the respect for elite values; and the stance of socialism towards religion and the churches (*o.c.*: 184-206). Reference to conflicts in Catholic countries is made when he analyses the impact of "intellectuals" and the position of laicists, legitimists, revolutionaries, Protestant denominations, and the Jews in the clash over religion.

It is clear from this summary that Martin has studied the different social groups involved in the spirals of hostility, the means they employed (*e.g.* pillarization and party formation), and the particular social situations that aggravated or alleviated conflict. Fenn also directs his attention to intergroup conflict over the issue of the boundary between the sacred and the secular. Various groups seek "either to expand or to contract the scope of the sacred in the pursuit of their own values and interests" (Fenn, 1978: viii). In other words, he argues "that individuals and groups are responsible for secularization: not impersonal or abstract forces like technology or education, but living and active human agents" (*o.c.*: xii).

He sets up a five-step theory of secularization (*o.c.*: 32-39):

*Step 1* – Differentiation of religious roles and institutions. Here religious and secular structures pull apart from each other.

*Step 2* – Demand for clarification of the boundary between religious and secular issues. Priesthoods are established and congregations gather, but the separation of religious and secular issues often takes longer than the separation of religious and secular structures.

*Step 3* – Development of generalized beliefs and values that transcend the potential conflict between the larger society and its component parts. Here he refers to the development of an overarching set of generalized religious and political symbols in a civil "religion", and to Sukarno's enunciation of Pantja Sila, the five general principles derived from the Hindu and Moslem cultures, that Sukarno used to foster the ideological integration of that society.

*Step 4* – Minority and idiosyncratic definitions-of-the-situation: groups and institutions, minorities and elites, struggle to extend or to limit the scope of the sacred in public life. Here he sees two contrary tendencies: on the one hand, the grounds of political authority are increasingly secularized; on the other hand, an increasing number of individuals and groups defend their rights on religious grounds.

*Step 5* – Separation of individual from corporate life. Here, too, he examines two contrary tendencies: the tendency towards privatization in which the sacred is contained in institutions of the private sphere; and the contrary tendency supplied by a religious culture that tends to expand the scope of the sacred to all areas of social life.

It is clear from this summary of his five-step model for analyzing the process of societal secularization that this process includes opposing tendencies and therefore is not irreversible. Fenn also makes it clear that the stages are seldom discrete but overlap (*o.c.*: xviii). "The dynamics of the process of secularization is supplied by opposing interest groups, ranging from sects to the state itself" (*o.c.*: 39). Since his focus is primarily American society, he limits his monograph to a detailed analysis of the last three steps.

Discussing the third step, Fenn criticizes Bellah's mythic conception of America, and conceives it rather in terms of opposing and cooperating individuals, groups, collectivities, and social categories (cf. *supra*). To the extent that people or groups are able to promote the view of America – or for that matter France – as a nation, civil "religion", or in my terminology a national ideology, is able to emerge and survive. Consequently, "civil religion" is the outcome of a conflict between people over definitions and ideologies. Fenn also points out that the use of religious symbols by officials arouses reactions from religious sects with deviant viewpoints and from individuals or groups engaged in a non-religious defense of their basic rights. This is the kind of struggle over the extension or restriction of the sacred in public life that emerges in the fourth stage.

In this "unstable and volatile stage" (*o.c.*: 54) groups and individuals challenge the nation on religious grounds, *i.e.* on the basis of sacred practices and values. They contest the grounds and limits of political authority in a process that strips away the religious elements of a nation's political ideology. As a result, the authority of the State is increasingly defined as resting on a secular base – cf. the verdict of the Supreme Court on the demand of the Jehovah's Witnesses to be exempted from the obligation to salute the flag – and limits are set on the authority of the State to act on religious issues and to circumscribe the activities of religious persons and groups, for example, with respect to conscientious objection. This is a step "forward" in the process of secularization; but it is also a step "backward". Indeed, an increasing number of individuals and groups – *e.g.* Mohammed Ali and Timothy Leary – enter claims to be taken seriously on religious grounds by other individuals, by their clients, by other religious groups, and by the state itself. Fenn (*o.c.*: 55) admits that he is

> Arguing a somewhat paradoxical thesis, *that the process of secularization increases the likelihood that various institutions and groups will base their claims to social authority on various religious grounds while it undermines the possibility for consensus on the meaning and location of the sacred.*

Most of these contests are fought out in the courts, and sectarian religious movements are primary factors in furthering this aspect of process of secularization (*o.c.*: 54-63). What is important for our discussion here is that Fenn makes it clear that he conceives societal secularization as a process that is the result of opposing interest groups and not of impersonal or abstract forces. Consequently, he suggests that the process is not irreversible, and indicates how in different phases it might be reversible. I shall return to this issue.

Fenn and Martin are very much concerned with the cultural and political context in which the secularization process unfolds. From his comparative perspective, Martin is able to indicate the impact of elements of the social situation such as "complete", "qualified" and "segmented" pluralism *versus* monopoly; the historical links between religion and the nation; and "external" dominance. Both he and Fenn are very explicit in referring to social actors and social means: the social actors being elites, religious groups (churches, sects and cults) and persons, *laïcistes* and clerics, legitimists and revolutionaries, people in the emerging social strata, social scientists, and members of the expressive professions; and the social means being, for example, associations and organizations, pillarization, political parties and changing alliances, education and mass media, legal and administrative measures such as subventions, appointments, and court orders. But it seems to me that the general theory of secularization is called "mechanical" when the processes of rationalization and *Vergesellschaftung* are at issue. These processes should also be related to persons and social categories. We need to focus our attention not only on societal and organizational secularization, but also on changes in the thinking and behavior of individuals to make clear that societal and organizational secularization is a process that is manifestly or latently set in motion by people, groups and quasi-groups. In recent studies of "pillar structures" in Belgium, the role of certain social categories in the process of organizational secularization was emphasized (Dobbelaere, Billiet and Creyf, 1978).

Different authors, especially Dutch historians, sociologists and editorialists, have argued that pillarization is linked to the emancipation processes of religious minorities, *i.e.* Catholics and orthodox neo-Calvinists. In Belgium, pillarization appears rather to have been a deliberate attempt to recover as much as possible of what was lost by the implementation of a liberal program of laicization, and the procedure for such recovery was the establishment of sub-structures, *i.e.* a multiplicity of organizations in which Catholics could be insulated from the secular or laic environment. Pillarization here was a defensive reaction and a typical process of segmented differentiation. It emerged in a context in which a separation was progressively being made – not only in principle but also structurally – between religion and other functional spheres, and to the extent that non-Catholics became a "fact", *i.e.* acquired real power to implement their views. In other words pillarization presupposes a process of laicization (Billiet, 1976: 247-248). This is very clear in the sphere of education in Belgium. The Catholic school system, which resulted from a de-laicization counter-movement, was only created after the liberals had seized power in 1878 and had put into effect the radical-liberal education program of laicization. This can be seen from the number of schools that were built and the increase of the Catholic school population from 13 per cent of the total school population in 1879 to 64 per cent in 1880 (Dobbelaere, Billiet and Creyf, 1978: 103-104).

In our study of some sub-structures of the Catholic pillar (the Catholic school system and the Catholic hospital system) we sought to evaluate to what extent the Catholic pillar was able to maintain a "Catholic state" within the secular Belgian state, in other words to what extent the de-secularization process was effective. Our hypothesis was that Church authorities and a Church elite, which had developed in the past an insulated Catholic pillar to perform such societal functions as socialization, the provision of information, health care, and social security, now sought to maintain it, but had failed in this effort. That they should have partly failed in our era of mass communication with television and radio invading the home with alternative ideas is easily understood. Our study, however, did not focus on this factor but rather on the process of organizational secularization resulting from specialization within the Catholic sub-systems – a process of change supported by lay professionals – as well as from diminished interest in religious and philosophical matters. Socio-economic and professional issues are considered to be more relevant to society, an attitude typical of young, university educated Catholics. Here, then, is the link with rationalization and *Vergesellschaftung*: the quasi-groups referred to are the carriers of these aspects of the organizational secularization process (Dobbelaere, Billiet and Creyf, 1978: 116-119; Dobbelaere, 1979a: 44-61; and Billiet and Dobbelaere, 1976: 283-289). Let us be more specific.

The consolidation of the pillar system ultimately required the professionalization of its role-players, which was also a state requirement. These professionals claimed a domain and defended it successfully against encroachment. What were the consequences of this in education and health care?

Our studies suggest that lay professionals (medical doctors, hospital managers, and teachers) with a professional rationale were the carriers of the secular tendencies. They determine the organizational structure of hospitals and schools. Christian hospitals, for example, are organized on the basis of differentiated and specialized services – *e.g.* the medical and pastoral – that function separately and develop according to their own rationale with their own trained personnel. There are very few exceptions to this mutual neutrality. Further, professionals marginalize religion even within the Catholic pillar. In Catholic schools, for example, religion is one class among others, taught by a special teacher; there are fewer religious services in the schools than previously; and the old custom of checking on pupils' attendance at Sunday mass has been abandoned. The professionals also reduce religion to the interpersonal level as a matter of private preference without overarching meaning. Appeal is made to the patient's individual freedom of religion, for example, in order to maintain private Catholic hospitals in competition with public ones. Meanwhile religion is privatized in such a way that, in the concrete activities of health care, it operates only on the inter-individual level. Christian values are so individualized that they no longer determine the concrete structures of the institution. The humane approach, that man and not the illness is the focal point of health care, is considered to be an important constitutional element of a Christian hospital. But it is regarded as something beyond the possibilities of formal organization, and staff restrictions, cost containment etc. are cited to justify a segmented and functional job-division in place of a total approach to the patient, which would require extensive, frequent, and sustained communication. Actual communication is segmented, formal, and authoritarian, because it is entirely determined by the medical rationale. Such a relationship is *gesellschaftlich*: the humane approach, on the contrary is *gemeinschaftlich*. Here we have clear examples of a latent process of organizational secularization: these professionals do not intend to secularize these Catholic organizations, but in professionalizing the services, organizational secularization occurs.

Professionalization is not only linked to the privatization of religion, the *Vergesellschaftung* of Christian organizations, and the marginalization of religion in separate and specialized services, but it may also conflict with traditional Christian values and ethics. In Catholic hospitals, medical doctors challenge the Catholic ethic by performing sterilizations, abortions etc. Social workers in Catholic organizations challenge the value of Catholic morality as a guideline for the solution of the specific problems with which they are confronted. More importantly, the Catholic school system, which is responsible for the socialization of the Catholic worldview and which is the cornerstone of the Catholic pillar, is challenged on the basis of pedagogical principles. The people, who support the professional rationale and take secularization for granted, are the professionals and, in general, young, university-educated Catholics who favor a re-alignment in the political and socio-economic field, *i.e.* a "progressive front" (Billiet, 1977: 45-47). They are opposed to the traditional mechanisms of problem solving in Belgian politics, which operates along ideological lines, *i.e.* through the pillar structure. Clearly, pillarization is not a permanent dike against secularization.

Other factors thought to be responsible for the decline in the strength of pillarization in Holland are "the integration of elites at the top of the system, the slow permeation downwards of objections by intellectuals to the system, and the successful conclusion of the emancipation process, making isolation unnecessary" (Martin, 1978: 190). Thurlings' analysis (1978: 170-181) is quite explicit about the last two points, especially the "crisis hypothesis". The "tottering" of the Catholic pillar was largely due to an internal threat, the crisis in the Catholic culture itself which started with the "nuclear" Catholics. Van Heek (1973: 205-257), on the other hand, stressed an external factor: "the permissive society", Dutch Catholics became disorganized under the pressure of the permissive society that surrounded them. In the second edition of his work, Thurlings (1978: 222) combined both hypotheses by suggesting that "nuclear" Catholics who were part of the elite, were the ones who were confronted the most by modern and reformatory theology and modern thought in general. Thurlings mentions other factors that helped to promote de-pillarization, but he does not elaborate on them: financial needs, which, for example, stimulated mergers in the world of the press; legal regulations, *e.g.* in the world of education; professionalization, *e.g.* in the social and medical sector; a greater self-confidence of Catholics, which stimulated open-mindedness; and an intensification of social and economic conflicts (*o.c.*: 224-225). Some of these factors are discussed in detail in our own studies.

The studies of Martin, Fenn, my colleagues and myself clearly demonstrate that secularization on the societal and organizational level is not a mechanical process to be imputed to impersonal and abstract forces. It is, on the one hand, carried out by people and groups who manifestly want to laicize society and its sub-structures. But, on the other hand, studies on professionalization in the Belgian Catholic pillar and of pillarization in the Netherlands also make it clear that certain social categories, if not explicitly, are secularizing the Catholic and Christian pillars. Once we have accepted that societal and organizational secularization is the result of opposing interest groups, then the outcome is clearly a non-linear process. The following studies have documented this.

## *Societal Secularization, De- and Re-Secularization*

Let me make it clear at this point, however, that I do not mean to imply that the secularization process is self-evident because certain professions are secularizing certain sub-systems within the religious pillars: there are also persons and groups who react, *e.g. Caritas Catholica* established an ethical commission to study bio-ethical problems in Catholic hospitals in Belgium. This commission maintains sub-commissions in pilot hospitals to advise the medical doctors of the teachings of the Church; to stimulate discussion on ethical problems; and to inform the bishops of the problems facing physicians, how they solve them, and on the basis of what principles. Reference might also be made to the Deontological Board established by the General Council of Catholic Education. Lay teachers in Belgian Catholic schools claim the right to a private life, but the General Council of Catholic Education reacted to the privatization of the out-of-school life of the staff members. It claimed that

> The staff member should be aware that this private life may have implications for his mission as an educator. [...] When a teacher's educational work is contradicted by an extra-scholastic life situation that openly contradicts the values that he or she is expected to demonstrate, a humane solution should be found with the knowledge and the assistance of the teacher concerned (Dobbelaere, 1979a: 53-54).

To this end, the Deontological Board was established. It is to be consulted if conflicts arise about "the specific obligations arising from the Christian orientation of the school" (*o.c.*: 54). Mention may also be made of Christian organizations for young adults where officers were compelled to resign for actions foreign to the Christian spirit of the organization. The outcome of such procedures largely depends, of course, on the influence and the power enjoyed by interest groups.

As Fenn has indicated, and as our studies confirm, the secularization process is not irreversible, there are contradictory tendencies. This is also what Archer and Vaughan (1970: 130-145) suggest by "secularization, desecularization and resecularization" in their study of educational systems. In the first place, they indicate that the prediction "about the decline of religious control over education and of its symbolic content" based on the logic of *rationalism* (Condorcet and Comte) and the logic of *industrialism* (Wilson and Parsons) is empirically not warranted. England and Germany "retained the religious control and the religious content of education after having developed an industrial economy", which is considered a manifestation of the diffusion of rationalism among the population and their enlightenment (Comte). On the other hand, France, which was outdistanced by England on a multiplicity of economic indices, had an educational system that "bore the characteristics attributed to industrial societies" (*o.c.*: 131-133). And secondly, the secondary proposition of the irreversibility of secularization cannot be sustained empirically. Counter-revolutions do produce de-secularization.

> While examples of a religious group regaining actual *control* over an educational system can be found, they do tend to be less frequent and further back in the past than cases where a religious *content* to instruction is reintroduced. [...] An almost classical example is the attempt of the English Utilitarians and the group they represented to legitimate the system of authority in industrial production by the incalculation of classical economic tenets in education. When this policy proved less than successful, Kay-Shuttleworth proposed the re-introduction of religion, with its concentration on a man's station in life, at the primary level. Thus, even if one were restricted to cases of supplementary legitimation where religious symbolism was reincorpo-

rated into secular instructions, this instance would be sufficient to indicate the possibility of institutional desecularization (*o.c.*: 139).

Berger's theory – contrary to the two previous types of theory is a prime example, according to Archer and Vaughan (*o.c.*: 144 and 135-137), of a theory that refers to the *interaction of structural and cultural factors*, at least "when discussing the causes of initial secularization: it succumbs to the logic of industrialism when discussing its continuation" and as such is susceptible to the same criticism about the so-called decisive trends in the secularization of education. De-secularization in Berger's view would be possible only if the course of industrialization were halted, and as the processes of Westernization and modernization have now become global, a reversal of these trends is, in practice, a "virtual impossibility". The possibility of de-secularization does not impair the central thesis of this theory. A comparison between counter-revolutions that reintroduced religion into education with those that did not allows Archer and Vaughan (*o.c.*: 140-143), preliminarily and roughly, "to specify the types of situations in which religion may be used once more to legitimate established *authority*":

(1) When the number of the "psychologically liberated" elite is small, it is easier to discredit them, and the existence of an alternative traditionalistic value system among the unenlightened and disadvantaged non-elite will provide not only a source of unity, but also a "rationale" by which the discrediting might be done.

(2) If there is a displacement of focal "concern" from the economic sphere to the political, as in times of political crisis and war, the reinforcement of value consensus is essential. Value-loaded instruction will then seek to ensure the solidarity of popular support.

> Although religious traditionalism has certainly no intrinsic superiority over secular ideology as a source for legitimizing opposition, it is more likely to be appealed to when (a) a "significant" portion of the population still holds to it [...]. (b) the policies of the secular power have demonstrably denied major tenets of the system of belief [...], and (c) the particular religious beliefs and practices are compatible with the secular political goals of the opposition or positively reinforce them (*o.c.*, 1970: 142).

(3) The closer the relationship between religion and national culture – religion being seen as the carrier, the *raison d'être* or the justifier of a culture – the more probable it is that it will be used as a source of legitimation and subsequently reintroduced in education. Other aspects of the form that religion takes are also important such as written *versus* oral traditions, hierarchically organized *versus* relatively undifferentiated structures, and the level of integration with the social structure. "it seems, then, that the complexity of the relationship between religion and the institutional variables that have been discussed pre-

cludes deterministic statements which assert the impossibility of desecularization" (*o.c.*: 143). The only theory that could accommodate this is Berger's, but the logic of industrialization fully persuades him to endorse the unavoidability of resecularization[1]. But Archer and Vaughan refer to Israel – a country, that they consider to have almost complete identification between culture, religion, and ethnicity – which has maintained a high level of economic, technical, and educational advance.

> It would seem [then], that one of the conditions stated as favourable to desecularization, namely extreme political crisis and particularly war, can often further a nation's economic and technical advance at the same time. Other things being equal, and other conditions specified being met; a society legitimated by tradition that was engaged in prolonged defensive or aggressive conflict would not be expected to undergo resecularization [...]. It could, of course, be argued that a decrease in political tension would favour resecularization, but both elements in the proposition remain at the hypothetical level (*o.c.*: 144).

It is clear from this study that variables other than industrialism and rationalism can influence the control and content of education. One of these is religion, varying with the forms that it takes, and its relationship to national culture.

## Theoretical Lines of Analysis

Looking back at the theories we have discussed, it seems to me that basically we have two variants of the secularization thesis: one, the Durkheimian approach which insists on the continuing importance of religion, of which Parsons and Bellah are prominent representatives; and another, in the line of Tönnies and Weber which insists on the diminishing impact of religion in societal life, with which I would identify Berger and Wilson. Luckmann combines both lines of analysis. It also seems to me that the dichotomous concepts used in the second approach give rise to some of the deficiencies and the one-sidedness of the theoretical analyses to which I have already alluded in the preceding section. Finally, I shall discuss some approaches to the process of societal secularization, which cannot be linked to the two main lines of analysis.

### *The Durkheimian Approach*

Sociologists in this line work with a functional – inclusive and nominal – definition of religion. They insist on the continuing importance of religion (Greeley) and oppose the idea of societal seculari-

---

[1]  It should be noted that Berger has revised his theory; we will come back to it in the second part of this book.

zation by pointing to the institutionalization of Christian values in modern society (Parsons) or to the emergence of a Civil religion (Parsons and Bella). My criticism of this type of definition has already been given (cf. *supra*) and also my opposition to Greeley's self-fulfilling prophecy. As far as Parsons' interpretation is concerned, the question is of course: What Christian values are institutionalized in modern society? His writings do not offer an answer. He simply states that a pattern of toleration, typical of the "denominational phase" in Christianity, "could not prevail were the secular part of the system regarded as radically evil", and he suggests "that in a whole variety of respects modern society is more in accord with Christian values than its forebears have been" (Parsons, 1967: 65) without specifying the "whole variety of respects" and "the Christian values" he is talking about. In conversation we had, he has referred to the "Protestant ethic" and "Christian love, particularly in the family". However, he states:

> This is of course very far from contending that the system of denominational pluralism is equally congenial to all theological positions or that all religious groups within the tradition can fit equally well into it. There are important strains particularly in relation to the Catholic Church, to Fundamental Protestant sects, to a lesser degree to very conservative Protestant church groups (especially Lutheran), and to the vestiges of really orthodox Judaism (*o.c.*: 63).

It seems to me that he underestimates the amount of religious dissent that is in opposition to the "world". The emerging new religious movements in their challenge to Western society also attest to its being far from religious and Christian ideals. My own contentions are, of course, no more fully demonstrated that his, but they do arise from inductions made fifteen years later. Bellah's studies tend to confirm my interpretation, at least as far as the Protestant ethic is concerned. In his evaluation of American society Bellah (1975: 157, italics mine) writes: "The dominant liberal utilitarian culture has been challenged many times but perhaps never by such an array of political and *religious alternatives*". It is this liberal utilitarianism that has evolved from the "nontotalistic social and political ideology of liberalism" and that has differentiated itself from "a basically pro-modern religious orientation", like ascetic Protestantism in the Anglo-Saxon culture (Bellah, 1970: 72 and 68). This is, it seems to me, the "iron cage" from which "the spirit of religious asceticism [...] has escaped", or a "worldly" and not a religious passion (Weber, 1958: 181).

Finally, reference was first made to civil religion when I presented the general value pattern that legitimates the wider variety of functions of the substructures (cf. *supra*). Discussing the differentiation process, Parsons suggests that it leads to an "adaptive upgrading": in the new structures, the primary functions are performed better, although the original structures undergo a loss of function.

First of all, how can we speak about the primary function or functions of religion? Different scholars give different religious functions such as salvation, integration, legitimation, comforting, challenging, providing meaning, identity and maturation. And how do we judge whether religion is now performing its function(s) better than hitherto? Who is to judge this? In addition, the "value pattern", according to Parsons, has to be general to legitimate the wider variety of functions of the substructures. Civil religion is just such a pluralistic religion-in-general (Parsons, 1974: 204-207; Martin 1978: 70). But such a religion is also more abstract, vague, indeterminate and feeble (Durkheim, 1964: 170-172). Parsons does not go into this problem. Durkheim does and according to him another type of solidarity must take over: "that which comes from the division of labour", *i.e.* organic solidarity (*o.c.*: 173). And here we are back at Wilson's and Fenn's argument that a religious basis to the normative order of modern industrial societies becomes less necessary (cf. *supra*), which means societal secularization after all.

Using a functional definition of religion as the transcendence of biological nature by the human organism, Luckmann (1967: 49, 101 and 108-114) also suggests the emergence of an invisible religion, an "institutionally nonspecialized social form of religion" of which he outlines the basic values.

> An important consequence of this situation [religion being defined as a "private affair"] is that the individual constructs not only his personal identity, but also his individual system of "ultimate" significance. [...] The "autonomous" consumer selects [...] certain religious themes from the available assortment and builds them into a somewhat precarious private system of "ultimate" significance (*o.c.*: 99 and 102).

This individual religiosity – of which the basic values according to Luckmann are "individual 'autonomy', self-expression, self-realization, the mobility ethos, sexuality and familism" (*o.c.*: 113) – extends Parsons "privatization of religion". In Parsons' view (1967: 62-63), the succeeding period of Christianity also resulted in a privatization or individualization of religion. In the denominational phase

> The individual is responsible not only for managing his own relation to God through faith *within* the ascribed framework of an established church, which is the Reformation position, but for choosing that framework itself, for deciding as a mature individual *what* to believe and *with whom* to associate himself in the organizational expression and reinforcement of his commitments. This is essentially the removal of the last vestige of coercive control over the individual in the religious sphere; he is endowed with full responsible autonomy.

84

Of course, individualization of religion also included "the freedom to abstain from formal religious participation" (Parsons, 1974: 203). But this participation is affirmed or rejected within an organization. According to Luckmann, (1967: 106) individuals build up an *institutional nonspecialized* social form of religion", supported by the family and groups evolving around the family, *e.g.* friends, neighbors, and cliques formed at work and around hobbies. As Luhmann states: "Die Sozialstruktur ist säkularisiert – nicht aber das Individuum" (1977: 172).

Individual religiosity was also predicted by Durkheim as a consequence of the collective religion becoming feebler, vaguer, more abstract and more indecisive (1964: 171-172). But according to him, this individual cult "would quickly weaken if it remained alone" (1965: 473). The weak structural basis of individual religiosity is also acknowledged by Luckmann. Indeed, the family, which is the most important catalyst of "private" universes of significance, has a relatively low degree of stability (1967: 106). This suggests a very weak plausibility structure for individual religion, and if this were what the future of religion depends upon, it might not survive. According to Durkheim (1965: 475), the future of religion will depend upon "those hours of creative effervescence" which our *societies* will know again, and

> [I]n the course of which new ideas arise and new formulae are found which serve for a while as a guide to humanity; and when these hours shall have been passed through once, men will spontaneously feel the need of reliving them from time to time in thought, that is to say, of keeping alive their memory by means of celebrations which regularly reproduce their fruits.

In this line of thought, we can conclude that the process of societal secularization will continue until such "hours of creative effervescence" occur.

## *The Weberian Approach*

I have just argued that in Luckmann's description of the "institutionally nonspecialized social form of religion" a secularization trend can be discerned. He himself is very explicit about the secularization process of the "institutionally specialized social form of religion" (churches, denominations and sects), which I have already discussed (cf. *supra*; and Luckmann, 1967: 79-106). In this analysis, he joins the line I linked to Weber and Tönnies, and uses, like the other representatives of this line, *a substantive definition* of religion based on the sacred cosmos, which is later carried by a special institution (*o.c.*: 61-62). What are the basic concepts of this line of theorizing?

We may sum up the juxtapositions used here to explain secularization as a process of societal secularization in three central concepts:

community/society, rational/emotional, and private/public. The dichoto-my *community/society* refers to types of interaction. In the community, social interactions are based on face-to-face relationships to known people, and these relationships are stable, total and affective. The hori-zontal and vertical bonds are strong, and they are regulated by moral habits that are based on traditional values and that are religiously sanc-tioned. In society, conversely, the social interactions occur between unknown, mobile role-players. Their relationships are utilitarian, for-mal, and contractual and are regulated by secular law. Social control is instrumental and technical. Anomie and class relationships, according to Martin, are prevalent. Conflict is contained by legal routines (Cf. Tönnies, 1963: 33-102). Once contractual relations occur, a *rational orientation* is present. Rationality implies that humans assess the em-pirical world in rational terms: actions and situations are thought to be controllable and calculable; and are conceived in terms of ends and means, which involves a calculation of costs and gains. In contrast, a magical-religious orientation implies a belief in the possibility of ma-nipulating the empirical world by extra-empirical or supra-natural means. Humans consider the social and physical world as determined by non-empirical forces and beings. Their attitude towards the empirical world is *emotional* (cf. Weber, 1973: 317). Luckmann does not oppose so much community and society, as the *private* and the *public* sphere, and Berger also uses these categories. The private sphere is "not yet pre-empted by the jurisdictional claims of 'secular' institutions". The public sphere contains segmented institutions that "became increasingly spe-cialized in their functions at the same time that the organization of the institutional areas became increasingly 'rational'" (Luckmann, 1967: 86 and 95). Weber's notion of rationality is sometimes combined with the dichotomy community/society, *e.g.* Wilson – which resembles Tönnies typology of *Gemeinschaft-Gesellschaft*, or is linked to the dichotomy private/public. If this evaluation is confirmed, then I would agree with Luckmann (1977: 17) that "most recent 'theories' of secularization are little more than reproductions and recombinations of earlier 'grand theories'".

A few questions are appropriate with regard to the three dichotomies and the fact that the theory states that religion is excluded from the rational sphere, be it in "society" or in the "public" institutions. First, to what extent can we maintain that the community and religion are non-rational, and, can we maintain that the public sphere is rational and the private not? Second, as the theory now stands are not these concepts too mechanical? Weber's notion of *Vergesellschaftung*, however, implies action, and allows an analysis in terms of social action. Third, is the distinction between the private and the public sphere not a social definition and does not that distinction differ according to social categories? Fourth, are the trends described irreversible?

### About the "Non-rationality" of Community, the Private Sphere and Religion

It should be pointed out that various theories of secularization and rationalization do not give sufficient attention to Weber's distinction between goal-oriented action or functionally rational action (*Zweck-rationalität*) and value-oriented action (*Wertrationalität*). It is clear that organizations are based on goal-oriented action, whilst religion remains essentially value-oriented. Therefore, religion cannot be reduced to non-rational action. The non-rationality of the religions based on revelation was put forward in the Enlightenment, and this view has been adopted by sociology under the influence of Montesquieu, Rousseau and Comte (with the law of the basic stages of progress: from a theological, via a metaphysical, towards a positivistic understanding of the world). Furthermore, it may be pointed out that *Zweckrationalität* has developed from religion (Weber, 1958) and, although from the point of view of functional rationality value-oriented action is always irrational (Lemmen, 1977: 42), such goal-oriented action is invariably based on at least implicit value options (Weber, 1964: 44-45; Lemmen, 1977: 45-46; and Lauwers, 1974: 78). In extreme cases efficiency and expediency become the core values. As a result, the evaluation of rationality will in the last resort depend upon one's values and consequently be relative. If categories of persons differ in value-orientation, they will see each other's actions as "non-rational" from their own point of view.

As a consequence, religion, on the one hand, and bureaucracy and industry on the other, are both "rational", but the latter becomes more and more functionally rational, while religion does not. The same can be said about Luckmann's opposition between the public and the private sphere. The public sphere is goal-oriented and consequently functionally rational. The private sphere is also "rationally" organized, but according to different principles.

The community-type organizations of the primitive and pre-modern societies relative to the *Gesellschaftlichkeit* of modern societies are not "non-rational", but, simply, non-functionally rational. They do not have a "public" goal-oriented sphere. But, as the bulk of cultural and social anthropology would attest, their "classification systems, taxonomies, and mythologies (early as well as classical) which are important elements in the organization of community life and of kinship bonds evidently have a logic" (Luckmann, 1976: 278).

### *"Vergesellschaftung" or Societalization*

Thus far it has been suggested that modern society is becoming more and more functionally rational and that there is less and less room for community relationships. This process is best described, I think, by Weber's notion of Vergesellschaftung (1973: 114-125) or Wilson's concept of societalization (1976a: 265-266) which express a process of decline of community. As was demonstrated in our study of the Christian pillar in Belgium, professionals organize the bureaucratic system according to their own rationales. The process of growing specialization determines the social structure of schools and hospitals: the classes are given by subject masters, and hospitals are organized in line with specialized medical services. In order to hire these subject masters the schools need sufficient students and so the schools grow; and to provide the specialized medical services with specialized personnel and up-to-date equipment hospitals need a large number of beds and so they also grow. Both schools and hospitals become mammoth like, and social interaction becomes more and more segmented, formal, utilitarian, hierarchical and shallow, to wit secondary or *gesellschaftlich*. In other terms, the professionals – *e.g.* medical doctors, economists, administrators and specialized teachers – *societalize* the schools and hospitals, as other professionals societalize industry and public administration. The decline of the community, the breaking of the bonds, is not a mechanical process, it is activated by people in powerful social positions, in particular the professionals.

### *The "Social Definition" of the Private and Public Sphere*

Now we come to the third question: do we have to consider that the public and the private sphere have evolved as the result of a mechanical process, or is it also the result of social action and social definitions? The opposition private/public refers, according to Luckmann, to the fact that in the public realm – the more or less autonomous economic and political institutions – the roles are determined by "secular" norms, which become increasingly functionally rational. These primary public institutions, in contrast with traditional societies, no longer contribute significantly to the formation of the individual consciousness and personality. Personal identity becomes essentially a private phenomenon.

> Institutional segmentation left wide areas in the life of the individual unstructured and the overarching biographical context of significance undetermined. From the interstices of the social structure that resulted from institutional segmentation emerged what may be called a "private sphere". The "liberalization" of individual consciousness from the social structure and the "freedom" in the "private sphere" provide the basis for the somewhat illu-

sory sense of autonomy which characterizes the typical person in modern society (Luckmann, 1967: 97; also Luckmann, 1980: 203).

And the relevance of specifically religious norms is restricted to domains that are not yet pre-empted by the jurisdictional claims of "secular" institutions, which is the "private sphere" (Luckmann, 1967: 86). This private religiosity is, according to Berger (1967: 133),

[L]imited to specific enclaves of social life that may be effectively segregated from the secularized sectors of modern society. The values pertaining to private religiosity are, typically, irrelevant to institutional contexts other than the private sphere. [...] It is not difficult to see that such segregation of religion within the private sphere is quite "functional" for the maintenance of the highly rationalized order of modern economic and political institutions.

Berger's suggestion of the functionality of the segregation of religion within the "private" sphere for the "public" sphere conveys the idea that this process is not mechanical but a consequence of social definitions and social actions.

At this point I cannot go into a detailed study of the rise and use of the concepts "private" and "public" (see *e.g.* Zaretsky, 1976: 56-77). In primitive cultures and in the feudal period, privacy and a private sphere were unknown (Luckmann, 1980: 203). One of the roots of the notion can be traced to a rule in British common law which became a proverb: "a man's home is his castle". It expresses the desire to protect wife, children and property from the king: "the rain may enter, but the King of England may not enter" (William Pitt). As a consequence of the Reformation and denominationalism religion was privatized, and the thinkers of the Enlightenment wanted to free the individual from "superstitions" and "prejudice" *and* from the authorities who supported them, especially the Church. In the private sphere, the person became increasingly free to structure his family life and to choose his own beliefs. The public sphere, by contrast, is well-organized; the individual has to take up given roles, with his usefulness becoming a central criterion of public judgment. But this public sphere is also the result of options and constructions. The type of political and economic systems in which we live were, and are, continually determined by options taken by people in power. And as we have seen in our previous discussions, in several countries the relationships between religion and politics are still in flux. In addition, it appears that conflicts resulting from attempts to expand the impact of the public sphere and to protect the private sphere are going on at different levels. From these we might gain a better understanding of the ongoing secularization process and of the parties involved.

Of the major institutions, two make up the "public" sphere – the polity and the economy – and two the "private" sphere – the family and religion. In several countries, the other major institution, education, is still the object of continual political struggle. Conflict over the rights and duties of the State to organize education and the rights of private bodies such as churches to do the same has, in some countries, resulted in a public or state school system, *and* a private religious educational system. The control over education, the content of the curriculum, the inclusion or exclusion of religion in state schools, and the rights and duties of both systems remain persistent political issues that depend on the socio-cultural and religious situation (Martin, 1978). Is education to be functionally rational for the public sphere or also related to the private sphere and its values? Who conducts this conflict, how does it evolve, and how is it resolved? These problems indicate the necessity of analyzing the composition of the parties involved and the way in which such conflict unfolds. Janowitz (1976) underscores the need to adapt the welfare sector to the community level, "to construct entities that would combine a geographic base with ethnic, racial, and religious, or just local, sentiments". He goes on to suggest that private effort is an essential part of the welfare system, and that the approach of the public sector is one of specialization, organized along functional lines. He mentions the typical tensions we have discussed: public *versus* private; specialization, fragmentation and societalization *versus* social and personal needs; community *versus* client participation; and he looks for links between the public and private social welfare institutions at the local and national level (*o.c.*: 126-133). Here again there is the obvious need to study the potential for secularization, and especially the possibility of adaptation involving functional differentiation: "Private welfare agencies are designed to perform services that the public agencies are unable to perform, to maintain higher standards of performance, and to carry out experimental programs", according to Janowitz (*o.c.*: 130 and 128).

Similar tensions and conflicts occur in the cultural sector, youth work, adult programs etc. Here the private sector, which in practice quite often means the churches, and the public sector compete with each other, and this allows us to study those who are involved and their leadership, their interests, the means they employ, and the forms of adaptation etc.

Discussing what he calls, "the pecuniary paradigm of utility", Gouldner (1971: 75-76) states:

> To the degree that a man's usefulness becomes a central criterion of public judgment, there is created a protected realm of privacy in which, we often say, his personal characteristic and his *personal* life are "no concern of ours". [...] As the occupational world becomes one of specialized experts

judged by their usefulness, we increasingly regard the traditional decencies only as private matters. [...] In trading virtue for freedom in private life we discover, however, that there is often less of both. There is less virtue [...]. And we have less freedom too, even in our private lives, because neither the Welfare State nor the private sector of the economy [what some call the "public" sphere] can permit this. The private sector, for example, wants to insure that the wives of its executives are of the right sort and will aid their husbands in their careers. The Welfare State, similarly, wants to he sure that the women for whom it provides "Aid to Dependent children" will not have further children out of wedlock, whom it will then have to support.

Gouldner is thus referring to the impact of the "public" sphere on the "private" sphere.

The family is the core of the "private" sphere, and this protected domain has become increasingly subject to the "public" sphere, *i.e.* governmental policies. Farber (1973), for example, indicates a shift from the "natural" to the "legal" family-model in family law in the USA. Some social scientists conceptualize the family as a nuclear (or conjugal) unit in which norms of interaction are governed by a set of universal functions (procreation and socialization of children, management of sex relations, and organization of the household economy). This sociological conception resembles closely the cultural model, which holds that the nuclear family is a "natural" entity, viable under all social conditions. In contrast, the alternative sociological conception envisages the family as a set of property rights and assumes that people exist as networks of relatives who have claims on one another; it then asks how people use these relatives (*o.c.*: 2-4). According to the first model, the natural or ascriptive nuclear family derives its authorization for existence "from a source outside the state – in religion, in the mystique of blood relationships, in the maintenance of estates, or in other sources of traditional values". Artificial family ties, by marriage or adoption, "in this context, are merely a creation of secular law and derive their legitimation from the state" (*o.c.*: 19). In the alternative model, the "legal" family model, the family is conceptualized as a mere legal entity: "since the only family relationships recognized are those in the law, the difference between natural and artificial family disappears. The state is then the only chartering agency for the legitimation of family relationships" (*o.c.*: 20). "The trends outlined [by Farber] [...] on marriage, adoption, illegitimacy, and inheritance law show the continual fading of the "natural" family as a cultural model in American society" (*o.c.*: 152). And,

[A]s the family in America has become liberated from the norms and functions associated with the natural-family paradigm, it has lost its status as a protected domain and has become increasingly subject to governmental policies governing educational and welfare activities, enforcement of criminal law, and economic stability. The legal-family paradigm heralds profound changes in modern family life which will be generated by the state in the course of its handling the vast array of problems facing it (*o.c.*: 157-158).

All these indicate the de-sacralization (see Becker, 1957) of the family, which in turn opens up possibilities for change since the family no longer rests on religion, "sacred" blood relationships, "traditional" values etc., and it opens the way for the rationalization of conjugal and family life.

The impact of the public sector on the family de-sacralizes it, but is this the only instance? A more functionally rational than moral approach to birth control (Wilson, 1979: 276), divorce and abortion, and today's stress on the technical aspects of eroticism, are other indications of a more secular approach *within* the so-called private sector, and especially the family. In several countries modifications have recently been made to legislation on birth control, divorce, and abortion, and elsewhere proposals for such modifications are being made by pressure groups. Whereas, until recently, these matters were usually exclusively sanctioned on the basis of moral and religious norms, attempts are now made to withdraw them from the sphere of religion, and to reduce these problems to their technical aspects, thus stimulating a functionally rational approach in this domain as well. Family planning is associated with a distinction, on the level of legitimation, between long-term intentions and short-term means. Discussion concerning divorce is no longer couched exclusively in terms of guilt but increasingly in terms of problem-solving. Thus, divorce becomes a means rather than an evil in itself. The facets of the family clearly require empirical study of real processes of change: role change, conflicts between groups, the wielding of power, the ideologies used etc., and such study would provide an opportunity to step out of a mechanical approach to the process of societal and organizational secularization.

Thus, not only does the "public" sector make inroads into the "private" sector, but the so-called private sector itself, and especially the family, becomes secular: a technical approach takes precedence over a moral one. This would suggest that the dichotomy "private/public" is not a fruitful sociological conceptualization. When we consider the so-called public sector to be secularized and the private not, we overlook tensions *between* particular institutions of both sectors – particularly between the polity and religion – and also processes of secularization *within* the so-called private sector. Should we, then, even use the terms "private" and "public"?

At least with respect to Catholic education in Belgium (cf. *supra*), those terms are social definitions used by social agents in conflict situations over the relationship between their so-called private life and their professional life. The social use of the terms, the different delineations of the "private" sphere by people in different social positions, and the interference of the "public" sphere in "private" life situation, and *vice versa*, are all instances in which we can study empirically the impact of processes like professionalization, specialization, segmentation, socie-talization and privatization and their secularizing potential. In so doing, we take into account that those processes are carried out by people, *i.e.* certain social categories, groups and quasi-groups. In sum, the "private" sector and the "public" sector are *socially* defined, they are continually in flux, and just what they constitute varies according to the social agents involved, the extension of leisure time, and the increase of per-missiveness. The so-called private sector is a social definition used by individuals and groups to protect aspects of their lives that they consider as professionally or civically irrelevant to authorities, *e.g.* their em-ployer or, in earlier times, the king. In such issues, religion can be part of the problem. Obviously, certain activities are not yet, or are only partially, incorporated into the so-called public sphere (*e.g.* education, welfare etc.). Other activities may never be so incorporated, and this may vary with the socio-cultural setting (Martin, 1978). Finally, the elaboration of a functionally rational approach is not limited to the "public" sphere: it has already made important inroads into the "pri-vate" sphere. These observations suggest that the conflicting aspects of the process of secularization might be particularly usefully studied in the cases suggested above and also that the use of the terms "private" and "public" should be the *object* of sociological inquiry, since these notions are social definitions and not sociological categories.

### Is the Process Irreversible?

Luckmann (1980: 204 and 206) underscores the "irrational auton-omy of the segmented and specialized social structure" (economy and polity), which seems to be subject to objective, functionally rational norms of economic-technological organization and development, in the face of which the individual feels a certain helplessness.

> In modern society we are faced with a curious reversal. Nature appears to be manageable rather than fateful, the social structure seems to have become unmanageable – a second nature. It can be seen today that we shall be obliged to revise the modern view of nature. But shall we be able to revise not only our *view* of society as a second nature (for that society is the result of human action, we do know after all), but also change what may have be-come a hard *fact*: that the modern social system has indeed become second nature? (*o.c.*: 206).

The "objective" economic and political institutions have only been challenged sporadically, *e.g.* in the late 1960s by the vociferous anti-institutionalism of the *jeunesse dorée* of the well-off industrial societies (*o.c.*: 203). Most people retreat into the "private", "free" spheres although, since the mid-1970s the functionally rational system has revealed its values and interests quite dramatically. As a result, people defend their "private" life against the functionally rational world. From the discussion of possible conflicts between the "private" and "public" sphere, it is clear that, depending on the balance of power, desecularization is a possibility. Archer's analysis also implies this (cf. *supra*), and Matthes suggests that in the late phase of industrialization the "private" sphere will gain importance as leisure-time increases. He refers here to new possibilities for primary groups (Matthes, 1967: 83). But we might also point to the commercialization of leisure-time activities, which is not at all favorable for the development of primary groups and primary relationships.

Sociologists of the family also describe trends in family life other than those already mentioned. The modern family is also highly privatized and couple-oriented, which emphasizes the importance of primary relationships in modern society (Dumon, 1977: 12-43 and 80-86). The parent-child relationship, inferred from an analysis of people's motives in deciding to have children by way of donor-insemination, and the evidence of a trend toward responsible parenthood, attest to the fact that children are more and more an internal family event (*o.c.*: 51-53 and 60-66). Children are evaluated with respect to the marital relationship and to the extent that they promote the chances of the development of the family as a group (*o.c.*: 81 and 62). This of course explains to a certain extent the need for birth control, and the functionally rational approach to having children. But, once they are part of the family, children also have an impact on the family, especially on the relationship of the family to organized religion. To explain the upsurge in church membership in America, Nash and Berger (1962: 91) formulated the hypothesis that it was "at least partly [due] to an increase in the number of children who enter the church *and* parents who follow", which was confirmed by other studies (Nash, 1968; and Hoge and Carroll, 1978). Children are sent to the churches because parents consider a religious education a necessary adjunct to the family in order to socialize them ethically (*e.g.*, Schreuder, 1962: 332-333 and Nash and Berger, 1962: 90). And for the church to perform its socializing function properly, parents feel that they, too, must commit themselves to it (*o.c.*: 90). So, it could be suggested that children are both a factor for secularization in the family as well as a factor for sacralization.

Of course, a certain affinity between the family and organized religion should also be stressed. "Of the principal institutions [...] the church is the only one to which people can commit themselves *en famille*" (*o.c.*: 90). "Salvation" and "love" demand very similar relationships. Religion offers "salvation" which is personal, total "an indivisible ultimate", unsusceptible to rational procedures or "cost efficiency criteria" and offered in a "community" (Wilson, 1976a: 266 and 269-274). Love is also considered to be personal, total, indivisible, and is offered in a community, but – contrary to salvation – aspects of functional rationality are introduced here: cost efficiency criteria are used to determine the number of children in relation to the promotion of marital happiness.

Families commit themselves *en famille* to organized religion, but love, unlike "salvation", has functionally rational aspects, and children, being a function of the marital relationship, sacralize and also secularize the family. The growing popularity of the ideal of marital happiness promotes secularizing attitudes in the family, but, on the other hand, the greater number of families being able to realize the social ideal of two to three children (Dumon, 1977: 63) is, if Nash, Berger, Hoge and Carroll are correct, sacralizing more families. In the family, the secularizing tendency is certainly not irreversible, at least during the child-rearing years.

Furthermore, it is not only the family sphere that attests to the importance of *gemeinschaftlich* relationships in modern society. These types of relationships are also highly valued in the service sector, which is very clear from the efforts to humanize hospital care (*e.g.* Deliège, 1978; Howard and Strauss, 1975; and Nuyens, 1971). Reacting against the existing professional relationships – which are functional, segmented, formal, authoritarian and brief – among doctors, nurses and other medical personnel, and especially with their patients, "bureaucratic" measures are paradoxically and ironically proposed and implemented to promote a more total approach to the patient, an approach that requires extensive, frequent, and sustained communication. Such a human approach is sometimes linked to a religious conception of caring for the sick: the institutionalization and effective realization of a *Christian* hospital (cf. *supra*; Rouleau, 1972; and Dobbelaere, Ghesquiere-Waelkens and Lauwers, 1975). Here we can speak of a process of re-sacralization. The relationship to the patient must be personal and total, which implies more than a somatic approach to the patient, and stresses the psychological, social and spiritual dimensions of the person.

We may conclude, then, that the chances of de-secularization of the economy and politics are very slim indeed. Outside the Western world, the Iranian revolution of 1979 offers us a counterexample, although the evaluation of what is going on there and of what the final outcome will be needs a longer time perspective. In the other institutions – the family and education – and in the service sector, a struggle is going on between the so-called private and public sectors, and between people advocating a functionally rational and those advocating a moral approach to problems. These oppositions attest to the possibility of a re-sacralization or de-secularization in those fields. Some of these measures are manifestly de-secularizing, *e.g.* when moral and religious norms are advocated; others are latently so, *e.g.* a humane approach to the sick offers more chance for the introduction of the spiritual dimension than does a technical approach. A study of such struggles would allow us more insight into the ongoing process of secularization and de-secularization and into the people and groups involved than the simple affirmation that the economy and politics are now secularized.

## Other Approaches to the Process of Societal Secularization

Outside the Weberian and Durkheimian approaches, I would like finally to discuss three other approaches to the process of secularization: Bell's cultural approach to religion, Luhmann's system-approach to secularization, and Matthes' pragmatically oriented interpretation scheme.

### Bell's Cultural Approach to Religion

Bell characterizes the secularization thesis as inadequate and misleading (1977: 419-449). Societies are disjunctive, he contends, and he sees a radical antagonism between the norms and structures of the techno-economic realm, the political system and culture. The process of rationalization in the economic sector reinforces secularization, the differentiation of institutional authority in the world. Thus, within the social system a process of secularization is at work: religions have authority "only over their followers, and not over any other section of the polity or society" (*o.c.*: 427). But apart from institutional change there is cultural change, and "there is no necessary, determinate shrinkage in the character and extent of beliefs" and the secularization process which has been taking place over the last 200 years (*o.c.*: 424-427). The dominant trend of disbelief occurring during this period Bell explains in terms of *profanation,* and this has, in his opinion, very different roots from those of the process of rationalization and secularization. Cultural change, of which this profanation consists, is based on, first, the demand for liberation, *i.e.* "to be free of all constraints"; second, the crossover from religion to the expressive arts in the problem of dealing with restraints on impulse, particularly of the demonic, and the elimination of boundaries: "the aesthetic is no longer subject to moral norms"; and, third, the decline of the belief in heaven and hell, and the coming to consciousness of nihilism (*o.c.*: 427 and 429-432). In the 19th and 20th centuries, culture, no longer tied in intellectual and expressive areas to the modalities of religious belief, took the lead in exploring alternatives to religion. Bell discerns five alternative responses to traditional religion: rationalism, existentialism, civil religion, aestheticism and political religion. The failure of the last two in particular has "opened up the beginnings of various searches for new, religious answers" (*o.c.*: 432-441). Bell goes on to suggest that three kinds of new religions will arise based on "the resurrection of Memory": *moralizing, redemptive,* and *mythic* religion (*o.c.*: 441-446). The ground of religion is, according to Bell, not regulative nor a property of human nature, but "existential: the awareness of men of their finiteness and the inexorable limits to their powers, and the consequent effort to find a coherent answer to reconcile them to that human condition" (*o.c.*: 447).

Bell defines religion functionally: "a set of coherent answers to the core existential questions", which are codified in a creedal form, celebrated in rituals and established in an institutional body (*o.c.*: 429). The changes in a religion can occur in any of these dimensions, but according to Bell the most crucial of all are the answers, since they go back to the common human predicaments that give rise to these responses. Bell is aware that his analysis rests on a study of high culture, in which religion was destroyed and which opened the way for a destruction in mass culture (*o.c.*: 442), but he does not confront the question of how this happened.

He is also aware that changes in culture "arise in reaction to changes in institutional life (to justify or to attack)"; and relate "to the changes in moral temper and sensibility, to expressive styles and modes of symbolization, to the destruction of old symbols and the creation of new ones". He limits himself, however, to the last level because changes in the character of religion "begin primarily at this second level" (*o.c.*: 428). This, of course, is an option that rests basically on his charge that sociologists of secularization start from the idea that the social structure and the culture are unified through "some inner principle of *zusammenhängen*" (*o.c.*: 424).

It is interesting, of course, to point out processes of profanation, but is it possible to analyze them and their impact without reference to the social structure? Bell himself relates the restructuration of new religions to social categories, *e.g.* moralizing religion will find its adherents among "the farmers, the lower-middle class, small town artisans, and the like" and redemptive religion will find them "in the intellectual and professional classes" (*o.c.*: 444). In the same way, an analysis of profanation without the incorporation of the study of social structure does not allow us to analyze the impact of "high culture" on "mass culture". The changes in the economy alone and the possibilities arising there from for the masses to come into contact with "high culture" and its vulgarization make this clear.

Wilson (1979) is absolutely correct in his rebuttal of Bell's criticism of secularization thinking. A sharp distinction between social structure and culture is untenable because the entire process of cultural activity, is very much affected by the values and norms of what Bell calls the institutional or public sphere, *e.g.* the instrumental values and the cost-efficiency criteria of the economic sphere. Wilson notes: "Far from being separate from the economic sphere, culture will be increasingly permeated by economic values, at the cost of all other intrinsic meanings" (*o.c.*: 273-274). But Bell does not see this, as he is only concerned with high culture and not with mass culture. His conception of culture is "too much of an agglomeration of cultural artefacts. It is too intellectual, and insufficiently emphasizes the prescriptions and proscriptions that constitute a range of shared collective evaluations" (*o.c.*: 274). And Wilson goes on to point out spheres in which structural changes have had an impact on regulative and moral aspects of religion (*o.c.*: 276-277): *e.g.* the moral issue of birth control is superseded by the technical solution, because the economic structure requires smaller families.

Bell's sharp division between social structure and culture is untenable. But the idea of studying the impact of elite culture on mass culture is challenging, and I hope that the larger work, of which his article is a *précis* (*o.c.*: 432), will meet that challenge.

## *Luhmann's System Approach to Religion*

Secularization according to Luhmann is a consequence of a change of the social system, called functional differentiation. This occurs when the religious system no longer presents itself to the individual primarily as *the* society but as a sub-system of society oriented towards a specific domain (1977: 227-228). As a sub-system, religion relates to society, the other sub-systems and itself. These relationships are called, respectively, the spiritual function, the ancillary function and theology.

The spiritual function is performed through a system of spiritual communications, which Luhmann calls "church" and which "makes available ultimate and fundamental reductions of complexity" or "solves contingencies". Religion offers fundamental laws for social life and makes sense out of seemingly senseless situations such as death, historical coincidences, and irregularities of nature and of human motivation (1977: 230 and 1972: 250-251). The central problem of this function is that the motives of private participants are no longer controlled by means of church membership. The church has to adapt to this, and it can offer possibilities, but it must realize that the results of its activities will be determined by the contingencies of the private lives of the people. Difficulties arise to the degree that spiritual communication is offered unsuccessfully and that the members of the church are marginal in society. As a result, the contingencies of consumption can have an impact on production: does the church have to adapt its message to enlarge its membership and to stimulate latent needs? In this way secularization could be a source of religious change. But, according to Luhmann (1977: 262-263), the chances are very slim, as the most important sub-systems – economy, politics, education and science – do not stimulate people to go to church, and the private sphere is too fragmented to allow religion to make a convincing synthesis of social life. On the other hand, religion is also quite different from the juridical subsystem, which intervenes only when there is a transgression of rules. Its own theological conception and its ethical orientation, which judges people as people, make it difficult for the church to realize itself if it may do so only in terms of ad hoc situations.

Hence it is understandable that the religious sub-system is more oriented towards secondary functions, and its spiritual function is reduced in favor of the ancillary function. The spiritual function is only relatively reduced, however, and not relinquished entirely, since it is still the crux of the church and that which gives it its identity. But the relative weakness of its spiritual function is compensated for by greater social activity. This is, according to Luhmann, the most important result of secularization (*o.c.*: 264). He corroborates the conclusions of our own research, namely, that the ancillary services have to adapt themselves to the wishes and norms of the clients and to the objective norms of the sector (cf. *supra*). As a result, the ancillary functions lose their specific religious character, and the question of what the specific religious character of these activities is leads to desperate confusion. In the end, the religious character of such activities is reduced to a readiness to do something, and the ancillary functions respond to the views and requirements of the environment (*o.c.*: 264-265). Luhmann finally suggests that theology should reflect upon this change from spiritual to ancillary functions, and should search for what secularization means for the identity of the religious sub-system (*o.c.*: 266).

In his analysis Luhmann also deals with the *Privatisierung* of religion, which he explains as a structural response to the problems of differentiation and inclusion. The functionally differentiated society breaks communal and hierarchical bonds. As a result, ascription becomes dysfunctional and each person has, in principle, equal access to functions, goods, and services – and also to the Holy – though not at the same time or in the same fashion. Total inclusion is of course impossible, because people are not all equally competent or have the same capacity to fill positions, so a professional structure emerged, which, in principle, provides everybody with one and only one profession. As a result, inclusion is only possible in *Komplementärrollen*, as a *Publikum*, *e.g.* as consumers, as the electorate, as students etc. In order functionally to differentiate these complementary roles in different "publics", role differentiation is necessary; otherwise functionally specific subsystems can neither emerge nor grow in society. Inclusion is only possible in function-specific systems. But is differentiation of complementary roles possible and can it be controlled? Luhmann suggests not, and therefore privatization of decisions becomes a functional equivalent. In other words, privatization emerges structurally as a consequence of functional differentiation and inclusion (*o.c.*: 232-240).

What is the impact of inclusion and privatization on the religious sub-system? (*o.c.*: 234 and 238-239). To what extent is a differentiation between clergy and laity acceptable? Is it possible to limit admission to the clergy on the basis of celibacy or gender? And is everyone eligible for salvation and on an equal basis? As far as privatization is concerned, this implies that belief becomes a private decision: previously unbelief was a private matter; now belief is. As a result, the institutionalization of consensus is forgone and can no longer be sanctioned as the truth. Consequently, dogmas and rites run the risk of degenerating into symbols. Moreover, religion becomes a leisure-time activity and liable to Gresham's law: activities of lesser value drive out activities of greater value. Today, obviously, the church has strong rivals in the competition for leisure-time.

Finally, I should like to discuss Luhmann's view on integration, which he conceives not as a problem of value integration, but rather, negatively, as "the avoidance of creating unsolvable problems in a subsystem as a consequence of actions in another sub-system". Integration is realized because all sub-systems are a structured inner-societal environment for each other, and not because they orient themselves toward shared meanings that are valid for all sub-systems (*o.c.*: 242-244). Consequently, self-governing and self-substituting sub-systems strive to specify their functions and relegate secondary functions to other specialized sub-systems. They are integrated in the societal environment by taking the other sub-systems into account, so there is no longer any need for an overarching sacred canopy. Religion then becomes a functional sub-system along with other specialized sub-systems (cf. *supra*; and *o.c.*: 244-247).

To the extent that secularization prompts the church to stress its ancillary functions, that it is not in a position to specify the religious character of these functions, and that such secondary functions are taken over by specialized sub-systems, it seems to me that religion as a self-governing and self-substituting subsystem has lost its future, especially as its primary function is reduced to being a private matter. Luhmann's approach does not contradict the major conclusions of the Weberian approach to secularization. But his way of thinking about self-governing and self-substituting sub-systems seems to eliminate people. I am inclined to stress, however, that people are the sacralizers or the de-sacralizers manifestly or latently, that they define the so-called private and the public world, and that they evaluate the consequences of the structuration of society, even though Luckmann warns us about the fact that the modern social system, and especially in the sphere of the economy and politics, has become a "second nature"; Weber had already spoken about the "iron cage".

Finally, I have one major question for Luhmann. Does he not, because of his implicit definition of religion and his conception of religion as a self-governing and self-substituting subsystem, reduce the religious sub-system to the churches? If so, how do sects relate to secularization? This is a question that will have to be taken up here, but before doing so, another approach to the secularization process needs to be analyzed.

## *Matthes' Pragmatically Oriented Interpretation Scheme*

In this section I have discussed from a social action perspective the theoretical lines of analysis used by sociologists in their study of societal secularization. I agree with Luckmann (1977: 17) that

> Secularization still denotes generally and vaguely a global process of transformation in religion and society [... I] t is a notion that has its roots in the common experience of an entire epoch: it is shaped by the need of the intellectuals to give a comprehensive account of the origins and of the essence of *their* time, of their unique place in history [...]. Although it has empirical points of reference [...] it is primarily a mythological account [a historical narrative that contains a number of fictitious elements] of the emergence of the modern world, a world that is felt to differ absolutely from what came before it.

But I do not quite follow Matthes and Lauwers, who, proceeding from the same evaluation, conceive the theory of secularization as a practical theory or an interpretation scheme that is pragmatically oriented (Matthes, 1967: 77 and 78), or as a social theory (Lauwers, 1974: 109). My reaction here would be to suggest a theoretical refinement of these theories and to make them amenable to historico-empirical verification, an approach akin to Glasner's (1977), although I agree that such theories can be used by certain groups or professions to further secularize some sectors of society.

Lauwers (1974: 109-110) conceives secularization theories as "social" theories, because they are ways of formulating and solving social problems, as was suggested by Matthes (1967: 84-85) who calls them practical theories or *Interpretamenten:*

> The secularization thesis seems to be a very elastic, historical interpretative scheme in which a multitude of experiences, of definitions of the situation, and of intentions are integrated into an explanatory system. Its extraordinary elasticity, its ability to unite controversial positions in one intellectual and interpretative vision, confers on this interpretative scheme a strong psychological cogency, and allows it to contribute to a continual confirmation and stabilization of the contexts which it explains.

This interpretation of social reality is multi-functional: it offers an epochal explanation of modern secularized society which has now become an "other", *i.e.* secular, reality by locating its origin in its Christian religious past. Second, it gives a description of and legitimation for the new autonomy and identity of society and sectors of society with respect to religion and church. Third, it explains causally the decrease in the number of church members and the decline of involvement in the churches on the basis of contemporary changes in the social structure of society, *i.e.* industrialization (with its functional rationality), mobility and urbanization which relegate religion and church to an irrelevant private structure. And, fourth, it offers to those who live in a ghetto of religion and church and to those who administer such a ghetto an identity as representatives of religion (*o.c.*: 77-84).

The validity of the secularization thesis and the value of its evidence lie, according to Matthes, in the fact that this interpretative scheme makes essential aspects of the socio-cultural changes of Western Christian society comprehensible and well-ordered for the different groups that are involved in it, and this in a double sense. On the one hand, certain facts and experiences, possibly loaded with diffuse and controversial evaluations, are brought together in a comprehensible framework, and, on the other hand, this framework offers room for widely divergent appeals for action and courses of action. The extraordinary multi-functionality of these interpretative schemes then becomes, in Matthes' view, very clear: it functions as a common frame of reference for those who are for, and for those who are against, secularization and it allows both to maintain and elaborate their controversial points of view within that common frame of reference. Furthermore, those who are neutral or indifferent are situated by reference to this polarized scheme of supporters and antagonists, who consider them as undecided or weaklings (*o.c.*: 85). Matthes concludes that such interpretative schemes are indispensable for the orientation of personal and social action as well as for the preparation of scientific hypotheses.

That such theories orient personal and social action is quite clear. Arguing from the secularization of society, young Belgian Catholic intellectuals opposed the separate Catholic and so-called neutral State school system, and advocated a new type of school to replace them: the "pluralistic community school". Here, pupils would be confronted with divergent views and stimulated to develop their own ideology. This is one possible attitude towards the secularization theories: to consider them as interpretative schemes used by participants as "social" theories that orientate their actions, and this is the perspective advocated by Lauwers (1974). In this option we would study how people use these theories to sacralize or secularize their society or aspects of it, how groups are mobilized, how communication takes place between leaders and followers etc. Secularization theories are then considered to be participant theories or ideologies. If this perspective is taken, sociological studies of ideologies might well be applied as models for the analysis of secularization theories.

The other option is the one advocated by Luckmann and considered to be a possibility by Matthes (1967: 87-88), although he seems very critical of its feasibility. This is the option adopted in this essay. First, the theories are stripped of their mechanical evolutionist implications: the secularization process is neither one-dimensional nor inevitable and varies in pace, incidence, and impact from place to place, depending upon such factors as the socio-cultural situation, the conflicting groups involved, and the impact of functional rationality on society and its different spheres. Second, use of "social" categories as "sociological" categories is rejected, because it obscures the sociological analysis and leaves certain institutional spheres outside the scope of secularization (*e.g.* the family) when it is situated in the sacred "private sphere". Indeed, the study of the family allows us to analyze empirically the *ongoing* processes of secularization and de-secularization. These processes can no longer be analyzed in economics except for studies of de-pillarization. Finally, to make empirical falsification possible, secularization theory must be cast in terms of clear concepts, must operationalize these concepts in a valid way, and must propose testable hypotheses. Replication will allow us to study structural and cultural differences between societies, and to evaluate the possibilities and limits of generalization.

It is clear that a process as complicated as secularization necessitates a high degree of caution. Simple explanations will not do, as Martin's complex categories show. And we should keep in mind Matthes' caveat about presenting an ideological interpretation as a scientific sociological analysis (1967: 88).

# CHAPTER 3

# Organizational Secularization

The decline and emergence of religious communities, changes in their organizational structure, and changes in beliefs, morals and rituals will be discussed here with regard to the functional differentiation of society and religion, the impact of religion on society or the process of societal secularization, the emergence of pluralism and civil religion, and the privatization of religion. First, I shall take up some ideas about religious evolution linked to individuation, privatization, differentiation, and argue that such processes should be considered not in terms of secularization but in terms of *organizational secularization*. Second, I shall discuss the relationship between organizational and societal secularization: What is the impact of religious pluralism on societal secularization? To what extent are the new religious movements to be considered indicators of secularization or of sacralization? And, how do the churches react to the processes of societal secularization?

## Religious Change and Organizational Secularization

I start with two studies of religious evolution, continue with a review of some studies on the evolution of religious organizations, and then link them to the problem of societal secularization.

### Bellah on Religious Evolution

In his detailed analysis of religious evolution, Bellah (1964: 373) sees a trend not towards indifference but towards individuation. He defines evolution at any system level as

> a process of increasing differentiation and complexity of organization which endows the organism, social system or whatever the unit in question may be, with greater capacity to adapt to its environment so that it is in some sense more autonomous relative to its environment than were its less complex ancestors (*o.c.*: 358).

He does not conceive of evolution as inevitable, irreversible or as a metaphysical phenomenon, but as "the simple empirical generalization that more complex forms develop from less complex forms and that the properties and possibilities of more complex forms differ from those of less complex forms" (*ibid.*). Religion is defined "as a set of symbolic forms and acts which relate man to the ultimate conditions of existence" (*o.c.*: 359). His scheme is based on several presuppositions: (1) that religious symbolization changes over time, *i.e.* becomes more differentiated and more comprehensive; (2) that conceptions of religious action, the nature of the religious actor, religious organization and the place of religion in society change in ways systematically related to religious symbolization; (3) that religious evolution is related to socio-cultural evolution; and (4) that stages can be represented in five ideal types – primitive, archaic, historic, early modern and modern – each having a temporal reference but only in a very general sense (*o.c.*: 360-361). For each stage, he examines the kind of religious symbol system involved, the forms of religious action, the type of religious organization and the social implications (*o.c.*: 361-374).

*Primitive* religion has a symbol system rooted in a mythical world that has two main features: it is to a very high degree related to the actual world and its structure is fluid and lacks precise definition. Religious action is characterized by identification, participation, and acting-out. It is ritual *par excellence,* and religious organization as a separate social structure does not exist. Socially, it reinforces tribal solidarity and serves to induct the young into the norms of tribal behavior.

*Archaic* religion has a mythical symbol system that is more objectified and conceived as actively involved in the world; the mythical beings become gods. The basic worldview is monistic: the world is one but hierarchically differentiated. Archaic religions tend to elaborate a vast cosmology in which all things divine and natural have a place. Religious action takes the form of cult with a much more definite distinction between men as subjects and gods as objects than in the primitive phase. Religious organization is still largely merged with other social structures, especially the functionally and hierarchically differentiated groups, which tend to have their own cult. The social implications are again Durkheimian: social conformity is at every point reinforced by religious sanction. But the notion of well-defined gods acting over and against men with a certain freedom introduces an element of openness. Through the problems posed by religious rationalization of political change new modes of religious thinking may open up.

The symbol systems of *historic* religions share the element of transcendentalism and are therefore dualistic. Religious concern now tends to focus on life after death, and salvation becomes the central religious preoccupation. Through the simplification of myth, historic religions represent a great "demythologization" relative to archaic religions. Religious action is above all the action necessary for salvation, and there emerges a clearly structured conception of the self. Religious organization is characterized by the emergence of a religious elite differentiated from the political elite, and on the level of the masses the distinction arises between the roles of believer and political subject. As a consequence, the probability of tension and conflict increases in the social sphere.

*Early modern* religious symbolism concentrates on the direct relation between the individual and transcendent reality. Religious action is now conceived to be identical with the whole of life, and salvation is not to be found in any kind of withdrawal from the world but in the midst of worldly activities. Stress is laid on internal qualities of the person rather than on particular acts clearly marked as "religious". The hierarchical structuring of both this and the other world as an essential dimension of the religious symbol system is abandoned. Hierarchy as an essential dimension of religious organization is also relinquished and replaced by a two class division between the elect and reprobates. The social implications are very complex and are among the more controversial subjects of contemporary social science, *e.g.* the controversy over the link between Protestantism and Capitalism.

*Modern religion*'s symbol system is "infinitely multiplex", and religious action in the world becomes more demanding than ever. "The search for adequate standards of action, which is at the same time a search for personal maturity and social relevance, is in itself the heart of the modern quest for salvation, if I may divest that word of its dualistic associations" (*o.c.*: 373). The symbolization of man's relation to the ultimate conditions of his existence, which Bellah defines as the great problem of religion, is no longer the monopoly of groups explicitly labeled religious – each individual must work out his own ultimate solutions. The most religious organizations can do is to provide the individual with a favorable environment for doing so without imposing a prefabricated set of answers. But in the modern situation, answers to religious questions can also be validly sought in various spheres of "secular" art and thought. The main social implication of the modern religious system as seen by Bellah, is that culture and personality themselves have come to be viewed as endlessly revisable. Thus the situation can be viewed as one offering unprecedented opportunities for creative innovation in every sphere of human action.

## Critical Reflections

Bellah concedes that a general theory of social evolution remains largely implicit in his scheme. Basically his theory is a "natural history of the aspects of religiosity which he has chosen" (Glasner, 1977: 31). Some authors even question the scientific validity of Bellah's analysis, and suggest that it is more an idealization of Protestantism fitting his own intellectual wishes and requirements (Drehsen and Kehrer, 1975:

194). Döbert contests Bellah's conception of the Protestant Reformation as a new stadium in evolution, namely, early modern religious symbolism, and conceives it rather as a *"Rückbesinnung"*, consequently *"nicht um ein Moment einer neuen Phase"* (Döbert, 1973: 127).

Furthermore, Bellah's "'theory' has little or no predictive power" (Glasner 1977: 31). In fact, it is a narrative of a differentiation process conceived as a development from less complex forms to more complex forms. It presumes that

> Everything already exists in some sense in the religious symbol system of the most primitive man; it would be hard to find anything later that is not "foreshadowed" there [... Or put differently,] neither religious man nor the structure of man's ultimate religious situation evolves, [...] but rather religion as a symbol system (Bellah, 1964: 359).

As a result of these claims, religion is defined functionally, and "every" set of symbolic forms and acts that relates man to the ultimate conditions of his existence is considered religious.

Consequently, Bellah (1971: 39-46) cannot differentiate between believers and unbelievers, as we have now passed the stage of dogmatic religiosity. "Religion, as that symbolic form through which man comes to terms with the antinomies of his being has not declined, indeed cannot decline unless man's nature ceases to be problematic to him" (*o.c.*: 50). Societal and individual secularization in his conception can be nothing other than dechristianization: "What is generally called secularization and the decline of religion appear as the decline of the external control system of religion and the decline of traditional religious belief" (*o.c.*: 50). Which of course is an implicit acceptance that a substantive definition is needed when we want to study secularization.

Very clearly his position is that there is no decline but only individuation of religion. This does not mean a personal escape from social and political exigencies, but rather a stress on inner authenticity and autonomy, which has profound social and moral consequences. Religion involves a personal quest for meaning: it must express the deepest dimensions of the self and in no way violate individual conscience. But it is not self-worship, for it is open to other selves and the universe itself (*o.c.*: 47-51). This personal responsibility for one's own ultimate meaning system can have anomic consequences for the person (Berger, 1967), a problem Bellah does not take up. He does, however, pose the question of the functionality of the churches in this matter and suggests that "the most the church can do is provide him [the individual] a favorable environment for [constructing an ultimate meaning system], without imposing on him a prefabricated set of answers" (Bellah, 1964: 373). It is this adaptation of the churches that Schelsky

(1965) analyses in his study "*Ist die Dauerreflexion institutionalisierbar?*"

Unlike Bellah, Schelsky sets limits to the Christian churches' potential for adaptation. The adaptation he advocates is a quest for new social forms for the eternal truth of Christianity, *i.e.* the adaptation of its social appearance to the social patterns of modern societies. The eternal and transcendental truths, the core values and beliefs of Christianity are not the objects of such adaptation. Rather, these objects are the organizational structure and methods of the Churches, their social ethics, adapted to facilitate their penetration of the modern social structures with a Christian ethic, and the forms of belief. Schelsky is especially interested in the last of them. In former times, the typical form of belief was the unconditional and unreflective acceptance of cultural truths including religious beliefs. Now *Dauerreflexion* – continual, intensive reflection about the truth – is the typical form of belief, and the churches should institutionalize it. According to Schelsky, the core of the adaptation should be the creation of the possibility of the conscious meeting of individual subjectivities as an organizational and communicative form. To achieve this, dialogue is the obvious method. Permanent conversation is fundamental for the life of a religious community of modern men. Dialogue stimulates permanent reflection, and dynamic subjectivity and subjective experiences reunite the community of believers. As a consequence, the "traditional house of prayer becomes the home of dialogue", and old forms of religious communication – rites, scripture reading, hymn singing and even sermons – recede. Schelsky's analysis and suggestions are narrower than Bellah's because he does not work with a functional definition of religion and because he incorporates the existence of eternal and transcendental truths of Christianity.

In Bellah's approach there is no explanation of the factors that promote the so-called process of differentiation. Döbert states that the evolution of religious consciousness is a process of reflection in which man progressively thinks out his own being and emancipates himself from the primitive coercion of prevailing norm systems. In so far as factors of the internal religious system are responsible, he suggests that it becomes possible only through innovations in the economic sector and that it is stimulated by the differentiation of religion from political institutions (Döbert, 1973: 140 and 109). His use of Lenski's (1966: 90-93) basic societal types classified in technological terms, indicates that he assumes that external factors are important in an explanation of religious evolution (Döbert, 1973: 84). As internal aspects of the religious system he distinguishes the structure of religious symbolism, the representation of God and man, the explicit themata and manifest functions of religion, the carriers of the religious system, the type of belief system, and religious actions. Methodologically, it is the consistency of the internal variables that allows us to see if the societal types also differentiate along religions lines (*o.c.*: 86). Döbert distinguishes four religious stadia: the religion of hunting, gathering, and simple horticultural societies; the religion of advanced horticultural societies; the religion of agrarian societies; and the modern "religion" of industrial societies (*o.c.*: 87-139). He states that the differences between these types are most explicit in the types of belief system (*o.c.*: 141) which are, respectively, direct living of natural life styles; coded, learned, and controlled belief; revelation, understanding, doubt, and dogma; and, finally, reason and understanding, with the personal God of monotheism becoming a superfluous metaphor (*o.c.*: 104, 115, 124-125 and 133-134). Döbert warns, though, that modern religion can only be outlined in a speculative and tentative way since a binding conception does not yet exist, and he explicitly refers to Luckmann's "invisible religion" and the "autonomy of the individual" to construct his own meaning system (*o.c.*: 131-132).

## *Luckmann on Social Forms of Religion*

The first and universal social form of religion is, according to Luckmann, *elementary and nonspecific*. It is a world view, a configuration of meaning underlying a historical social order, in which human beings are socialized. This world view transcends the individual as an historical reality, and, through socialization, the human organism transcends its biological nature, and the historical objective (transcendent) reality becomes a subjective (immanent) reality. The human organism becomes a Self. Luckmann (1967: 49-56) calls the transcendence of biological nature by the human organism a religious phenomenon.

But sociological theory is interested in specific forms of religion in society, not simply in establishing the religious function and social "objectivity" of the world view. The question then becomes what additional and distinctly articulated forms may religion assume in society and how they are to be derived from the elementary nonspecific social form of religion (*o.c.*: 56).

The social form of religion typical of *relatively* "simple" societies is, according to Luckmann, *specific and historical.*

> The hierarchy of significance which characterizes the world view as a whole and which is the basis of the religious function of the world view is articulated in a distinct superordinated layer of meaning within the world view. By means of symbolic representations that layer refers explicitly to a domain of reality that is set apart from the world of everyday life. This domain

may be appropriately designated as a sacred cosmos. The symbols which represent the reality of the sacred cosmos may be termed religious representations because they perform, in a specific and concentrated way the broad religious function of the world view as a whole (*o.c.*: 60-61).

Such a religious form is typical of societies with a low degree of "autonomy" of separate institutional areas, where the sacred cosmos is, in principle, equally accessible and equally relevant to all members of society.

By contrast, in a "complex" society it is more likely that a distinct institution will develop, an institution that supports the objectivity and social validity of the sacred cosmos. Such a social form of religion is called *institutionally specialized*. It is "characterized by standardization of the sacred cosmos in a well-defined doctrine, differentiation of full-time religious roles, transfer of sanctions enforcing doctrinal and ritual conformity to special agencies and the emergence of organizations of the "ecclesiastic" type" (*o.c.*: 66). Only in such a situation does an antithesis between "religion" and "society" develop that is the basis for the secularization process. Preconditions for the development of such a social form are some degree of articulation of the sacred cosmos in the world view and the formation of specifically religious roles that support one another. The latter presupposes an increasing complexity of the division of labor and large surplus above the level of subsistence to allow the growth of specialized bodies of experts (*o.c.*: 62-66). It is the process of societal secularization (cf. *supra*) that undermines this social form of religion, and that, according to Luckmann, stimulates the emergence of a private, invisible religion which he tentatively calls an *institutionally nonspecialized social form of religion* (*o.c.*: 101).

Luckmann attributes the changes in types of religion, which are very similar to the ones I have already discussed, to a process of institutional and cultural differentiation, to the division of labor, to a large surplus above subsistence level, and to the development of specialized bodies of experts, religious experts among them. He situates the process of societal secularization in a society where a particular social form of religion prevails, *i.e.* the "institutionally specialized social form". At the same time, he suggests that a new form of religion is emerging in modern society: an invisible, individual religiosity, *i.e.* an "institutionally nonspecialized social form of religion". But it seems problematic to me how one can call individual religiosity a "social form" of religion.

## Social Types of "Institutionally Specialized Social Forms of Religion"

Luckmann does not attach great importance to the different institutionally specialized social forms of organizational religion: cults, sects, denominations, and churches. Pfautz and Herberg do, and they develop a theory of secularization based on them.

According to Pfautz (1955-56), five types of religious groups demonstrate an "order of increasing [organizational] secularization": cult, sect, institutionalised sect, church, and denomination. He analyses these types according to five sociological perspectives: the demographic, ecological, associational, structural and socio-psychological. His concern is to indicate how factors such as size, composition, and rate of growth, together with diffusion and segregation, influence the development of social types of religion. Other factors that he invokes include internal, external, social and cultural differentiation; the basis of social interaction and recruitment; the type of authority and leadership; and the type of social action and interaction.

Pfautz holds that the church is the most developed form of religious social organization, and hence the most able to survive – the best example being the Catholic Church of the 13th century. However, "the denomination is one extreme of the secularization process", and the cult, being the least secularized, is the other. It seems implicit in his theory that secularization is a function of differentiation, with the cult being the most primitive and most elementary religious form (*o.c.*: 121, 123, 124, 126-128). Secularization is also a function of the following phenomena: types of social interaction, which vary from fellowship (in which affectual motives are primary) to association (in which secondary relationships and purposeful-rational orientations predominate) (*o.c.*: 123-124); the relationship to the larger society, which varies from conflict to assimilation and accommodation (*o.c.*: 127); and the primary basis of the interactional characteristics, which may have both symbolic and non-symbolic elements (*o.c.*: 123, 124 and 126).

Herberg (1967b: 515) follows Pfautz in suggesting that the cult is the least secularized form of religious group, since, for the member of the cult, there is very little distinction between conventional, operative and existential religion. Herberg (1967a: 471-472) distinguishes three usages of the term "religion":

> In the first place, "religion" is properly used for the system of attitudes, beliefs, feelings, standards, and practices that in the particular society, generally receive the name of religion. For our purposes, we will designate religion in this usage as "conventional religion". We can speak of Christianity, Protestantism, Lutheranism, Judaism, Islam, Buddhism, Roman Catholi-

cism, and the like as examples of conventional religion. In the second place, "religion" may be taken to signify that system of attitudes, beliefs, feelings, and practices that actually *does in fact* provide the society with an ultimate context of meaning and value in terms of which social life is integrated and social activities are validated. This I will call the "operative religion" of a society. It may or it may not be the same as the conventional religion. German *Rassen-* or *Volksgemeinschaft* and the American Way of Life are two very different examples of operative religion in this sense. In the third place, "religion" may be understood existentially as the structure of one's being oriented to one's ultimate concern.

According to Herberg, the sect follower has already advanced on the road to organizational secularization, and in America, where denominationalism became the established religious pattern, this represents a further and very advanced stage of secularization. "For denominationalism, in its very nature, requires a thorough-going separation between conventional religion and operative religion, and this is the mark of secularization" (1967b: 515-516).

With denominationalism, religious groups abandoned their overarching claims and fitted themselves into an overarching profane value system. The *conventional* religions have been compelled to transmit to the "American Way of Life" their legitimizing function, *i.e.* providing an ultimate meaning system for the integration and validation of social life, and so have lost their status as *operative* religions. In American society, the conventional religions fulfill only the functions of social identification and social integration: they offer the individual a socio-religious community. This functional shift diminishes the importance of the differences among the denominations and makes for a more "ecumenical" attitude, leading to a grouping of many denominations into three socio-religious sub-communities: Protestants, Catholics and Jews (Herberg, 1967a: 470-478). Of course, he recognizes points of resistance to and counter-currents against secularization, for example among the sects and older ethnic churches – all of which are aware of their marginality and therefore have a strong sense of their own distinctiveness – and churches with a strong creedal or confessional tradition (*e.g.* the Missouri Synod Lutherans), and theologically concerned people (*ibid.*).

"Divergence between operative religion and conventional religion: that is substantially what secularization implies" (*o.c.*: 477). This divergence sometimes gives rise to opposition and conflict, but in the USA there is no hostility between them: operative religion is expressed in the traditional vocabulary of conventional religion, while conventional religions see themselves as functioning within the operative religion, serving its purposes and implementing its values (*o.c.*: 477). This is also the thesis of Berger's *The Noise of Solemn Assemblies* (1961: 38-104).

What occurs in the younger generation, according to Herberg, is the disappearance of tensions between the religious sub-communities. This results especially from the fact that conventional religions "are grounded in the 'common' religion of American belonging–, 'After all, we're all Americans'". The weakening of tensions between religious groups is the result of progressive secularization of American life and American religion. "The conventional religions – Protestantism, Catholicism and Judaism – are typically understood as variant expressions of the 'Common faith' which all Americans share by virtue of their participation in the American Way of Life" (Herberg, 1967b: 519-522). Consequently, the progressive line of organizational secularization according to Herberg is cult, sect, denomination, socio-religious community, and the tri-faith system.

The line of organizational secularization drawn by Parsons was quite the reverse. As we have seen, he attributed the emergence of denominationalism to an increasing institutionalization of Christian values in secular society. This is related to the trend toward ascetic Protestantism and its call to establish the Kingdom of God on earth. The creation of a new American nation was the climax of this process (Parsons, 1974: 204-205). The value pattern or collective conscience which, in more general and vaguer terms, legitimizes the wider variation of the substructures is civil religion or Herberg's operative religion. In this way Parsons traces an anti-secularization tendency: "The fundamental changes in the religious constitution of Western society which culminated in the later 18th century thus did not lead to the destruction of the influence of religion but rather to the development of two striking important new types and levels of religion" (*o.c.*: 208-209). Parsons identifies them as America's civil religion and, typical for Europe, Marxist Socialism (*o.c.*: 207-208 and 210). At present he sees, particularly in the USA, a possible new phase in Western religious traditions: the new religion of love, which is this-worldly and non-theistic, and has a strong emphasis on the community (*o.c.*: 210-221).

## Conclusions

Yinger's reaction to the thesis of Herberg and Berger is that one should distinguish clearly between secularization and social change. Secularization as used by Berger and Herberg, as well as by Luckmann (1967: 36-37), when writing about "internal secularization" is identical to social change, *in casu* religious change (Yinger, 1962: 69-74 and 1967: 19):

If one thinks of religion [...] as an ongoing search, subject to changed forms and revised myths, then lack of orthodoxy does not mean the weakening of religion. It can be a sign of strength [...] it is an indication of an expected *churchlike* response to dramatic changes in the conditions of life among the middle and upper classes in a prosperous society (Yinger, 1962: 73).

For Yinger, religion is the dependent variable to be explained by social differences. This may clearly be seen from his explanation of America's distinct religious groups. "Such differences as exist are still to be explained, to an important degree, not as existing in spite of drastic reduction of secular differences but because of the continuation of significant secular differences" (*o.c.*: 80).

Yinger does not speak about organizational or "internal" secularization, he prefers the notion of religious change, a point of view that is clearly dependent upon his functional definition of religion. What Bellah, Döbert, Luckmann, Pfautz, Herberg, Parsons and Berger are describing are clearly forms of religious change, but some of them call these changes forms of organizational secularization or do not, which depends upon their definition of religion. Calling such changes "religious changes" is neutral, to call these changes "organizational secularization" or not, is an evaluation based on a substantial definition of religion.

Bellah and Luckmann describe a general process of religious change, suggesting that in the modern world a new form of religion is emerging, which according to Döbert (1973: 131) is not yet clearly conceptualized and which might probably be described most clearly in terms of "the characteristics of traditional religion which are eliminated". Such eliminations could of course imply that what is socially considered to be the essence of religion – *i.e.* the transcendental reality, the supra-empirical reference – is eliminated. Then we should ask ourselves, of course, if this is not the elimination of religion *per se*, to wit organizational secularization. Second, individuation, privatization, individual religion or whatever it is called, can hardly be called a "social form" of religion.

Pfautz, Herberg, Parsons, and Berger are concerned with organizational types, which are characteristic of what Luckmann calls the "institutionally specialized social form of religion". Determination of a secularization trend in such an organizational pattern is based on a definition of the cult (Pfautz) or the type of religious function involved (Herberg and Parsons). Pfautz stresses the structural characteristics of the cult such as its primitive, elementary form, its fellowship and its conflictual relationship to society. Herberg is more concerned with its functions and the fact that the cult combines "conventional, operative and existential religion". Parsons, on the contrary, stresses the impact of ascetic

Protestantism and the increasing institutionalization of Christian values in secular society, which I have already criticized. Martin's criticism of "Catholic utopianism" in reference to the historical "base line" used by Sorokin and others who evaluated the degree of societal secularization (cf. *supra*), can be applied here to Bellah, Parsons and others who use Protestantism as a criterion to evaluate the religious change: "Protestant utopianism". Of course, Herberg and Parsons extend the trend of organizational types of religion when they introduce notions such as "the tri-faith system", "civil religion" and "the new religion of love".

Finally, Yinger's suggestion that religious change be explained in terms of social differences is supported when we bring together elements from the different studies that I have discussed. The basic idea is that religious evolution is related to socio-cultural evolution, and that in so far as internal religious factors are specifically responsible for religious change they became possible as a result of technological and economic innovations, the differentiation of political from religious institutions and demographic and ecological factors. Changes in the division of labor and economic surpluses allowed the emergence of specialized bodies of experts, including religious specialists, and stimulated the development of institutionally specialized bureaucratic organizations, including religious organizations. Religious specialists working in the context of religious organizations favored the articulation of a sacred cosmos in the world view.

Pluralism of religious forms and content had important effects. Herberg refers to the fact that they lost their status of "operative" religion and were replaced by the co-called "American Way of Life", which was subsequently called "civil religion". The conventional religions, according to Herberg and Berger, even came to function within this operative religion and offered, on a sub-societal level, a social identity to those individuals whom they integrate in socio-religious communities. Comparing the functions of religions in America and Europe, Wilson (1969: 124) suggests that "In a society in which there was, apart from the long-settled areas, much less stability of community life than Europeans had been used to, the role of the Churches was increasingly that of providing an agency for community orientations and loyalties".

The next question I shall take up concerns the kind of relationship that exists between societal secularization and religious change. I shall suggest a tentative answer on the basis of research reports.

## Societal Secularization and Religious Change

The relationship between religious change and societal secularization suggests several questions: What is the impact of pluralism on the secularization of society? What is the impact of societal secularization on the emergence of religious and functionally equivalent secular movements? What is the impact of societal secularization on the internal adaptations of churches and denominations? And how do different religious organizations react to societal secularization, *i.e.* do they stimulate it or do they try to counteract it?

### *What is the Impact of Pluralism on Societal Secularization?*

According to Yinger (1967: 25-26), religious pluralism poses serious problems from a societal perspective:

> A society needs not only flexibility, diversity, and tolerance; it needs also an underlying unity, agreement on procedures and basic goals, and a sense of coherence. In societies where separate religious communities are important elements in the social structure, the unifying task may be transferred to quasi-religious institutions in some ways antithetical to the religious values. In the United States, "the American Way of Life" has [...] become the operative faith to a substantial degree.

Here, Yinger regards *religious change* (*o.c.*: 19) as necessary for the integration of American society. But religious pluralism can also stimulate secularism. Yinger uses the term secularism "to refer simply to beliefs and practices related to the 'non-ultimate' aspects of human life. It is not anti-religion, it is not a substitute religion; it is simply another segment of life" (*o.c.*: 19). According to Yinger (*o.c.*: 26), pluralism can spill over into anomie,

> [N]ot from a clash of religious values, but from a desire on the part of the separate religious communities to maintain themselves and to preserve advantages [... W]here dissensus paralyzes action, supports a cycle of interaction that progressively weakens the structure necessary for intergroup discourse, or weakens the efficacy of culturally approved means to shared goals, it leads toward anomie.

This process is illustrated by the enormous difficulties over integration into which the schools of virtually every city have fallen, without anyone intending or wanting it. And these sharp conflicts over school integration are partly due to religious pluralism. Therefore, Yinger (1967: 27) suggests that

> [T]he conflict can be reduced only by transferring the issue entirely into the secular arena [...] Pluralistic societies that do not have a substantial amount of secularism are generally unable to develop the mutual tolerance that religious diversity requires. If almost every question of life is a religious ques-

tion, there is too little shared neutral ground on which to stand. If there are secular interests – economic, political, educational – that the members of different religious communities can share, they have a basis for mutual respect and accommodation in religious matters. In varying amount, Holland, Austria, and South Viet-Nam, for example, would profit greatly by a growth of secularism, by the removal of many questions from the religious arena. This indicates the important connection between pluralism and societal secularization.

The transfer of issues into the secular arena also requires the building up of a secular moral doctrine. According to Lidz (1979: 196), secularization is "more than the displacement of religious factors from the moral or normative regulation of social life"; it is also "the building up of a secular moral doctrine ... operating on the basis of new kinds of ethical resources and moral constraints". Lidz holds that American secular moral doctrine is largely based on principles of the Enlightenment, and that it emerged through ideological debates about the moral foundations of practically all social institutions. Rationalism, individualism, progressive optimism, achievement, civil liberties and "other elements of what Hartz termed the 'liberal tradition'" are the core values of American moral culture.

> The core of the American liberal tradition, and a chief factor in its persistence, has been a pattern of accommodative integration between differentiated systems of religious culture and of secular moral culture. The secular morality has sustained a pragmatic, rationalist, technical manner of orientation [...] Yet, liberal morality has also proved able – some delimited, largely fundamentalist episodes aside – to defend its functional autonomy against intrusion of particularistic religious standards [...] However, more positive integration between the secular and religious spheres has also been present and has been an important factor in religious toleration of the autonomy of secular moral culture (*o.c.*: 207).

Comfortable accommodation between religion and secular morality, as in the pluralistic USA, is not always the case. Lidz writes also about ardent secularism in Marxist countries as, for example, in the Soviet Union where the secular moral doctrine, Marxism, may be transformed into a "secular or political religion" when "central principles and ideals of the ideology are placed above the possibility of rational criticism" and are "viewed as sources not just of practical legitimation but of truly ultimate resolution of problems of meaning" (*o.c.*: 210). He also mentions the restrictions on "the autonomous functioning of Enlightenment or secularized moral culture" imposed by established traditions grounded in one of the world religions: in Latin American societies Roman Catholicism, in Asian countries Islam and Theravada Buddhism (*o.c.*: 210). It is important to see that opposition to secular morality occurs in rather homogeneous religious cultures. Well-integrated relations between ongoing religious traditions and secular ideologies seem to be more prevalent in religiously pluralistic countries. In France, a Catholic country, there are deep-seated and enduring tensions between an institutionalized secular morality and an institutionalized religious tradition (*o.c.*: 208).

To prevent dissension arising from religious pluralism, issues have to be transferred to the secular arena, and this promotes societal secularization, more specifically laicization. Pluralism also breeds religious change: a political ideology is construed from conventional religions and could become the "operative faith" that integrates the political institution, at least as long as the civic society is considered to be a nation (cf. *supra*). Religious pluralism also stimulates the building up of a secular moral doctrine to legitimate the social institutions of such a society, while monopolistic situations prevent the development of a secular moral doctrine or generate opposition between the religious tradition and the secular morality. Consequently, religious pluralism stimulates the stripping of religious qualities from social problems in order to reduce tension and conflict, and it also promotes the development of a secular morality. In other words, it secularizes society through a process of laicization.

## *What is the Impact of Societal Secularization on the Emergence of Religious Movements*

Analyzing the emergence of Pentecostalism in the USA and Great Britain, Wilson (1970: 69-74 and 1958: 149-150) suggests that this was linked to the development of functional rationality, *Vergesellschaftung* and anomie typical of the rapid changes in the early part of the 20th century and the development of cities. The migrants lost the warm association of rural communities: the American cities were impersonal and the relationships shallow and dominated by role performances. The normative structure of life was confused; crime flourished; there was no received tradition of custom and convention; and anomie was prevalent. These migrants were also "hindered by poor verbal skills in a society that coined neologisms, and conducted its affairs in constantly changing jargon" (Wilson, 1970: 72). Pentecostalism, "the tongues movement", promising power by supernatural acquisition of verbal facility (the gift of tongues), was well fitted to appeal to the first generation of city dwellers. It symbolized their difficulties as well as the solution to them. Unlike other sects which could provide community life, Pentecostalism offered these people the possibility of running away from their social experience "sobbing and screaming". "Primitive religions often re-enact the day-to-day concerns of the tribe, particularly in fertility rituals: so Pentecostalism re-enacted the traumas of daily life for many of their adherents" (*o.c.*: 72). Pentecostalism fitted their social conditions; its demands were light and its gratifications immediate:

> The religion they needed had to be group-centred. They needed social support, and they needed a permissive context for expression of their emotional troubles. Pentecostalism was the fullest manifestation of a faith sanctifying, expressive emotionalism. It provided instantaneous relief (*o.c.*: 73).

Pentecostalism was more than group therapy, however, it was part of the evangelical tradition, and it communicated standards to its adherents. "Converts drawn in for emotional gratification, and little acquainted with formal moral injunctions, steadily learned – often by rigorous injunctions and taboos – the styles appropriate for the ideal moral man in the modern West" (*o.c.*: 74).

Describing a similar situation in Great Britain, Wilson (1958: 149-150) concludes, the members of the sects of the 20th century, especially of the Pentecostal groups,

> [H]ave abandoned Paul's insistence on "work out your own salvation" for the benefit of "Jesus saves", or the exhortation "only believe". They reject the desire to understand intellectually God's commands, in order to give preference to an extra-rational quasi-mystical belief in Jesus. For one part, without doubt, this insistence on the mysterious and near thaumaturgical aspects, reflects the mysterious nature of the social problems for the members of "sects": the social process is mysterious because it is complex and situated above total comprehension. The despair of its members in the face of the social situation is not a despair resulting from economic dispossession, which stimulated the resentment and the indignation of some sects of the nineteenth century. Rather, it is the despair emerging from a less tangible problem: that of man deprived of roots in the midst of a depersonalized society. The difference in the points which these "sects" emphasize might reflect a difference in the tensions of a changing social order: the substitution of tensions centred on economic inequality by tensions emerging from the rapidity of social evolution, the rupture in the traditions, the general anomy of social life in modern cities, the development, to put it in Weberian terms, of functional rationality (*Zweckrational*) to the detriment of value rationality (*Wertrational*) [...]. In all this may not these contemporary sects illustrate the social disorder of our times?

Closer to the present day, "sects with the imprint of secularity" emerge and flourish. They are congenial to the prevailing secular culture, and Wilson calls them "manipulationist sects". They "are secularized sects, for which only the *means* to salvation are religious: the *goals* are largely those of secular hedonism" (Wilson, 1970: 141). These sects emphasize a special knowledge, a *gnosis* that gives the diligent believer power to manipulate the world. Emerging in metropolitan centers, they reflect the impersonality of city life. Participation in these sects is segmentary, not total, and they celebrate the benefits and the optimism of the future. Movements of this type are self-consciously syncretistic, blending ideas taken from the Christian repository with secular metaphysical speculation, psychotherapy and other religious ideas. These movements have increasingly adopted the styles of educational and therapeutic agencies and lack community life and worship (*o.c.*: 141-144). However, some groups in this category which are mentioned in *The New Religious Consciousness* (Glock and Bellah, 1976), would not fit my definition of religion. Let me simply mention a few: Scientology, Transcendental Meditation, Est, Psychosynthesis, Encounter Groups, Transactional Analysis, and Esalen.

According to Wilson an analytical distinction may be made between "those movements in which salvation is offered through learning a new body of teaching", *e.g.* Scientology (Bainbridge and Stark, 1980), "and those in which men are taught to seek to discover new potential within themselves", *e.g.* Human Potential Movement. But, he goes on,

> in practice cults combine these things. Often the way in which inner capacities are said to be released is by the application of specific techniques. The theoretical distinction is worth maintaining, however, since so many new movements focus on the redemption of the self, by the self, and for the self, that one must take their emergence as itself a significant comment on the ideological individualism of our age, and on the contemporary process of individuation. Their attraction suggests that many people have lost all faith in external systems of knowledge, whether science, political theory, ideology, or religion. The cults suggest that you can save yourself; and no one else, and nothing else, can. They are, in this sense, profoundly anti-cultural movements: not merely are they against the existing culture, but their basic thrust is against *any* culture (Wilson, 1976b: 67).

A third group of new religious movements emphasizes the importance of the sacred community as the location of salvation. They have a strong sense of their boundaries and their monopoly on salvation, and demand total commitment of the members. Examples are the Unification Church of Rev. Moon, the Divine Light Mission of Maharaj Ji, the Hare Krishna movement, and the Happy-Healthy-Holy Organization. The emphasis of these movements is on self-realization, the means to which is not service to the wider society on its terms – their deviant subculture totally rejects society – but, service of their own community on terms which deviate from the general social norms, and which are indeed counter-cultural (*o.c.*: 70-78).

For some sociologists, the new cults represent a religious revival (Greeley, 1974: 159-170). For others, like Wilson (1976b: 96), they are a confirmation of the process of secularization:

> They indicate the extent to which religion has become inconsequential for modern society. The cults represent, in the American phrase, "the religion of

your choice", the highly privatized preference that reduces religion to the significance of pushpin, poetry, or popcorns. They have no real consequence for other social institutions, for political power structures, for technological constrains and controls. They add nothing to any prospective reintegration of society, and contribute nothing towards the culture by which a society might live.

The sources of secularization and the appeal of the new cults are themselves to be found in the contemporary social situation [...] Secularization is intimately related to the decline of community, to increased social mobility, and to the impersonality of role-relationships. The new cults and the eclecticism that is indebted to them stand in direct continuity with the protest against all these developments which is misleadingly called "the counter-culture" (*o.c.*: 99).

[Indeed,] the cults reject the instrumental rationality of modern society and the large-scale impersonal social order. They pronounce their distrust of the scientific, routinized and bureaucratic procedures on which modern social systems depend, and demand a rediscovery of the self by avenues of exploration previously forbidden. But whereas earlier religious revivals. revivalism within a religious tradition, led to reintegration of the individual within the social order, the new cults propose to take the individual out of his society, and to save him by the wisdom of some other, wholly exotic body of belief and practice (*o.c.*: 98).

In fact, we are talking here about "magical and occult religion" which, as Fenn puts it, limits the scope of the sacred and has a low degree of integration between corporate and personal value systems. These types of religion are compatible with societal secularization, and, according to Fenn, societal secularization may foster them (cf. *infra*).

Wilson's studies, first of all, support the conclusions of the first part of this chapter: religious change and the emergence of new religious groups are consequences of social changes. Pentecostalism was linked to societalization of urban life, and it helped its followers by re-enacting the traumas of their daily life; but it was also part of the evangelical tradition. This new type of sect was not born out of economic dispossession, like some sects of the 19th century, but out of anomie following ruptures in communal traditions.

In contrast with the other sects, the modern manipulationist sects continue to emerge and thrive. If societal secularization means a reduction of the social impact of religion and the restriction of it to the personal life, then these new sects and their secular equivalents fit the pattern. They accept the secularized world, and they emphasize a special knowledge, a *gnosis* that allows the individual to manipulate the world. They are like therapeutic agencies and generally lack communal life and worship, although one type of cult does emphasize the importance of the sacred community. But they all stress self-realization and are inconsequential for modern society. They do not affect the societal institutions, nor do they contribute to the reintegration of society. They are a protest against this society with its decline of community and increased impersonality of social life. But they do not reintegrate the individual within the social order, and they do not build up a new social ethic. Instead, these new cults propose to take the individual out of this world: they offer occasional or permanent escape. In fact, they have accepted a secularized society and have adapted to it. Recent religious changes confirm the secularization of society; they certainly are not an indicator of a religious revival.

## *What is the Impact of Societal Secularization on the Internal Adaptation of Churches and Denominations?*

Consciously or unconsciously, and quite often by force of circumstance, churches and denominations adapt to the secularized world. A few recent studies allow me to suggest some trends in theology, ethics, rituals, church policy and ecumenism.

It is clear that religious and cultural pluralism – different religious cultures competing with each other and with world views that do not specifically contain religious representations – stimulates the privatization or individuation of religion. Luckmann (1979: 136) suggests:

> As for religious themes one is tempted to say with some exaggeration: anything goes. In the global interpenetration of cultures, a vast – and by no means silent, although perhaps imaginary – museum of values, notions, enchantments and practices has become available. It has become available "directly" but primarily through the filter of mass media rather than social relations. The choice is determined rather less by social conditions – although evidently they continue to play a kind of screening role – than by individual psychologies. Originally the statement "religion is a private matter" has a political meaning. Now it has an essentially psychological one.

Berger (1967: 151) stresses the same point when he writes:

> [T]he pluralistic situation multiplies the number of plausibility structures competing with each other. Ipso facto, it relativizes their religious contents. More specifically, the religious contents are "de-objectivated", that is, deprived of their status as taken-for-granted, objective reality in consciousness. They become "subjectivized" in a double sense: Their "reality" becomes a "private" affair of individuals [...] And their "reality", insofar as it is still maintained by the individual, is apprehended as being rooted within the consciousness of the individual rather than in any facticities of the external world – religion no longer refers to the cosmos or to history but to individual *Existenz* or psychology. On the level of theorizing, this phenomenon serves to explain the current linkage of theology with the conceptual machineries of existentialism and psychologism.

Confronted with the secularized world, the religious organizations have, according to Berger, two basic options open to them, accommodation and resistance, each having practical and theoretical difficulties. The difficulty of the accommodating posture, both practically and theoretically, lies in deciding "How far should one go?"; and that of the resisting posture lies in deciding "How strong are the defences?" The practical difficulties are to be

> [M]et by means of "social engineering" – in the accommodating posture, reorganizing the institution in order to make it "more relevant" to the modern world; in the resisting posture, maintaining or revamping the institution so as to serve as a viable plausibility structure for reality-definitions that are not confirmed by the larger society. Both options, of course, must be theoretically legitimated. It is precisely in this legitimation that the "crisis of theology" is rooted (Berger, 1967: 155).

In a chapter on societal secularization and the problem of legitimation, Berger analyses Protestant theological development as prototypical (*o.c.*: 156-168). Important stadia in this development are pietism and rationalism which eroded orthodoxy and mixed contemporary psychologism with theology. Important schools were "theological liberalism" in the 19th century, the orthodox reaction of Barth, and the theological reaction to neo-orthodoxy by Bultmann, Tililich, Gogarten, Bonhoeffer, *et al.*, which Berger calls "neo-liberalism". "The contemporary eruption of what may well be called – neo-liberalism – thus takes up where the earlier liberalism left off, and just because of the intervening period does so in considerably more – radical-ways" (*o.c.*: 165-166). The new liberalism "subjectivizes" religion in a radical fashion and in a double sense (cf. *supra*). In this enterprise various conceptual machineries derived from neo-Kantian philosophy, psychologism, existentialism and sociology have been employed (*o.c.*: 138).

Another study of the "internal secularization of Christianity", and particularly religious change in the Catholic Church, is presented by Isambert (1976). His study first of all deals with the changing moral attitude towards contraception in the Protestant Churches, the Anglican Church and the Catholic Church. In the Catholic Church, even if opposed by the Pope, a reorientation of moral attitudes, similar to Reformation ethics as analyzed by Weber, is largely accepted: the Church is no longer accepted as the judge of each and every act, but only of the general orientation of the action. Individuals are considered to be responsible for deciding on the best means to achieve the goals proposed by the Church. In other words, the churches can still propound values, but their competence to promulgate detailed rules is diminishing (*o.c.*: 581-583). Isambert also suggests that the specificity of Catholic rituals seems to become blurred as a result of the rationalization process. There has been a reduction of symbolic gesture in rituals, and a reduction of the expressive function in these rituals in favor of the teaching function – as indicated by the development of the liturgy of the Word in the Mass and the administration of the sacraments. Increasing numbers of Catholics reject the official point of view concerning the efficacity of the sacraments, thereby reducing them to symbolic acts. All of these tendencies in the Catholic Church are clearly in the line of the Protestant reformation (*o.c.*: 581-583). In fact, the Protestant "disenchantment" of the sacraments is extended to other domains where contemporary Catholicism also draws nearer to the Protestant position as analyzed by Weber. In this line of reasoning, Isambert talks about the demythologization of the Scriptures, referring to the impact of Bultmann, among others (*o.c.*: 586-588). Here we return to Berger's analysis. Both Isambert and Berger, in fact, point to the influence of secular thought on theology and the undermining of its credibility. Berger (1967: 159-160) also explicitly refers to the impact of the social and cultural context, "the 'golden' age of bourgeois capitalism" and the great shocks that have jolted this world (see also Lidz, 1979). Both mention counter-movements, *e.g.* the neo-orthodox school of Barth and the profoundly anti-secularist charismatic movement.

Wilson's analysis of the contemporary transformations of religion also takes into account charismatic renewal and the church's espousal of rationalization (1976b: 32-37 and 88-89). But he also defines the limits of the process of rationalization: religion, being communal, personal and concerned with ultimate ends, defies functional rationality. Nor does he regard the charismatic movement as de-secularizing with its attempts to cut through formal routines, its dependence on subjective feeling reinforced by group-engendered emotions, and its inconsequentiality for society (*o.c.*: 86-87 and 96). The charismatic movement, and what is called *déritualisation* by Isambert (1976: 584), Wilson considers to be "voluntary 'destructuration'" (1976b: 85-88). It is "the conquest of faith by the artful techniques of the world". People demand to see religion "working". He also refers to the challenge to authority on the basis of radical democratic principles, which has stimulated so-called "dialogue" in the churches as it has in society.

Charismatic renewal, voluntary destructuration and rationalization are three of the five ways in which Christians have responded to societal secularization, according to Wilson, the two other ways being eclecticism and ecumenism (1976b: 85). Eclecticism "is an attempt to incorporate into worship elements from other cultures and sub-cultures, or from other social contexts". He refers to the attempt to embrace political issues, and to the impact of the so-called "counter-culture", exotic cultures and other religions, which has relativized Christianity. He

125

points out in particular that in "an experimental liturgy, each exotic bauble is divorced from its context, from its cultural significance, [and] is wanted only for its brightness, to deck out a jollification". It produces ecstasy; a few people may be high for a few hours, but it lacks significance in the long-run (*o.c.*: 90-95).

Wilson, Séguy (1973) and Berger consider ecumenism to be another response to societal secularization, and Berger (1967: 137-144) explains it in terms of market economics. The key characteristic of all pluralistic situations is that the allegiance of the members is voluntary. As a result, religious traditions must now be marketed, or "sold", to a clientele, and consequently the question of "results" becomes important. The pressure to achieve these in a competitive situation entails a rationalization of the socio-religious structures, *i.e.* the buraucratization of churches, denominations and established sects.

> The contemporary situation of religion is thus characterized by a progressive bureaucratization of the religious institutions. Both their internal and their external relations are marked by this process. [... Furthermore], bureaucracies demand specific types of personnel. [...] This means that similar types of leadership emerge in the several religious institutions, irrespective of the traditional patterns in this matter. [...] The individuals conforming to this type in the different religious institutions speak the same language and, naturally, understand each other and each other's problems. In other words, the bureaucratization of the religious institutions lays a social-psychological foundation for "ecumenicity" (Berger, 1967: 139-140).

Wilson (1969: 163) also underscores the growing importance of rational bureaucratic organizations in the religious field and the role of the threatened religious professional, who sees his activities undervalued and his functions becoming superfluous. "Their real power [...] is in their administrative control and the fact of their full-time involvement". A clergy which increasingly shared a modern rational economic spirit, in command of religious bureaucracies, fostered ecumenicalism in the 1950s and 1960s (*o.c.*: 151-167). Indeed, according to Berger, the socio-psychological affinities only ensured that religious rivals were regarded not so much as "the enemy" but as colleagues with similar problems, which made collaboration easier. And as free competition without restraints becomes irrational and too costly in purely economic terms, the rationalization of competition by means of cartelization is one obvious way to reduce costs and risks. And this is what ecumenicity does: "the number of competing units is reduced through mergers; and the remaining units organize the market by means of mutual agreements" (Berger, 1967: 142-143).

With regard to the ecumenical hope of the 1950s and 1960s, Wilson notes in a later work that these "early hopes ran into the sand of difficulties between, and divisions within, the Churches". There was opposition over social activism and other problems between laity and clergy, and between conservatives and liberals. The clergy was "less successful in working out the details of organizational amalgamation" than establishing theoretical and doctrinal agreements, even if they were "achieved with a certain deviousness and [...] a deliberate obscuration of difficulties". To younger people, and perhaps particularly the younger clergy, the idea of the emergence of ever larger monolithic religious institutions has become less attractive in a period when existing structures have been assaulted as alienating and inhuman. Paradoxically, writes Wilson (1976b: 30-36), the most vigorous grass-roots ecumenical movement of recent years, the charismatic movement, is also potentially the most divisive. It brought together Christians of very diverse denominations, but it also created sharp differences within individual churches and denominations.

In a discussion of Berger's and Wilson's analysis of ecumenism, Séguy (1973: 41-42) points out that they concentrated their analysis too much on institutional forms in the Anglo-Saxon world, and they too strongly equated ecumenism with institutional unity based on institutional fusion. He turns, instead, to the "protesting" ecumenism of small groups, and suggests, in the French context, three types of ecumenism linked to three different groups of intellectuals. *L'oecuménisme sauvage* in the Catholic setting represents the protests of "liberal intellectuals" who are linked to the traditional university. This represents the scientific and positivistic ideals of the 19th century and classical culture, and is linked to the bourgeoisie. The ecumenism of the *groupes informels actuels* – ranging from the political left to the right, including charismatic Catholicism – which developed later than the first group, represents the "revolt of intellectual technicians". They represent technical knowledge and apply the policies devised by the technocrats with whom they do not share power. May 1968 marks their revolt against technocracy. *Le système oecuménique officiel* is linked to the emergence of the "technocrats" who are linked to the leading sectors of advanced capitalism, if not by birth, then by education, function and social relationships. According to Séguy, the future of "protesting" ecumenism depends on the "intellectual technician"; the "liberal intellectual" is *passé* and more retrogressive than progressive. As a result, the "third man" in ecumenism is not the unbeliever, as proclaimed by the churches and certain sociologists but "the intellectual technician" of the *groupes informels actuels* who is still a believer and a church-goer (*o.c.*: 104-112).

This analysis of ecumenism suggests the importance of studying the groups and quasi-groups involved: the clergy, the types of intellectuals, the young, the younger clergy, etc. I must stress again the importance of studying the groups and quasi-groups involved in religious change, as suggested above in the review of the studies on the process of societal secularization (cf. *supra*).

Last but not the least, I would like to draw attention to Coleman's study (1978) of the evolution in Dutch Catholicism. This study of the Catholic Church in the Netherlands offers an example of what he calls reactive differentiation. For a long time Catholicism failed to face the problem of function-loss and functional specialization. It lost its function in economics, politics, education and welfare, all of which became separated from the Church, and civil religion also moved away from Christianity. In the span of a couple of decades the Dutch Catholic Church succeeded in adapting itself to the secularized world by functional specialization. It differentiated itself gradually as a community of faith from its own organizational apparatus, *i.e.* its pillar structure (*o.c.*: 9).

Coleman analyzed the organizational change of Dutch Catholicism with the help of Vallier's typology of strategies for church influence: the traditional missionary strategy as opposed to the cultural-pastoral strategy. These models are differentiated on the basis of several factors: the level of church ambition, the dominant ideology, the major and secondary bases of influence, the church-society relationship, the religious action principle, the priest's primary role, the laymen's role, the target group, and the organizational mode. Since in both models church ambitions are high, the differences are to be found in the other factors.

In the *traditional missionary* strategy, the dominant church ideology seeks to block or overcome societal secularization; the Church's major base of influence upon society lays in its differentiated organizations, the Catholic pillar; and its secondary base rests upon the ideological formation of the laity in Catholic schools or Catholic Action cells. The church-society relationship is characterized by separation and controlled contact through the dominant religious action principle of penetration in strategic secular spheres *en bloc*. The priest's primary roles are those of missionary, militant organizer of Catholic Action cells or confessional organizations, and political middleman and spokesman for Catholic economic minorities. The prestige and authority of the priest are diffuse. The layman's role is that of a passive hearer and doer of the Church's word, and in more active phases he is a hierarchical auxiliary: the agent of the bishop in the secular sphere. The primary target-categories for Catholic strategy are the workers and the middle class; intellectuals are tolerated and even encouraged, but they do not set the tone for Catholic strategy. Finally, the international Church is strongly organized to control orthodoxy; its pastoral, liturgical, and catechetical planning and co-ordination are poor. At national and diocesan levels, planning and co-ordination are decentralized.

In the *cultural-pastoral* strategy, by contrast, the dominant ideology accepts a co-operative role; the bishops forego informal political roles and speak to more than their own faithful. The church provides socio-ethical leadership within the wider community, and the locus for the secondary influence over its own membership is the local congregation. The church-society relationship can be characterized as integrated co-operation. The church aims at a condition of integrated autonomy wherein both the church and the secular world remain independent of each other, and its dominant action principle is secular involvement by emancipated yet conscientious Catholic laity. The primary role of the priest is that of spiritual advisor, liturgical leader and counselor to the laity. He also has a task in the formation of a local sense of community. The laity are autonomous in their role as Christian citizens: they are expected to be responsible co-participants as committed Christians within both the church and society. The primary target-categories are the Catholic intellectuals and youth. While the Church has reduced its efforts at conversion, it retains ambitions of influencing the moral and ethical persuasion of non-Catholics. Here new strategies for dialogue and ecumenism can be ascertained. Organizationally, national Episcopal Conferences emerge which entail coordination of the micro-units at the congregational level through central bureaucracies.

According to Coleman, the structural changes, in the last couple of decades, in the roles of bishops, priests and laity, and the implementa-tion – in the Netherlands, of these in new institutional arrangements – which also implied a change in the normative and the sanction systems was deviant within the Catholic world only as far as tempo was con-cerned. Reactive differentiation, in other words, the adaptation of the religious subsystem to changes in society and its other subsystems, is imperative, but is occurring in other national settings at a slower tempo. In order to analyze these swift changes, Coleman used, in addition to Vallier's typology of strategies for church influence, Smelser's reading of the sequence of change and his list of explanatory variables, thus setting the stage for international comparative work (*o.c.*: 2-10).

What provoked such swift changes in the Netherlands? Coleman takes into account the international setting – the *nouvelle théologie* and Vatican II – but he also searches for typical Dutch elements: Dutch socialism shed most of its ideological dogmatism, and there were also the war experiences which called separatism in question. But, more importantly, there was a growing dissatisfaction among Catholic elites, both lay and clerical, with the missionary strategy of triumphal separatism, and in the 1960s, Dutch society was primarily addressing itself to the high costs of the pillarized structure. The first reaction of the authorities was to hold the line: the bishops attempted to contain the dissatisfaction in their Mandatory Letter of 1954. But the pressures of pillarization surfaced again in 1957 over the question of Catholic membership in and support for the Netherlands Organization for International Assistance, an organization that tried to amalgamate the various pillars in an effort to provide joint development aid to underdeveloped countries. Archbishop Alfrink was asked to mediate in the disagreement concerning this co-operation, which, according to some Catholics, was forbidden by the Mandatory Letter. Instead of repeating the bishops' 1954 decision, he entrusted the question to a study commission of experts, which issued a series of six volumes entitled *Welfare, Well-being, and Happiness: A Catholic Viewpoint on Dutch Society.*

The commission proposed greater Catholic openness, pointed to the pastoral problems of preaching and catechism as crisis points within the Church, and emphasized a change in the roles of the laity and the clergy. By the mid-1960s, the bishops realized that a holding-action would not work. The Catholic Church in the Netherlands was unique, compared to other national churches, not in having a groundswell from the bottom – from the lower clergy, intellectuals, journalists and Catholic youth – but by virtue of having a body of bishops that was tolerant enough and decisive enough to help to determine the directions of change (*o.c.*: 99-101). The changes were then taken up in 1966-70 with an élan, enthusiasm, intensity and self-confidence that Coleman considers unusual for the Dutch. He uses Durkheim's notion of collective effervescence to explain this swiftness of change based on a collective élan (*o.c.*: 157-165). He then goes on to describe the collective redefinition: the new institutional forms and the contestation and conflict that surrounded them in 1966-74. Finally, he analyses the consolidation of the new institutions, taking the appointments of Bishops Simonis and Gijsen and Archbishop Willebrands as his test cases.

Coleman's empirical analysis is an important example of a study of a church's reactive or adaptive differentiation in the face of the secularization of a modern society. Moreover, its use of theoretical categories is to be commended since it makes international comparative studies possible.

## What is the Reaction of Religious Organizations to Societal Secularization?

Here we are concerned with the positive or negative attitudes of religious organizations – cults, sects, denominations and churches – toward the secularizing tendencies in modern societies. Fenn (1978: 65) suggests a tentative answer in his monograph on secularization: *"The more a religious group narrows the scope of the sacred and reduces its demands for integration between corporate and personal values and standards, the more adapted is such a group to a secular society"*. His answer is based on two factors: the scope of the sacred, and the degree of integration that religious organizations promote between corporate role-behavior and personal ideals, values and norms. The combination of those two dimensions results in four "ideal types":

> Each type of religious culture [...] presents a model of how social life should be organized, i.e. with or without the integration of personal and corporate systems of action. And each type of religious culture limits its mission to the communal life of the religious groups or extends its mission to include, perhaps, secular education, work or politics (*o.c.*: 69).

In his typology the most outstanding examples of religious cultures approximating the combination of his typological dimensions are situated and discussed (*o.c.*: 68-77).

**Table 1. Classification of some outstanding examples
of religious communities according to Fenn's typology**

| Dimensions | | The scope of the sacred | |
|---|---|---|---|
| | | Wide | Limited |
| Degree of integration between corporate and personal value-systems | High | A Catholicism and mainlaine Protestantism | B Sectarian religions *e.g.* Mormons, Jehovah's Witnesses |
| | Low | C Evangelical religion *e.g.* Charismatics, Pentecostal movements | D Magical and occult religion |

According to Fenn, mainline Protestantism and Roman Catholicism (Type A, in Table 1) represent religious cultures in which personal and corporate values are highly integrated, and Catholicism in particular assigns a very broad scope to the sacred, *i.e.* religious authority extends to a wide range of social and political issues. Occult and magical religion (Type D), in contrast, separate personal from corporate systems of action and place an exceedingly sharp boundary between the sacred and the profane, in part because the sacred is limited to relatively few subjects and objects. As a result, Catholicism and the dominant model of the mainline Protestant denominations may find affinities with "civil religion", but the drive to extend the sacred in a broad array of social institutions may on occasion lead to tensions between the values of the churches and the values of the secular institutions. The religions of the occult and magical type encounter fewer areas of opposition with the larger society. Because ecstatic or magical activities are confined to the personal level of action, they do not threaten the values and standards of the corporate level. Occult and esoteric religious movements may, as Fenn suggests, provide people with a conviction that they are free to achieve new identities and personal growth regardless of the "iron cage" in which they are living.

Sectarian religion (Type B) does not extend its demand for the integration of corporate and personal systems of actions beyond a limited sphere that is defined as having religious significance. The Mormons, for example, place all communal relationships under the guidance of religion, especially those of the family; but they also include economic and social ties that exist between members of the sect. The larger society is defined as secular, and only when it intrudes upon the physical or social space with which the Mormons identify their religious beliefs, *e.g.* in their former defense of polygamy, do they enter into conflict with other groups or with the state. Like the Mormons, Jehovah's Witnesses engage in evangelistic proselytizing rather than fraternal relationships with outsiders. Both conflict with the larger society on a limited set of issues. The Witnesses, for instance, reject participation in national ceremonies and service in the Armed Forces – both highly strategic issues. Conflicts between this type of religious group and the larger society clarify the boundaries between the religious and the secular in areas especially salient to them. As a result these groups are agents of the process of societal secularization in that they demand that political authority be based on secular grounds and observe limits asserted by religious culture.

> The process of secularization, then, is compatible with esoteric or occult religious culture. In fact, secularization may foster these forms of religion as a reaction to pervasive routinization and rationalization in social and political organization. Conversely, religious cultures of the second type [sectarian religions], of which the Mormons and Jehovah's Witnesses are paradigmatic cases, foster the secularization of political authority (*o.c.*: 72).

Finally, then, what is the relationship of societal secularization to evangelical religion (Type C)? Pentecostal, evangelical and charismatic variations emphasize the wide scope of religion in the life of the individual without at the same time providing a model for the ideals of large-scale corporate actors.

> The whole of the society may be thoroughly secularized at the corporate level without frustrating the goal of this type of religious culture which is to permeate all areas of personal life with religious influence and meaning [...]

The evangelical program thus represents religion under the conditions of advanced separation between personal and corporate systems of action. It promises personal, spiritual power to individuals who are at a disadvantage in the balance of power with institutions and organizations (*o.c.*: 72).

According to Fenn, this type of charismatic and populist religious culture may come into conflict with the authority of corporate actors and reject the special knowledge of various experts, elites and holders of high office at points of significance to personal ideals and values, *e.g.* in education and medicine. Cases in point are the right of believers to rely on spiritual sources of healing or to teach their views on evolution.

Fenn's typology is illuminating as far as the relationship of particular religious organizations with societal secularization is concerned. Possible de-secularizing tendencies can come, he suggests, only from the main Christian churches and denominations. But such an expectation appears utopian since the critical or prophetic activity of these religious organizations has diminished, probably as a result of their confrontation with the authority of professionals (cf. *supra*), and the sharp decline in membership and in the involvement of those who have remained members (cf. *infra*). The de-secularizing impact of the main churches is also limited, since, in consequence of pluralism, conflicts over religious issues can be resolved only by de-sacralizing the issues (cf. *supra*). Sectarian religion furthers the process of societal secularization in the limited range of issues that seem to impinge upon the sacred, and especially so in the field of politics in which sectarianism seeks to limit the sacralization of political authority. Evangelical religion appears to accept a separation of religion from the secular along a boundary that divides personal from corporate goals and ideals. It will engage in criticism and action only in areas of the sacred that are of primarily individual concern, since religious beliefs and orientations are limited to the personal domain. Finally, magical and occult religion completely accepts the secularization of corporate action, and seems to be able to offer the individual strategies for coping with existential and social sources of uncertainty (cf. also Glock and Bellah, 1976).

## Conclusions

In the first part of this section I stressed that organizational secularization is a particular type of religious change and I related this to socio-cultural changes. The analysis of the evaluation of the type of religious change, whether or not a form of organizational secularization, was clearly dependent on the definition of religion which authors were using In the second part, I tried to answer some questions on the relationship between religious change, c. q. organizational secularization, and societal secularization. In the first part, the impact of pluralism on the secularization of social problems was stressed along with the emergence of a secular moral doctrine. Second, Wilson's studies allowed us to see how a secularized society stimulates the emergence of religious communities that are inconsequential for modern society. These are, in Fenn's terms, magical and occult sects. On the basis of Fenn's analysis I would suggest that the chances of a re-sacralization of society, *i.e.* de-secularization, are very slim, as this could come only from the main Christian churches and denominations, but they are losing members and their remaining members are becoming less and less involved in church life. Moreover, Berger's, Wilson's, Isambert's, and Coleman's studies attest to the adaptation of denominations and churches to the secularized world, and this supports my thesis.

But Coleman's study also makes us aware of a new trend in church strategy. Churches still retain ambitions of influencing the moral and ethical persuasions of non-members by initiating dialogue networks and inviting them to co-operate with trans-confessional aims (Coleman, 1978: 14-15 and 200-204). A problem quite often referred to the churches is the quest for meaning. Not a quest for institutional ideologies, but for a system of meaning that transcends them and that has a more general validity (Dahm and Hoerner, 1975; Dobbelaere, 1979a; and Wuthnow, 1976: 77-81). Stauffer (1973) and Helle (1975) have argued against Luckmann's thesis that our modern societies do not have general meaning systems and that individuals only have private ones, and especially against Fenn's thesis that such societies do not need overarching cultural legitimation systems of any kind and, indeed, that such systems would rather be divisive. Stauffer suggests that our modern societies have their own meaning systems that emphasize technocracy, functional rationality, professionalization and the incompetence of the lower classes. It is a meaning system that maintains consensus among the powerful and actively discourages a deviant consensus from emerging among the relatively dispossessed. But, according to Stauffer (1973: 418-423), such technocratic legitimation is precarious. It will work as long as social problems can be solved, but it may be threatened by the slowing down of economic growth, which could provoke widespread discontent among the middle and lower classes by increasing life-style dissatisfaction resulting from demographic and environmental problems and rising structural unemployment. As a result, sociologists should

(1) recognize that both persistent and new forms of overarching cultural legitimations, including technocratic beliefs and values, do exist; [... (2) ...]

(3) become sensitive to persistent or emergent social structural problems or contradictions within modern societies and analyze the degree to which and

ways in which consequent strains give rise to open ideological debate or more explicit articulation of cultural symbols and myths (*o.c.*: 423-424).

Helle suggests that belief in the technocratic meaning system was indispensable in promoting the economic development of the industrialized countries. But in today's welfare state such a value-orientation is no longer a basis for future projects. This explains why more and more people become disillusioned with a value position that only legitimates what has already been achieved. The churches could play an important role in responding to recurrent and new quests for meaning, but in this case they should not be organized as bureaucratic, hierarchical societies. According to Helle (1975: 69-75), hey should offer informal and non-hierarchically structured occasions for communication. However, according to Dahm and Hoerner (1975: 88-89), in a differentiated society, theology cannot build up such a new overall meaning system, as religion is only a subsystem of society, and meaning can only be restored if a broader dialogue emerges. Such a meaning system will have to confront the questions of whether and, if so, how we shall be able to control meaningfully the evolving process of differentiation. And from this analysis we shall have to develop criteria that will enable us to give the world a more responsible orientation.

CHAPTER 4

# The Process of Declining Religious Involvement and Individual Secularization

Religious involvement refers to individual behavior and is a measure of its degree of normative integration in religious bodies. It is an index of the accord between the norms of religious groups imposed by the religious authorities and the opinions and conduct of the members who can simply reject all religious beliefs and practices, which is evidence of a decline in religiosity; or they can re-compose their beliefs and practices neglecting religious authorities, which points to a transformation of religion. Two of the three theses that are typical of the sociological approach to the relationship between religion and society, according to Fürstenberg (1968: 13-20), are used to explain disengagement from churches or denominations and involvement in cults and sects. These are, the secularization thesis and the compensation or comfort thesis. The third thesis, the integration thesis, is not relevant to our problem.

## The Comfort Thesis

Charles Glock has reformulated the comfort or compensation thesis to account for the rise and development of religious groups. He suggests that a necessary precondition for the rise of any organized social movement, whether religious or secular, is a situation of felt deprivation which continues to be important to the development of these movements and to their potential for survival (1965: 242-259). Relative deprivation – defined as "any and all of the ways that an individual or group may be, or feel disadvantaged in comparison either to other individuals or groups or to an internalized set of standards" – has, according to Glock, five forms: economic, organismic, social, ethical and psychic (o.c.: 246-249). "In the case of ethical and psychic deprivation [...] a religious resolution may be as efficacious as a secular one in overcoming the deprivation directly". In the case of economic, social and organismic deprivation, however, "religious resolutions are more likely to occur where the nature of the deprivation is inaccurately perceived or those experiencing the deprivation are not in a position to work directly at eliminating the causes". Where these conditions do not apply, the resolution is likely to be secular (*o.c.*: 249). *Sects* are likely to arise out of economic deprivation: they transform society symbolically, but in actuality leave it relatively untouched. *Cults* take up a religious solution to psychic deprivation, and *churches* emerge out of social deprivation (*o.c.*: 250-254). Sects and cults are short-lived: they most often disappear, though a cult can become a sect and a sect can evolve into a church. Churches have a substantial chance of survival because of the persistent nature of social deprivation. Glock suggests that

> Participation in a church functions to provide individuals with a source of gratification which they cannot find in society-at-large. Since there are always individuals who are socially deprived in this sense, there exists a continuing source of new recruits to the church. Furthermore, church participation only compensates for the deprivation; it does not eliminate it. Thus, [...] the primary reasons for the existence of the church are not likely to be dissipated over time (*o.c.*: 255-256 and 259).

Here discussion is confined to the emergence of sects, which arise out of economic deprivation, and the involvement in the churches that follows from social deprivation.

We may note in passing that Glock fails to substantiate his theory with empirical data and that it is a more limited theory than Smelser's theory of collective behavior which suggests four levels of structural strain. Glock also fails to resolve the methodological difficulties that result from Merton's concept of relative deprivation being a "provisional-after-the fact-interpretative concept". Then, too, his theory is a special case of reference group behavior theory, which suggests that a large number of groups and individuals can be a referent, some being "cosmopolitan" and others "local". The major criticism of Glock's thesis, however, is that he does not take into account the process of societal secularization (Laeyendecker, 1967: 232-242).

Religious resolutions of social, economic and organismic deprivations reflect, according to Glock, an inaccurate perception of the nature of these deprivations and/or a lack of power. However, as a result of the development of functionally rational thinking in the social, economic and medical world, supported by the advance of the human and natural sciences, a more accurate perception of the nature of these deprivations is developing. The awareness that solutions to problems in these fields are within human capacity stimulated the emergence and expansion of such secular agencies for remedial action as labor unions, co-operatives and political parties. These agencies improved the social power of the lower social classes of society. As a result, religious sects based on economic deprivation, which were typical of previous centuries, are receding and are being replaced by sects that offer *Gemeinschaftlichkeit* and an irrational, emotional belief system in reaction to a mechanical, rational and depersonalized world (Wilson, 1958: 148-150). Of course, the medical, social and economic worlds are confronted with problems that they cannot solve, *e.g.* uncertainty, powerlessness, scarcity and the absence of meaning. But here too, the societal secularization process allows the development of alternative meaning systems. Pluralism offers us a plethora of religious and secular worldviews (Laeyendecker, 1967: 237-242).

Turning more specifically to studies of social deprivation and the involvement of church members, Glock and his associates conducted an empirical study that supports his theory. In a study of the Episcopal Church in the United States, the degree of social deprivation – based on sex, age, family status, and socio-economic status – was found to be positively associated with mean church involvement and its composite indexes: ritual, organizational and intellectual involvement (Glock, Ringer and Babbie, 1967: 13-102 ). This allows the authors to conclude that the comfort hypothesis "provides one important avenue toward the explanation of religious differences". "Parishioners whose life situations most deprive them of satisfaction and fulfilment in the secular society turn to the church for comfort and substitute rewards" (*o.c.*: 109 and 107).

Unfortunately for the deprivation-compensation theory their study stands alone in reporting a negative association between socio-economic and family status on the one hand and church involvement on the other. Even the use of subjective indices to measure deprivation does not confirm the theory (Hobart, 1974; Hoge and Carroll, 1978: 112-117; Hoge and Roozen 1979c: 48-52; McNamara and St. George, 1978: 303-320; Roof, 1978b: 61-62; and Roof and Hoge, 1980: 413). This could be because Glock's team studied the Protestant Episcopal Church, which is largely made up of urban and suburban middle-class Americans. Thus, lower-class members could be "over-involved" in order to prove themselves in the eyes of the middle- and upper-class members. But for our argument, the idiosyncrasy of Glock's study need not be a matter of concern. What is important is that the deprivation-compensation theory does not generally hold empirically. Roof accounts for this by referring to the process of societal secularization: "it is unlikely in a highly secular culture that deprived persons will find sufficient compensation in other-worldly rewards. As the plausibility of traditional religion for many people declines, so does the likelihood that they will turn to it as a source of gratification" (Roof, 1978b: 62-63). In a recent reappraisal of the deprivation theory, Stark (1972: 500) underscores the same point:

In order for economic deprivation to result in certain kinds of religious commitment it is necessary first that a religious perspective is a *plausible option* for the deprived person in question [...] In society generally, economic deprivation operates mainly to shut persons off from religion rather than to drive them into faith as means of compensation.

What then is the empirical validity of the secularization thesis as an explanation of the disengagement from churches or denominations?

## The Secularization Thesis

In order to study stability or change in church involvement, researchers have used such factors as church membership, parochial day school and Sunday school enrolment, church attendance, church contributions, trends in religious beliefs, and saliency of religion according to the polls. Demerath (1968), in a comprehensive survey of religious indicators, has reviewed and criticized most of these measures. Fluctuations in the figures depend upon the churches' definition of membership, their registration zeal, the impact of social definitions like "religious revival" or "religious decline" on the polls, and even the date of the poll interviews *e.g.* being close to the Christmas season or not. Using the most reliable data, however, certain cautious generalizations can be made.

In the USA, most religious indicators suggest a peak of religious involvement in the 1940s and 1950s and thereafter a decline (Roozen and Carroll, 1979: 21-41) that seems to restore some of the characteristics of the 1930s and perhaps earlier (Demerath, 1968: 352-391). Studies of religious "switchers" in the USA and the Netherlands indicate that the highest percentage moves out of institutional religion altogether, and that males, young adults, the more educated, and those more committed to the new morality are more prone to switch to "none" rather than to "another denomination" (Kluegel, 1980: 37-38; Newport, 1979: 538 and 549; Roof and Hadaway, 1977: 409-412; Roof and Hadaway, 1979: 373; and Van Hemert, 1979: 15 40, 54, 68, 72-73 and 95-96). According to two German studies, German Churches are still predominantly *Volkskirchen,* and are astonishingly stable (Hild, 1974; and Schmidtchen, 1973b). But here, too, the level of education is negatively related to stability. As far as church attendance is concerned, even if it is impossible to study the decline over a long period of time, recent studies document that church involvement in the Western world is now considerably weaker than it was twenty or thirty years ago, and that this decline has been especially dramatic since the mid-1960s (Bibby, 1979: 13; van Hemert, 1980: 10-11). In the last decennia the number of people who believe in God and life after death has also fallen (see *e.g.*, Bibby, 1979: 13; Schmidtchen, 1973b: 257 and 266), and in several countries even the rites of passage are being celebrated by fewer and fewer people (see *e.g.* Wilson, 1976b: 21-27 and 36; and Van Hemert, 1980: 24). Wilson (1976b: 99) reports, and other studies (van Hemert, 1980: 24) could be cited in confirmation, that the number of religious vocations is also sharply declining, which is very indicative of the declining social significance of the churches. More and more people are becoming aware of these developments, since the figures are published and commented upon in the daily newspapers and on radio and television.

Berger (1967: 4-7) links the decline of church religiosity to the "secularization of consciousness". On the basis of church practices and the evacuation of meaning from traditional religious beliefs, he suggests that "*today* the supernatural as a meaningful reality is absent or remote from the horizons of everyday life of large numbers, very probably of the majority, of people in modern societies, who seem to manage to get along without it quite well". This seems to be substantiated by Bibby's study of religion in Canada (1979: 5-13). In West Germany, Schmidtchen (1972 and 1973a), studying Lutherans and Catholics, diagnosed the growth of a perceived discrepancy between societal and churchly value patterns. Churches have the reputation of promoting irrelevant values, and of not promoting and even of preventing the realization of relevant ones. As the societal value pattern becomes dominant, cognitive tensions resulting from such a perceived dis-crepancy are generally solved by opting for the societal value pattern.

Others link the decline in church involvement to societal seculariza-tion by indicating that it is produced by the same processes: urbaniza-tion, industrialization, social and geographical mobility, rhythm of life, the sensual and material culture, modern technology, etc. (Acquaviva, 1979: 133-161). Analyzing the social correlates of the decline of church religiosity, Luckmann concludes that the degree of involvement in church-oriented religion correlates negatively with the degree of in-volvement in the work processes of modern industrial society. Talking about the differences between country and city, he suggests that changes in the distribution of church-oriented religion are linked to an increasing economic interpretation of country and city, the growing functional rationalization of farming, and the diffusion of urban culture to the country through mass media. Discussing the participation of the various occupational groups, he concludes that "Farmers, peasants, and those elements of the middle classes which are basically survivals of the traditional bourgeoisie and petit bourgeoisie are marked by a degree of involvement in church-oriented religion which is disproportionately higher than that of the working class". And comparing the findings in America with those in Europe he states that, in view of the historical differences, "it is surprising that they exhibit so much similarity" (Luckmann, 1967: 30 and 33). According to Berger (1967: 108) "the European and American cases represent two variations on the same underlying theme of global secularization". With regard to Europe, he concludes on the basis of data collected by sociologists working mainly in the line of Le Bras, "that church-related religiosity is strongest (and thus, at any rate, social-structural secularization least) on the margins of modern industrial society, both in terms of marginal classes (such as the remnants of the old petty bourgeoisies) and marginal individuals (such as those eliminated from the work process)".

A great amount of empirical material has been published in support of the preceding conclusions, but let it suffice here to refer to a few recent studies done in Canada, the USA, West Germany, Belgium, and the Netherlands, and a synthetic study done in France (Bibby, 1979: 13-15; Schmidtchen, 1973b: 268-271, 274-277 and 292-295; Wutnow and Christiano: 257-276; Voyé, 1973; Voyé, 1979: 162, 182-185, 197-201; van Hemert, 1980: 12, 16 and 18; and Isambert and Terrenoire, 1980: 33-167 and 180-186). These studies indicate that urbanization, industrialization, rationalization, societalization, mobility, etc. induce declining involvement in religious bodies. According to Wuthnow (1976), however, these processes of modernization do not account for the recent sharp decline of religious commitment. Counter-cultural events – reflected in such indicators as favorable attitudes to legalizing marijuana; the experience of being "high" on drugs; the approval of unmarried couples living together; a favorable disposition toward increased freedom for homosexuals; and the experience of taking part in a demonstration – account, in his opinion, for significant variations in religious commitment beyond that explained by the trend variables that measure modernization. These counter-cultural events are largely produced by the younger generation. This could imply that "as successive age strata mature, not having experienced the counter-cultural contagion of the 1960s, there may well be a return to more traditional religious commitments" (*o.c.:* 862).

A more recent study by Rigney, Machalek, and Goodman (1978), taking into account Demerath's criticism of the indicators used by Wuthnow, tries to assess Wuthnow's discontinuity thesis on the basis of refined *and* expanded measures of religious commitment. They suggest that whether the secularization process "is to be regarded as discontinuous depends largely upon which behavioral, attitudinal or cultural indicators we are considering" (*o.c.:* 386). Although a return to more traditional religious commitments is possible, it seems to me that the results of both studies suggest only that we might have had a temporary acceleration of the decline of religiosity, but they provide no evidence for believing an opposite process to be equally likely. The data conform to the modernization process. Conscious of the situation in which they lived, young people reacted; but did so outside the churches. Religious bodies, having already lost much of their significance, were not considered adequate to channel their protest, and this accelerated their decline.

It seems to me that the preceding studies point towards the impact of an underlying modernization process – *i.e.* functional differentiation, rationalization, societalization, industrialization, urbanization, mobility, bureaucratization etc. – on the disengagement of modern man from religious bodies. The processes have also had an impact on cultural trends: researchers have noted a growing absence of the supranatural as a meaningful reality in the consciousness of modern man, along with a felt discrepancy between societal and religious values. Counter-cultural trends even accelerated in the golden 1960s, especially among the younger generation.

All these arguments also emerge in a recent study of major Protestant denominations in the USA conducted under the general direction of Hoge and Roozen (1979a). The researchers wanted to evaluate the impact of national and local institutional and contextual factors on the declining membership of some denominations. Institutional, *i.e.* church-internal factors, can only explain 30 to 50 per cent of the changes; an estimated 50 to 70 per cent of the changes occurring in the 1960s can be explained by contextual, *i.e.* church-external factors (Hoge and Roozen, 1979b: 326). The important contextual factors considered were: the impact of the natural sciences; the rising standard of living; the rising educational level; the greater amount of free time; the impact of the mass media; geographical mobility; urbanization; and the like. But these cannot explain the dramatic short-term developments. Changes in value commitments loom as the most important national contextual factors. Trends toward individualism, personal freedom, tolerance of diversity, and a greater distance from traditional institutions, especially the family, which have been most evident among young adults, contribute particularly strongly to decreasing involvement (see *e.g.* Hoge 1979b: 120; and Hoge and Roozen, 1979b: 321-323).

Of course, there are also fluctuations in involvement resulting from the impact of such factors as the link between the churches and nationalism or regional nationalism, the cleavages in society, and the differences between denominations (Martin, 1978: 151-161). Hoge and Roozen (1979b: 323-324; see also Hoge, 1979a: 193-197) also indicate that the conservative denominations are still growing. This is explained as a result of maintaining a unitary set of beliefs, emphasizing local and community evangelism, keeping themselves apart in morality and lifestyle from the cultural mainstream, and de-emphasizing social action and ecumenism, with the first three factors having the more direct and stronger impact on denominational growth or decline. The impact of what Mol (1970) calls the degree of institutional secularization – what I have called organizational secularization – *i.e.* traditionalism, and institutional cohesion, also explain to a large extent the different hold which denominations have over their members in New Zealand and Australia. But van Hemert (1980: 27) suggests on the basis of data from the Netherlands that this is rather a cultural lag and that sooner or later even orthodox denominations lose their hold over their members.

Concluding his overview of the data and trends, Martin (1978: 160) wrote:

> In general the disorientations of industrial society in terms of conceptual, geographical and social mobility, all militate against the roots and the sense of the familiar and familial which support Christian images of the world. But alongside this general mobility certain fundamental facts stand out: insofar as work takes place in a personal setting where people own their homes, or their farms, or their own individual skills and professional abilities, in contexts which are familiar and on a human scale they are more likely to practice Christianity and be sensitive to it. Insofar as they are submerged in a mass, dominated by vast enterprises and large scale private or state undertakings, subjected to a soulless process based on mechanism, they are less likely to practice Christianity or to be aware of its meaning. The intelligentsia varies. If sensitized to forms of control inimical to its own expressionist sensitivity it may revert to highly personal religiosity, in particular either a free, unbound mysticism or aesthetic ritualism. But if the intelligentsia is deployed as the agent of technical exploitation carried out under the aegis of state power it succumbs to a materialistic ideology.

This last remark brings us to Marxist secularism. Most of the studies of religion and secularization in Communist countries point to changes of involvement in religious bodies (cf. *supra*). They refer, on the one hand, to *objective conditions* that produce "the death of religion, secularization and the function of atheist ideas" – *i.e.* technological development and material-economic conditions, involvement of individuals in political and other public activities, and cultural and educational levels – and, on the other hand, to *subjective factors* – *i.e.* processes that facilitate the acceptance of scientific atheistic philosophy, of which atheistic propaganda, atheistic education, and the development of materialistic philosophy are important components (De Neve, 1973: 596-599). In these empirical studies, such variables as cultural level, education level, type of education, professional level, social class, degree of urbanization, involvement in socio-political organizations, sex, and age, are used to explain variations in religiosity as indicated by church affiliation, regularity of church practice, religious self-definition, the frequency with which men pray, the acceptance of dogmas and moral principles etc. (*e.g.* Bahtijarvic, 1971; Cimic, 1971; Flere, 1978; Lutter, 1966; Paweczynska, 1971; Roter, 1971; and Vrcan, 1977). For an extensive analysis of Eastern Europe, I refer to Martin's analysis of the pattern of secular monopoly (1978: 209-243), and for the religious Situation in Russia also to the work of Lane (1978) and of Ethel and Stephen Dunn (1975). It is interesting to note that the Dunns explain religious behavior in Soviet society as a response to actual social conditions on the part of persons who are, or feel themselves to be, excluded for structural reasons from the mainstream of Soviet society: women, the rural population, and various categories excluded from education because of differential availability. In other words, they stress objective conditions and state that "The most obvious threat to the believer today is not so much a particular political system to be viewed as the antichrist as an inexorable process taking place all over the world – secularization" (Dunn and Dunn, 197.: 142-143; see also Berger, 1963).

In Eastern Europe, of course, there are also fluctuations in the level of personal commitment to the churches. As in the West, they result also from differences in the churches themselves – the resistance of the Orthodox and Lutheran state churches is weaker than that of other religions (Martin,1978: 152-153 and 235) – and the link between church and nationalism *(o.c.:* 153, 229 and 237; and Swiecicki, 1971). But fluctuations depend as much upon differences in the church-state relationship prior to the advent of Communism, the freedom of the church with regard to religious socialization and catechetics (cf. *supra;* and Martin, 1978), and the presence of a strong church-related intelligentsia (Swiecicki, 1971: 95-96; and Martin, 1978: 223 and 236).

Martin (1978: 151-164 and 234-239) gives a detailed and comparative analysis of differences between and among the Eastern and Western European countries. What is important to stress is the tenacity of certain rites of passage, especially baptism and religious funerals, in Communist countries including Russia (*o.c.:* 154-155 and 220). Martin suggests that the ruling ideology of Eastern Europe is an intellectualist formation originally expressing the position of, in particular, ethnically or religiously marginal intellectuals in a state of partial disintegration (*o.c.:* 161). This ideology served them in their confrontation with the old administrative élites, and it also helped to mobilize and solidify an "untheoretical sector of the deprived" which had already achieved positions of relative power and affluence within the system.

> Once in control [...] the intellectuals and the sectional working class oligarchies found themselves confronted by the remorseless imperatives of power, made doubly remorseless by their own ideology, which disallowed conflict and claimed a monopoly of power and ontological rectitude. Thus armed and constricted they set about to control in terms familiar to them: the ma-

145

nipulation of culture through socialization, education and the rejection of all verbal dissidence. Creatures of the word they feared the word more than the rite (*o.c.*: 162).

We may then conclude that the disengagement of individuals from the churches in Eastern Europe is linked to a policy of laicization of society, which is extended to private persons as a consequence of what are considered to be objective conditions and subjective factors. The important difference with the West is the last factor, which facilitates the acceptance of a scientific atheistic philosophy (cf *supra*). In the West, the societal value pattern, which is also conceived as opposed to religious values, is rarely propagated consciously as an attack on religion. In the Communist countries, the Communist atheistic philosophy is propagated by the state, its school system and the mass media. Second, in the Communist countries, some factors that provoke fluctuations in involvement, such as the freedom of religious socialization and the impact of the intelligentsia, are also manipulated to promote the extinction of private religion. But, according to the Dunns (1975), these factors are not as important as the objective conditions.

## The "Secularization Thesis" and Some Other Theories

In addition to the secularization and the comfort or deprivation theory, other theories are also used to explain commitment and participation in the churches (Hoge and Roozen, 1979c: 48-62). Together with the deprivation theory, Hoge and Carroll (1978) investigated some of them: the child-rearing theory, the doctrinal beliefs theory, the status group theory, and the localism theory. I have already discussed the deprivation theory in the first part of this section. According to their study, the status group and localism theories seem hopeful starting points, and the child rearing theory found some support.

It is my contention that these theories do not contradict secularization theory, but are extensions of it. These three theories specify the plausibility structures that, in our modern society, are potentially supportive of denominational commitment: the family, local groups (especially those upholding traditional local culture) and, in the USA, the "status churches" or denominations which bring together people of similar social status. This contention will be argued here using Roof's theory of local-cosmopolitan plausibility (1976 and 1978a) and its links with the so-called value structure theory.

Roof started off from Luckmann's, Fenn's and Berger's position and looked for plausibility structures for church religion.

Because traditional beliefs and values are less and less capable of furnishing overarching symbols unifying society, religious plausibility is increasingly restricted to smaller "subworlds" of social experience. The latter are associated more with the private than with the public sectors of life; and structures such as family, ethnic group or some other limited social sphere play a crucial part in sustaining personal religious loyalties. One such sphere in modern society, curiously neglected in studies in religion, is the local community (1976: 197).

Using Merton's conceptualization of localism-cosmopolitanism, which describes a scale of social experience and participation ranging from one's immediate social networks to the broader society (Merton, 1957: 393-409), Roof (1976: 206) argues that locals are more committed to institutional religion than cosmopolitans. According to his exploratory research in North Carolina where he studied adult church members of the Episcopal Church:

> Local community attachments undergird both socio-religious group participation and personal beliefs and practices. [...] In much the same way as [the family and the ethnic group], the local community in modern mass society offers individual opportunities for nurturing and maintaining the "private life", set aside and somewhat distinct from the public sectors of society. Institutional church-type religion, both as a belief system and as a set of organized rituals, retains greater plausibility within these private, more restricted sectors and no doubt functions to symbolize and legitimate traditional values and life-styles.

Additional support for local community attachments as the social basis for church commitment was uncovered by confronting the localism theory with the doctrinal beliefs theory. According to the data, it appears that declining community attachment, more than erosion of traditional beliefs *per se* is the critical factor in accounting for the decline in church attendance and church support, *i.e.* financial contribution (Roof, 1978a: 133-136). Furthermore, not only does the analysis of his data show that orthodoxy's relation to church attendance and financial support for the church is partially spurious, it also indicates that among locals the influence of social status and parental religiosity on church attendance and financial support are considerably stronger (*o.c.*: 136-143). "The results underscore the critical role that local cognitive orientation plays in predisposing church members to traditional beliefs and participation in the liberal Protestant denominations" (*o.c.*: 144). According to Roof's research, localism would also be a precondition for the impact of the family and social status, suggesting that localism is a primary plausibility structure and family and social status secondary plausibility structures.

More recently, Roof and Hoge (1980) tried to test the different theories of church commitment on a random sample of Americans. Once again localism seemed to serve as an especially important plausibility structure for church commitment among liberal Protestants and to a lesser extent among Catholics, but not among conservative Protestants. Roof and Hoge speculated that the difference between types of Protestants could be explained by the fact that the liberal denominations are located closer to the individualistic and secular sectors of American culture than the conservative Protestant denominations, so the plausibility structures are more crucial for the maintenance of church involvement in liberal denominations (*o.c.*: 415).

The reference to the secular culture links this theory to the value structure theory (Hoge and Roozen, 1979c: 57-61). People who are committed to the churches in present-day America hold "conventional values, including preference for traditional sex roles and family roles, non-involvement with drugs, definite moral codes, and emphasis on private concerns rather than broader political concerns" (Roof and Hoge, 1980: 408) . The so-called "New Morality", to which younger persons, the more educated and the more cosmopolitan adhere, predicts nonmembership and less active involvement in the churches (*o.c.*: 420). Roof and Hoge's study emphasizes a link between cosmopolitanism and the "New Morality". "The result is a widening cleavage between the traditional culture and a growing cosmopolitan-modernist subculture. The latter is sometimes called the 'New Morality' or the 'do your own thing' subculture" (*o.c.*: 423). The decline in church membership, especially in liberal Protestantism, is partly attributable to the identification of institutional churches with the local-traditional subculture and to the growing importance of the cosmopolitan-modernist subculture. Thus a theory of two life-styles is proposed by Roof and Hoge to explain changing church commitment of Americans today (*o.c.*: 423-424). At the very least, their research opens avenues in the study of plausibility structures that support church religiosity in a secularized society. Further research incorporating data from other countries and other religious dimensions is needed to validate these findings.

## The "Secularization Thesis", "Invisible Religion", and "Alternative Meaning Systems"

Luckmann (1967: 27) has suggested that the question should be asked "whether, in contemporary society, any socially objectivated meaning structures but the traditional institutionalized religious doctrines function to integrate the routines of everyday life and to legitimate its crises". He himself suggested that a new form of religion is emerging, an "institutionally nonspecialized social form of religion" that is privately constructed. This he calls "invisible religion" (*o.c.*: 101, 103-106 and 113-114. Yinger (1969: 90) starts off from Luckmann's argument that much of contemporary religion remains invisible and suggests "rather than asking *if* a person is religious, we ask *how* he is religious". In order to do so he suggests studying the basic, permanent and presumably universal questions that give rise to religious expressions. His approach is functional, and like Geertz (1968: 14) he thinks that religious belief systems are shaped in great part by the experiences of meaninglessness, suffering and injustice (Yinger, 1977: 68). Yinger (1969: 91 and 1970: 33) has called for greater attention to indicators that can diagnose "*awareness of and interest in the continuing, recurrent, 'permanent' problems of human existence*". Apart from awareness and interest, which is the individual character aspect, there is also a cultural aspect (shared rites and beliefs), and a socio-structural aspect (group formation), which are constitutive of religion and which should be studied (Roof and Hoge, 1980: 91). The items he uses to study awareness and interest are non-doctrinal statements about the persistent and intractable problems of meaninglessness, suffering and injustice that reflect the conviction that these problems can ultimately be dealt with by our beliefs and actions (Yinger, 1977: 68).

Yinger gathered data from college and university students in Japan, Korea, Thailand, New Zealand, Australia, the United States and the Netherlands and secondary school students in England and found that nearly three-quarters of the responses were in the "religious" direction. They expressed the belief that behind day-by-day experience there is another kind of reality that supersedes or redefines it. These beliefs, as reflected in the responses to the set of non-doctrinal statements, occurred with roughly the same frequency among adherents to the major religions as among those who professed no religious identity (*o.c.*: 77) . In the analysis of the effects of social variables on "non-doctrinal religion", sex and social status were found to be unrelated; nationality and religious identity were only weakly related; and level of education and age proved to be most significantly related, older students being more "religious" than younger ones (*o.c.*: 78-85) . Roof (1979: 32) is probably correct in suggesting that a lack of strong social correlates implies the widespread existence of these basic concerns across heterogeneous groups of people.

Yinger's lead was followed in studies conducted by Nelsen and associates (1976), Roof and associates (1977), and Machalek and Martin (1976). The first two studies used a student sample; the last one sampled an old, middle-to-working class white neighborhood. Machalek and Martin (*o.c.*: 317-318) found support for the existence of privatized religion outside an institutionalized religious context: 18 per cent of the respondents had transcendent ultimate concerns; 33 per cent of the coping strategies mentioned were transcendent in nature, and 43 per cent had formally organized transcendent or humanist coping strategies. But their study did not relate people's ultimate concerns to traditional institutionalized religious forms. The studies by Nelsen, Roof and their associates provided evidence that "doctrinal" and "non-doctrinal" religion, or "institutional" and "invisible" religion, covary together (Nelsen *et al.* 1976: 266-267; and Roof *et al.*, 1977: 407).

Nelsen and associates subjected the Yinger items to factor analysis, using a student sample from the Southern United States; similarly, Roof and associates used a student sample from the Northeast. They concluded that the items do not form a unidimensional scale and suggested two and three factors respectively. One factor is the same in both studies, with Nelsen calling it "value of suffering" and Roof calling it "value of difficult experience", the latter name indicating that the items stress a broader concern than simply suffering. This factor emphasizes that beliefs may be a means of coping with such experiences and that they may be sources of increased understanding and powers of endurance (Roof *et al.*, 1977: 406; and Nelsen *et al.*1976: 266). Nelsen's (*o.c.*: 265-266) other factor is called "acceptance of belief and order" and closely approximates Yinger's concept of non-doctrinal religion. Roof and associates (*o.c.*: 406) label their two other factors "value of religious efforts", which is a form of non-doctrinal commitment, and "belief in order and pattern", which emphasizes "religion as a means of dealing with threats to the social order". Roof's latter factors seem to be a specification of Nelsen's second factor, stressing, on the one hand, religion's potential for integrating life in some personally meaningful way, and, on the other hand, its social function. Both studies indicate that the factors are related to traditional religion. Nelsen's factors (*o.c.*: 206) are positively correlated with devotionalism, orthodoxy, sectarianism, and associational involvement; Roof's (1977: 406-407) with belief in God, attendance at religious services, personal prayer, meditation, bible reading, and self-rated religiosity.

In sum, the above studies suggest that privatized, "invisible", "non-doctrinal" religious structures exist, which points to the transformation of religion on the individual level. But, according to Roof, Nelsen and their associates, such a religion may not form a unitary belief system. It seems instead to be multi-dimensional. They also indicate that non-doctrinal religion is related to traditional religiosity, which is not contradicted by Yinger's recent research. As the samples are mostly based on students, Yinger's ideas should be studied using a broader population.

Another line of research, based on secularization thought and especially that of Berger and Luckmann (1967), is related to the construction of reality. How do people make sense of their worlds? How do they structure reality? Or, as Roof (1979: 33) puts it: "How do they interpret experiences and events in their lives that call for some kind of judgment about the nature of reality?".

Glock and Piazza (1978) asked the question: How do people deal with *experiences* (*e.g.* their own life experiences), *situations* (*e.g.* a hypothetical situation of twin brothers growing up very differently), and *conditions and events* (*e.g.* suffering, poverty, and social inequality) that call for a judgment about how the world works? They found that the adult population of the San Francisco Bay Area conceived of reality as being structured, in decreasing order, by: latent social forces, *i.e.* social arrangements created by historical social forces operating now independently of conscious human control; individuals; culture; supernatural forces, *i.e.* God, luck or fate; conspiratorial social forces, *i.e.* social reality as manipulated by those in power; and finally heredity. According to their research the modes of structuring reality vary according to age, college education, and religious background. The *environmentalists*, who explain experiences and events by latent social forces, are young or middle-aged, college educated liberal Protestants or people with "no religious beliefs". The *individualistic* mode predominates among middle-aged people who have no college education, and who are conservative and moderate Protestants. The *culturalist* mode tends to recruit among older people, but from the more educated among them, and it is over-selected only by those outside the churches. The *supernaturalists* are especially older, relatively uneducated people; they are generally conservative Protestants, but also Catholics and moderate Protestants. The *conspirationalist* mode attracts younger people of less education and middle-aged people with a college education. Agnostics or atheists rather than the blander "no religious belief" are conspiratorialist, but Catholics also show a tendency to over-select this mode. The *hereditarians*, finally, represent only two per cent of the population and were omitted because of the paucity of cases.

Glock and Piazza suggest that their data, juxtaposed with earlier data on the political and moral correlates of the different modes, raise the possibility that a generational shift is occurring in the distribution of the different modes of reality construction.

McCready and Greeley (1976) are not so sure about a generation gap. Analyzing how people respond to ultimate questions of good and evil, they found five basic responses in the American population: religious optimism, hopefulness, secular optimism, pessimism, and diffusion. "If there is any difference in ultimate values between adolescents and adults, it would seem that adults are more likely to be religious optimists and adolescents more likely to be hopeful" (*o.c.*: 177). But they were not able to determine if this is a life-cycle difference or a generational change.

A more sophisticated and very systematic approach to this question is given by Wuthnow (1976) in his study on conscious reformation done in the San Fancisco Bay Area. He started out with four theoretical meaning systems circumscribed by the items in brackets: *theism* (belief in God, creation, and afterlife; influenced by God; God causes poverty and suffering; devil causes suffering), *individualism* (work hard and equality; blame self for failure; influenced by will power; poverty and suffering caused by self; and failure is own fault), *social sciences* (influenced by environment and childhood experiences; evolution; suffering caused by society and class; and the American way of life causes poverty), and *mysticism* (experience nature, the sacred, and harmony; live in fantasy world; influenced by new insights; learn from the arts and the woods; feel deeply; and suffering caused by lack of inner space) (*o.c.*: 229-230 and 237-239).

Empirically, seven meaning systems seem to flower in the San Francisco Bay Area. As only 50 per cent of the sample could be classified as adhering to only one of the four theoretical meaning systems with a greater degree of likelihood than any of the other three, the remainder were divided into three categories: *traditionalism* (people holding both individualistic and theistic meaning systems), *modern* (people with an equal likelihood of holding the social scientific and mystical meaning systems), and *transitional* (people holding simultaneously to one of the more traditional and one of the more modern meaning systems). More than 25 per cent adhere to the transitional meaning system; around 15 per cent adhere to the theistic, social, mystical, or modern meaning systems; about 10 per cent are individualistic; and about 5 per cent are traditional (*o.c.*: 144-145 and 242).

On the basis of age, maturation characteristics by age, phase of life. cycle, education and related factors, and background characteristics (*o.c.*: 153-171) Wuthnow is able to demonstrate that trends may now be under way or have been taking place during the past generation: "theistic and individualistic understandings have witnessed a noticeable decline in the past several decades while social-scientific and mystical ideas have shown an equal increase in importance" (*o.c.*: 172). This change seems to be very gradual, however. The analysis of the generation gap prompts him to suggest that whatever long-range changes may endure, they will be relatively small, as the likelihood that youths will return to the views of their parents as they grow older seems great. Similarly, the impact on the culture of people with a higher level of education has been extraordinarily gradual thus far, and appears likely to remain that way in the future (*o.c.*: 172).

## Conclusions

The decline in the number of church members, the disengagement of those still in the churches, the emergence of new forms of religion outside the scope of religious authorities, and the development of non-religious meaning systems all bear witness to individual secularization. These changes are best explained by the same processes that prompted the secularization of society. And here, too, as for the process of societal secularization, there are fluctuations depending upon the particular socio-cultural complex within which individual secularization occurs: the state ideology; the link between churches and nationalism or regional nationalism; the differences in denominations; the freedom of churches to organize religious socialization and their access to the mass media; the position of the intelligentsia etc. All these similarities suggest the following questions: Are individual secularization and societal secularization parallel developments? Are they independent? Or do they have a bearing on one another? I shall deal with these questions in the concluding section and Part II.

This section confirmed the existence of transformations of religion on the individual level beyond the range of influence of the religious authorities: a so-called "invisible" or "non-doctrinal" religion, although we should realize that some questions remain unanswered. According to Yinger, Machalek and Martin, non-doctrinal religion exists quite independently of institutional religion, and (according to Machalek's and Martin's research) both as a private and as a formally organized religion. Roof and Nelsen and their associates established that non-doctrinal religion need not be uni-dimensional in content. What are the basic dimensions in invisible religion? Three dimensions were established: "value of difficult experience", "value of religious efforts", and "belief in order and pattern". They also ascertained that these dimensions co-vary with dimensions of institutional religion. What then is the relationship between non-doctrinal and institutional religion? Does non-doctrinal religion as operationalized simply refer to an anthropological universal, *i.e.* an expression of ultimate concern, which is answered in a typical way by institutional religion? If so, we should expect to find a relationship between non-doctrinal and institutional religion. However, what other answers are there? And what is their relationship to institutionalized religion. What are their rites and beliefs, and what social groups support them? These last questions bring us to the symbolic constructions that Wuthnow, Glock, McCready and their colleagues studied as meaning systems defining and ordering reality.

It is clear from their research that between 25 per cent (McCreay and Greeley, 1976: 212) and more than 50 per cent of people (Glock, and

Piazza, 1978: 62) cannot be classified as adhering to only one meaning system. This raises the question of what ultimate concerns are defined and ordered by what meaning systems. Up to now research has not gone into this problem, although Glock and Piazza (*o.c.*: 62) refer to two facets of it. They suggest that people may refer to events as being multiply caused or may see "one agent being responsible for some events and another as cause of others".

The symbolic constructions that were studied were also built along different dimensions. McCready and Greeley's (1976: 177) categories were construed along a line of optimism-pessimism, but as they called both religious optimists *and* hopefuls religious, their types implicitly also included the religious-secular dimension. Glock and Wuthnow built their types on the basis of symbolic content: each has a supernaturalist or theistic, and an individualistic meaning system. Wuthnow's social science meaning system is probably equivalent to the meaning systems of Glock's environmentalists, culturalists, and conspirationalists. Wuthnow's mystical meaning system is new, and he also has three mixed types. All this indicates that meaning systems can be studied along different dimensions – optimism-pessimism or supernaturalist-secular, for example – and that they can be specified according to types of supernatural or secular explanatory principles.

What then, finally, is the relationship between types of meaning systems and institutional religion? And between types of meaning systems and life-styles? (Cf. *supra*). Wuthnow (1976: 169 and 171) has data only on parental religion, and people's religious background shows interesting differences in their relative tendencies to choose different meaning systems. People with a Protestant background are disproportionately likely to be traditionalists while those whose parents were Catholics are more likely to be theists. A Jewish background seems more conducive to the socio-scientific assumptions or a modern meaning system, *i.e.* a mixture of socio-scientific and mystical assumptions. A non-religious background seems most conducive to the socio-scientific and the mystical assumptions, or a mixture of them. McCready and Greeley's (1976: 48-49) study linked the type of ultimate values that people hold to their religious affiliation. Protestants are more likely to be either religious optimists or hopefuls, and in the authors' terms this means that they are over-represented in the religious types. Catholics are over-represented in the pessimist and diffuse types, but to a lesser extent than Jews and non-religious people. Those who claim to be religious, but who do not claim any religious group, are not only over-represented in the pessimist and diffuse types, but also in the secular optimist type. Glock and Piazza's (1976: 65) findings largely confirm this. Catholics are the most prone to select a supernaturalist and a conspiratorialist mode. Conservative and moderate Protestants show a tendency to over-select the supernaturalist and the individualistic mode; liberal Protestants tend to be environmentalists. Non-religious people are often environmentalists and culturalists, and agnostics and atheists over-select the conspiratorialist mode. This suggests that religious background and affiliation pre-dispose people more to certain meaning systems than to others. It would be interesting to pursue this line of research, taking into account not only affiliation but also involvement in different religious dimensions. The question concerning the relationship between types of meaning systems and lifestyles cannot be answered with the available data.

# CHAPTER 5

# Conclusions

I have tried to make two points in this trend report: first of all, that we should distinguish between societal, organizational and individual secularization; second, that secularization is not a mechanical evolutionary process, but one that depends on the cultural context in which it unfolds and on the persons, groups, and quasi-groups involved. Such a view of secularization is supported when one recognizes that the subprocesses of functional differentiation, functional rationalization and societalization are reversible. They are activated by persons, groups and quasi-groups who, manifestly or latently, secularize or sacralize society and its social institutions. Reading the process in terms of a private and a public sphere blurs the issues.

In functionally differentiated social institutions, social action has been organized in accordance with functionally rational principles, and in these institutional spheres social interaction has been based primarily on the role-performances of unknown role players. This type of relationship, which started in the work sphere, has extended into the social world: city life, neighborhood, family life and leisure. The impact of traditional religion has declined as it is incompatible with these functionally rational principles and the *Gesellschaft*, which is based on technical and bureaucratic controls and has downgraded all moral controls. Religion has become less and less operational in modern societies.

As religion lost its societal functions, religious pluralism developed. The religious tradition, which prior to the advent of modern society could be authoritatively imposed, lost its monopoly position and a pluralistic situation developed. In such circumstances, religion had to be marketed. This of course further de-objectified the sacred cosmos, which allowed non-religious rivals to emerge and to compete. Our analysis of the literature suggested that a pluralistic situation promotes secularization of society in order to reduce social conflicts by transferring social issues out of the religious arena to more neutral grounds. This, of course, stimulated the building up of a secular moral doctrine and promoted the emergence of "operative faiths" by which the political institution was integrated.

On the other hand, religions also adapted to the secular world. New religious faiths of the magical and occult type emerged, which accepted the secularized world and functioned as therapeutic agencies offering a permanent or occasional escape from that world. Surviving sectarian religious groups, wishing to restrict the scope of the sacred, consequently promoted the secularization of the world; and evangelical and charismatic religions, which adopted the secular ideology of the "private" and the "public" sphere, restricted their prophetic clashes with the secular world. Only the traditional churches and denominations emerge as possible challengers to secularized agencies. But, for different reasons, their impact seems to be minimal. In fact, they also adapted to the world by subjectivizing their theology, by promoting ancillary functions, which in the long run relinquished their typical religious qualities, and by submitting to the pressures of their members, who have increasingly rejected traditional morality and rituals. A process of de-objectification of the sacred cosmos and rituals set in, and, at the same time, different forms of ecumenism emerged. Coleman's comprehensive study of Dutch Catholicism suggests ways in which the churches adapt to the secularized world.

Present research does not enable me to suggest clear links between, on the one hand, societal secularization and religious involvement and, on the other, between organizational secularization and religious involvement. Most researchers suggest that the same processes that promoted the secularization of society – *i.e.* functional differentiation, functional rationalization, societalization, and the accompanying processes of specialization, professionalization and migration – also stimulated a decline of involvement in churches, denominations and sects. But are the diminished participation in religious organizations and the secularization of society parallel developments? Do they change independently, or do they have a bearing on one another? Does the secularization of society as such have an independent impact on personal involvement in religious organizations? Does the fact that people work in settings reflecting different degrees of secularization result in a different degree of participation in religious organizations? And, inversely, what is the impact of a decline in participation in churches, denominations and sects on the promotion of a secularized world? Manifest processes of secularization, *i.e.* laicization, sometimes seem to be supported by former church members, as is the case with the proposal to secularize the Catholic schools in Belgium. In these cases, religious organizations become negative reference groups. This could be an example of what Merton (1957: 295) called the ambivalence of ex-members, who become more hostile toward their former groups than are their new-found associates.

Another unknown factor is whether religious bodies change their doctrine, ethics and rituals, in response to the secularization of the world or to the disengagement of their membership? Nor do we know what the impact is of changes in church laws on membership involvement. Does a change in certain rules – *e.g.* in the Catholic Church, about fasting before communion, Friday abstinence, or the observation of Lent – stimulate doubts about the rightness of other church laws – *e.g.* about weekly church attendance? And what is the impact of church conservatism in a particular area such as birth control or divorce on the involvement of people in the church?

Greeley and his associates (1976: 103-154) have tried to answer these last questions by studying American Catholics. They analyzed the impact, on the decline in Catholic religious involvement of, on the one hand, the Second Vatican Council as a "well-intended exercise in modernization and liberation" and, on the other hand, the birth control encyclical, *Humanae Vitae*, as a "reaffirmation of traditional teachings, despite widespread expectations to the contrary". Their data indicate that the impact of the conservative teachings of the encyclical and the connected loss of respect for papal authority on the decline of involvement in the Church was the greater, although they admit that the modernization and liberation of the Council stimulated a high level of expectation for change that was frustrated and that produced religious alienation.

My problem with this explanation is that it is too particularistic. It does not take into account that in the same period religious decline also occurred in most Christian denominations without "papal encyclicals". Are the frustrations at the lack of change produced by the Council and the reactions aroused by the conservative encyclical, *Humanae Vitae*, not simply indicators of a deeper change that took place in the Western world? This change was described as a trend toward individualism, personal freedom, tolerance of diversity, and a greater distance from traditional institutions, especially the family. It was found among cosmopolitans and accelerated a modernization trend that had begun some decades ago. Most recent research indicates that the traditional Christian meaning system functions only in very restricted "sub-worlds". The local community and the family, as far as they are impregnated by traditional values, are still plausibility structures for traditional religion. The value system of cosmopolitan modern society conflicts with traditional Christian values.

It is clear that our research endeavor should more and more shift toward an analysis of different competing meaning systems, a research design suggested by Berger, Luckmann and Yinger, and initiated by Glock, Greeley, and Wuthnow. What meaning systems are used by people to make sense of, on the one hand, just which "permanent" human conditions and, on the other, of "quotidian" events? Which of these events, conditions, situations and experiences are considered to be multiply caused, and which are explained by one cause? Is there a difference in this respect according to social categories? And what is the relationship between types of meaning systems, life-styles and religious backgrounds? Answers to these questions would further our understanding of the function of religion as a particular meaning system, and broaden our understanding of the relationship between secularization and operational meaning systems including religion.

# PART II

## SECULARIZATION: THE THREE LEVELS AND THEIR INTERRELATEDNESS

# Presentation

In my Trend Report of 1982, the first part of the present work, I set forth the need to differentiate between three levels of analysis in our studies of the secularization process – the societal, the organizational and the individual level, and on the study of their interrelatedness. Secondly, throughout the chapters on societal and organizational secularization, I have pointed out that secularization is not a mechanical, evolutionary process, which implies that we have to study the impact of actors – among others: religious and lay collectivities, groups and quasi-groups and professionals, politicians and church leaders – on latent and manifest attempts to secularize or to sacralize organizations and society.

Since 1982, a new synthesis of the secularization paradigm has been published (Tschannen, 1992); new empirical studies have become available; and the discussion pro and con the secularization theory has continued, especially animated by representatives of rational choice theory (RCT), who proposed RCT as an alternative, at least in the USA (Young, 1997). In this second part, I address some of the issues raised, refer to recent empirical studies – without pretending to be exhaustive, and take up a position in the ongoing discussion; whilst trying to make clear what I consider to be the advantages of distinguishing the different levels of analysis. Study of the relationship between the societal and individual levels dominates the discussion, but I do not neglect the impact of the raising level of religious pluralism in our regions.

# CHAPTER 1

# The Interrelatedness of Societal and Individual Secularization

During the last decade, several studies have analyzed the effect of societal secularization on individual church commitment. Evaluating these studies, I suggest a methodological approach to analyze this impact by introducing a comprehensive secularization-index and a compartmentalization-index in longitudinal studies. However, my analysis also suggests that the causal link is not unidirectional: church commitment also has an impact on compartmentalization, which may have repercussions on the process of societal secularization. The use of the term interrelatedness expresses better the possible reciprocal effect.

To measure the degree of secularization of the different countries studied by the European Religious and Moral Pluralism (RAMP) study (Billiet *et al.*, 2002), I tried to use Chaves and Cann's measure of deregulation of church and state (1992). However, it did not sufficiently differentiate between the eleven countries being studied and forced us to look for a proxy variable based on the analysis of the societal and organizational secularization process.

## The Secularization Process: A Partial Recapitulation

In assessing the secularization theories (Dobbelaere, in press), I started from the "exemplars" developed by Tschannen (1992) using the analytical distinction between segmentary and functional differentiation (Luhmann, 1982: 262-265). Modern societies are primarily differentiated along functional lines and have developed different sub-systems (*e.g.* economy, polity, science, family and education). These are similar – since, so to speak, society has equal need of them all – and dissimilar – since they perform their own particular function. Their functional autonomy depends of course upon their communication with other functional systems and the environment. To guarantee these functions and to communicate with their environment, organizations (enterprises; political parties; research centers; families; schools and universities) have been established (the meso level). Each of these organizations functions on the basis of its own medium (money; power; truth; love;

information and know-how) and according to the values of its sub-system and its specific norms.

Regarding religion, these organizations affirm their autonomy and reject religiously prescribed rules, *i.e.* the autonomization of the sub-systems. In this context, Luhmann speaks about secularization in the sense of a specifically religious conception of society as the environment of the religious sub-system (Luhmann, 1977: 225-232). In other words, secularization describes the effect of functional differentiation for the religious sub-system and expresses the interpretation of this experience by religious personnel. Thus, the sociological explanation of societal secularization starts with the process of functional differentiation: religion becomes a sub-system alongside other sub-systems, losing in this process its over-arching claims over the other sub-systems. In fact, societal secularization is only the particularization of the general process of functional differentiation in the religious sub-system.

The declining religious authority over the other sub-systems, *i.e.* their autonomization, allowed the development of functional rationality within the organizations. The economy lost its religious ethos (Weber, 1920: 163-206). Goals and means were evaluated on a cost-efficiency basis. This typical attitude implying observations, evaluations, calculation and planning – which is based on a belief that the world is calculable, predictable and controllable (Wilson, 1976b and 1985) – is not limited to the economic system. The political system was also rationalized, leaving little room for traditional and charismatic authority, as modern states developed their rational administration. Since these economic and political organizations needed more and more people trained in science and rational techniques, the educational curriculum had to change. A scientific approach to the world and the teaching of technical knowledge increasingly replaced a religious-literary formation. The development of scientifically based techniques also had its impact on the life-world: domestic tasks became increasingly mechanized and computerized. Even the most intimate human behavior, sexuality, became governed by it. This is also the case of the so-called natural method of birth control proposed by the Catholic Church. The Ogino-Knauss method, for example, is based on the basal temperature of the woman registered when waking, which has to be plotted on a chart. On the basis of the temperature-curve, the fertile and infertile periods can be calculated. Thus, it was on the basis of observation, calculation and evaluation that sexual intercourse could be planned to prevent pregnancy.

# Studying the Effect of Societal Secularization on Individual Religiosity

Referring to the effect of the functional rationalization process, also called the Weberian secularization thesis, Jagodzinski and I used the Gross Domestic Product (GDP) *per capita* as a proxy for the degree of societal secularization. If the Weberian secularization hypothesis is correct, the effects of the GDP *per capita* on church commitment for the different countries[1] would be increasingly negative the higher the GDP *per capita*. The results of the regression analysis, controlling for the church context – Protestant *versus* Catholic dominance – in the different countries, allowed us to conclude that the "comparisons between the countries offer[ed] the most convincing evidence in favour of the Weberian secularization thesis" (Jagodzinski and Dobbelaere, 1995: 101). We warned however, that our regression analysis should not be taken as a statistical test but as a parsimonious description of the relationship.

Referring to our theoretical reasoning – functional rationalization being a consequence of functional differentiation and the autonomization of the subsystems – we used Gross National Product *per capita* as proxy for societal secularization in our analysis of the RAMP data (Billiet, *et al.*, 2002). Examining the impact of GNP *per capita*, as a context variable, on church commitment for the eleven European countries in the study[2], controlling for church commitment in childhood and present denomination, on the basis of a multilevel regression model, we found also a significant and negative relationship: the higher the country's GNP *per capita* the lower individual church commitment was (standardized parameter -.189 and t-value -3.23).

Halman and Pettersson (1999) used GDP *per capita* as an indicator of economic development, which they used as an indicator of deprivation, but, which Jagodzindski and I had used as an indicator of the level of functional rationality in the economic field in the countries under study. Their study based on the survey data from the 1990 European Values Study (EVS) in 23 European countries[3], allows for a distinction between Western and Eastern European countries. The main ranking of the levels of religious involvement was fairly similar to the level of

---

[1] Belgium, Denmark, France, Germany, Great Britain, Ireland, Italy, the Netherlands, Spain, and Norway.

[2] Belgium, Denmark, Finland, Great Britain, Hungary, Italy, the Netherlands, Norway, Poland, Portugal, and Sweden.

[3] Austria, Belgium, Bulgaria, Czech Republic, Denmark, East Germany, Estonia, Great Britain, Hungary, Ireland, Italy, Latvia, Lithuania, Northern Ireland, the Netherlands, Norway, Poland, Portugal, Romania, Spain, Slovak Republic, Sweden, and West-Germany.

GDP *per capita* but in reverse order: the higher the GDP *per capita*, the lower the level of religious involvement and this was the case for all 23 European countries taken together (significant rank order correlation: -.35), also for the 15 Western (-.77) and the 8 Eastern (-.60) European countries taken separately (*o.c.*: 55). They assert that "from the magnitude of the rank correlations, it can be concluded that [...other factors also determine] the national levels of religious involvement" (*ibid.*) and point to the level of Catholics in the country, calling it a Catholic-Protestant divide in Europe. The afore-mentioned studies came to the same conclusion about the effect of Catholicism on the level of church commitment compared to Protestantism.

Indeed, the level of societal secularization is not the only factor that explains the level of church involvement of individuals. However, the studies referring to the GDP *per capita* use a proxy for the level of societal secularization. As long as we are unable to measure the level of functional differentiation between religion (churches, sects and NRMs) and the other sub-systems, we will be forced to use such proxies. We should work towards an index of societal secularization, *i.e.* the functional differentiation of religion and the other sub-systems. Chaves and Cann (1992) have shown how to start measuring de-regulation of church and state, however, their items for differentiating church and state should not be dichotomous but should scale the differentiation and their scale should be extended. The secularization-index should also include the differentiation of the various sub-systems, among others religion and education, *e.g.* the degree of financing denominational schools and the existence of classes in religion in primary and/or secondary schools; the medical sub-system and religion, *e.g.* laws about abortion, euthanasia and experiments with embryos; the family and religion, *e.g.* the mores relative to contraception, the divorce rate, the legal status of heterosexual and homosexual cohabitation; and also the legal system and religion, *e.g.* religious symbols in courts of justice and the oath referring to God or the Bible. By these means, we shall obtain a more comprehensive index of societal secularization.

Halman (1991) tested the impact of societal secularization on individual religiousness in a different way. He calculated the degree of correlation between, on the one hand, the religious values of individuals, and, on the other hand, their political and moral values and those related to the life-world, in reference to the level of structural modernization in ten European countries[4], Canada, and the USA. The data used were assembled with the questionnaire of the European Values Study. In general, the political and moral values, and those related to the life-

---

[4]   See footnote 1.

world of individuals were the most independent of their religious values in the more modern countries. (*o.c.*: 258-259).

All these studies do not solve the methodological difficulty that is similar to the study of Glock who used Merton's concept of 'relative deprivation', which is a "provisional-after-the fact-interpretative concept", as I pointed out in Part I (*supra* p. 138). Indeed, a correlation between two objective data sets, *e.g.* GNP *per capita* and level of church commitment, lacks an intervening variable: the secularization-in-mind, that I have called *compartmentalization* (Dobbelaere, 1999: 241).

## Compartmentalization

To test validly the impact of societal secularization on the individual we need international comparisons between countries. Consequently, we should first establish the degree of societal secularization using a comprehensive *secularization-index*. This will allow us to distinguish between countries according to their degree of societal secularization. Then, we should be able to build a *compartmentalization-index*: *i.e.* an index based on secularization-in-mind. Do people *think* in terms of the separation of religion and the juridical, the educational, the economic, the family, the scientific, the medical, and the political systems? In other words, do they think that religion should not inform the other sub-systems, that the sub-systems are autonomous and that any interference of religion in these sub-systems should be eradicated and disallowed? If we can establish a link between the societal secularization-index and the compartmentalization-index, then we have to go still one step further and link the compartmentalization-index with the beliefs and practices of individuals.

In my research, I was able to measure the association between compartmentalization and church commitment. On the basis of the Belgian data from the EVS of 1999, a compartmentalization-index was built on segregation between religion and the political subsystem[5], there were no data available to build a more comprehensive index. A church commitment index was built with the available indices on church membership, church practices, orthodoxy, importance of rites of passage, private practices and self-evaluation of religiousness. Using a regression model for church commitment, we found that compartmentalization had the

---

[5] How much do you agree with each of the following: Q30 - C - It would be better for the country if more people with strong religious beliefs held public office; - D - Religious leaders should not influence government decisions; and Q39 - A - Politicians who do not believe in God are unfit for public office; - B - Religious leaders should not influence how people vote in elections.

strongest significant total negative effect: the lower the church commitment, the more compartmentalized a person was (-383), compared to generation, level of education, urbanization, gender combined with work situation, and post-materialism (Dobbelaere and Voyé, 2000: 150).

We were able to build a more comprehensive compartmentalization-index[6] using the RAMP-data (Billiet *et al.*, 2002). Church commitment was operationalized using multiple indicators of the ritual dimension, the belief dimension, and the consequential dimension – saliency and the perception that one's religion has moral consequences. Using multi-level regression models for compartmentalization, we found that church commitment had the strongest negative significant t-value -57.46 (the higher the church commitment the more a person was against compartmentalization of religion and subsystems), compared to level of education, geographical mobility, and science as a meaning system. The other individual explanatory variables (gender, generations, degree of urbanization, church commitment in childhood, and actual denomination) and contextual explanatory variables (GNP *per capita* and religious heterogeneity of country) had no significant effect whatsoever.

Both studies indicate that church commitment and compartmentalization are strongly negatively related. However, the causal line cannot be established with such studies. To do that we need longitudinal data, which follow a sample of individuals over a long period of time and measure at regular intervals, *in casu*, the changes occurring in church commitment and its impact on compartmentalization, or *vice versa*. Do historical data help us to determine the causal direction of this relationship?

## The Causal Link between Church Commitment and Compartmentalization

In France, a manifest policy to laicize the country was put into effect by the republicans against the reactionaries, with whom the Catholic Church was allied, as a result of the French revolution. This conflict produced a profound split in the country over religion *per se*, on the national level as well as on the local and family level: republicans *versus intégristes*, schoolmaster against *curé*, father against mother

---

[6]  (1) State recognition of religion: agreement (Yes/No) with prohibition of religious symbols in (State) schools, agreement with financial support of none, some, or all religions, and degree of financial support of religious schools that meet the normal educational standards; (2) swear with religious reference; (3) State consulting religious leaders at the occasion of making laws on moral questions; and (4) the desirability of religious influence in politics.

(Martin, 1978: 36-41). The schoolmaster was the "priest" of the laicized republican faith and Balandier (1997: 124-127) depicts the impact of the ecclesiastical model on the laicized school: its laicized catechesis, its republican hymns, and its proper rituals, where the speeches replaced the sermons. Laicized values were sacralized, and the laicized virtues honored (see also Baubérot, 1997: 115-284). Such a directed internal scenario from national authorities, Demerath would call "coercive secularization" (2001a: 219, 221-223).

Was it always an anti-religious attitude that stimulated the process of laicization, as in France and in the communist regimes (see Part I)? In Belgium the process was different. Wils (1977 part 12: 267-304, and part 13: 164-206) has convincingly demonstrated that liberal politicians wanted to establish an independent political power. They opposed the authoritarian Church authorities and were against the tutelage of the Catholic clergy in cultural matters – education, science, art, literature, theatre and leisure – and poor relief. At the outset, they were anti-clerical, but not anti-religious. They considered religion an integrating factor of society, functioning as a civil religion, and an important element of socialization to be taught in school. In fact they only wanted to laicize some sectors of society. However, during their campaign, supported by the emergent Belgian Socialist Party, the radical liberals became anti-religious since fighting the power of the Catholic Church implied that they were combating religion *per se* – a consequence of the equation between the Catholic Church and religion in Belgium. Here religion was on one side of the conflict and not on both sides as was often the case with conflicts in the United States (Martin, 1978: 30-31 and 62-63).

A century later, the laicization of Belgium goes on, but at the end of the 20th and the beginning of the 21st century, the driving forces were anti-religious free masons of the socialist and the liberal parties. A liberal abortion law was adopted, which led to a constitutional crisis. The Catholic King Baudouin, not being able to make a distinction between his role as king and his personal conscience, refused to sign the law on the grounds of his conscientious objections to killing. A juridical trick – declaring the king temporarily incapable of governing – allowed the law to be enacted. In 2002, a law was voted by parliament legalizing euthanasia, which has been condemned by the Belgian Cardinal and partially by the Association of Catholic Hospitals, Psychiatric and Geriatric Institutions. Consequently, we may conclude that non-religious people who have the power, initiate legislature to change laws reminiscent of a Christian past. In contrast, the opposing groups – wanting to preserve the remaining religious mores in the institutions and the laws of the society – are largely composed of persons highly involved in their churches, and to a lesser extent by less integrated church members who are still marked by a Christian culture.

The latter deduction we may confirm referring to a study – based on data from fourteen Western European countries[7] covered by the EVS (1990) – that extends the field of the public sub-systems by focusing on the family, a so-called private sub-system (Dobbelaere, Gevers and Halman, 1999). Has religion still an impact, and if so to what extent, on motivations, options and behavior in the life-world, more specifically on conceptions of family values? The conclusions of this study were that "Core church members appear to have indeed in general a more integrated view of religion and family than less involved church members" (*o.c.*: 78).

This overview allows the conclusion that a major causal chain is: the degree of church involvement is positively related with an anti-compartmentalization attitude, or, a pro-compartmentalization attitude increases concomitantly with the degree of decline in church commitment. This implies that societal secularization has had an impact on the vision that people have about the relationship between religion and the other sub-systems, even the family, and this holds all the more so when they are estranged from the churches.

---

[7] Belgium, Denmark, France, Great Britain, Iceland, Ireland, Italy, the Netherlands, Northern Ireland, Norway, Portugal, Spain, Sweden and West-Germany.

CHAPTER 2

# Individual Secularization

In the recent literature, discussion is not so much on the question of whether the society is largely secularized, but whether the individual is secularized. With "a decline in the social power of once-dominant religious institutions [...] other social institutions [...] have escaped from prior religious domination", Stark (1999: 252) agrees. But he adds that, what is at issue is the contention "that secularization predicts a marked decline in the religiousness of the individual"(*o.c.*: 253), which he calls a myth, "the myth of religious decline", based on "the myth of past piety", and "the persistence of religion" (*o.c.*: 253-264).

Stark is not the only one who takes this position: Berger (1999) refers to the world and points out "thriving religious movements" (*o.c.*: 7-9), *i.e.* those that "rejected an *aggiornamento* with modernity" (*o.c.*: 6). However, he recognizes an exception to his desecularization thesis: Western Europe. But even there he suggests, without references, "strong survivals of religion, most of it generally Christian in nature", which leads him to suggest a "shift in the institutional location of religion [...] rather than secularization" (*o.c.*: 9-10).

Stark and Berger reduce individual secularization to the *decline* of religion. Stark's arguments go back to Woolston, Frederick the Great, Voltaire, and Jefferson all of whom predicted the end of religion (1999: 249-250). I am sure that more such so-called "secularization prophets", who to my knowledge are not sociologists, might be found. Indeed, their projections are not the fruit of sociological analysis, they are rather based on personal "beliefs" and "hopes". But, when Stark is confronted with an analysis of sociological theories about secularization processes in modern societies, he calls it "revisionism", an "evasion", "insincere" and "historically false" (*o.c.*: 252). However, as Yamane (1997: 110) correctly states "the *decline* of religion [...] has never meant the 'extinction' of religion, as Stark *et al.* are fond of claiming" (see also Hellemans, 1998: 70). Furthemore, another aspect of individual secularization stresses the *transformation* of religion: the individual *bricolages* or re-compositions that occur *outside the scope of religious authorities*, which is another facet of what Chaves (1994: 757) calls the "decrease in the extent to which individual actions are subject to religious control". I have called combinations of decline and transformation of individual religiosity: "religion *à la carte*", to which a newly installed Belgian bishop in his first interview with the press retorted that a religion *à la carte* was unacceptable for religious authorities, since they, and they alone, were able to define true beliefs and practices. If one accepts that the transformation of religion is an aspect of individual secularization, then Berger's suggestion of a "shift in the institutional location of religion" is also individual secularization. For these reasons, let us study not only the decline but also the transformation of individual religiosity in our analysis of the current discussions.

The core argument for defining Western Europe as the exception is the comparison with the USA: a modern country that is secularized on the societal level, but where church practice on weekends is considered to be much higher than in Europe and where religious beliefs are said to be widely held:

> Europe stands out as quite different from other parts of the world, and certainly from the United States. One of the most interesting puzzles in the sociology of religion is why Americans are so much more religious *as well as* more churchly than Europeans (Berger, 1999: 10).

Davie (1999 and 2001) has argued along similar lines:

> Secularization was a necessary part of modernization, and as the world modernized, it would automatically secularize. But if this was so, how could the very different situation in the United States be explained? The answer lay in trying to understand American exceptionalism. [...] But not everyone has continued down this path. Berger and Martin, for example, have suggested that the argument be reversed. [...] Exceptionalism undoubtedly exists, but it is rather Europe than the United States that is exceptional [with its] healthy and competitive market of religious institutions (1999: 76).

Demerath replied to the idea of American exceptionalism in a chapter on "Taking Exception to American Exceptionalism" (2001b: 220-223). Confronting American survey data with counts done in the churches on weekends give another image of the States. "This study [Hadaway, Marler, and Chaves, 1993] and subsequent replications and extensions show that actual levels of church attendance are about half of those that are so widely cited" (Demerath, 2001b: 221), which certainly questions the exceptionalism of the States compared to Europe, or *vice versa*. Again, the high percentage of people in the USA claiming to believe in God is based on a very simple question, without specification of the type of God they believe in. According to the European RAMP-study[1], 31 per cent believe that "God is something within each person rather than something out there", 16 per cent believe in a "spirit or life

---

[1]    See footnote 2 of Chapter 1, Part II.

force", 33 per cent in a God "with whom I can have a personal relation-ship", the others did not believe in God or were agnostic. This clearly reveals that one must probe deeper than the question "do you believe in God" to evaluate the level of individual secularization, since this belief may imply an important transformation of beliefs.

The issue of beliefs is also taken up by Davie. Concentrating on Europe, and using EVS-data of 1990, she distinguishes between:

> Two types of variable: on the one hand, those concerned with feelings, experience and the more numinous religious beliefs; on the other hand, those which measure religious orthodoxy, ritual participation, and institu-tional attachment. It is [...] the latter (the more orthodox indicators of religious attachment) which display, most obviously, an undeniable degree of secularization throughout Western Europe. In contrast, the former (the less institutional indicators) demonstrate considerable persistence in some aspects of religious life (2001: 266).

This distinction allows her to suggest:

> [I]t seems to me more accurate to suggest that Western Europeans remain, by and large, unchurched populations rather than simply secular. For a marked falling-off in religious attendance (especially in the Protestant North) has not resulted, yet, in a parallel abdication of religious belief. In short, many Europeans have ceased to belong to their religious institutions in any meaningful sense, but they have not abandoned, so far, many of their deep-seated religious aspirations (*o.c.*: 267).

However, these so-called "deep seated religious aspirations" are based, among others, on the 70 per cent who believe in God according to the 1990 EVS (Davie, 2001: 268), a percentage that reaches more than 77 per cent according to the 1999/2000 EVS (Davie, 2002:7; and Halman, 2001: 86). This latter percentage is based on data assembled in a larger group of European countries than in 1990, to wit, 32 countries from Central, Eastern and Western Europe. However, only 40 per cent believe in a "personal God", to wit, the Christian vision of God, and 33 per cent believe in "a spirit or life force" (Halman, 2001: 94), which attests to the transformation of the beliefs in God, one aspect of individual secularization.

I am not suggesting that this is occasioned only by the secularization of society. Let me make it clear that I agree with Berger (1999: 3) that "secularization on the societal level is not necessarily linked to secul-arization on the level of the individual consciousness". Other factors also play an important role in defining the beliefs of the people. For example, the process of individualization (Hervieu-Léger, 2001) – which in its modern version is linked to functional differentiation (Luhmann, 1977: 233-242; Beyer, 1990: 374-376), and the particular cultural circumstances within which the societal process of secularization operates, see Martin (1978) and the discussion of his theory (*supra* Part I). Contrary to France, religion never was on one side of societal conflicts in the USA, a cultural context that also partially explains differences between the level of secularization between France and other Catholic countries.

On the other hand, I do not agree with Berger that:

> The religious impulse, the quest for meaning that transcends the restricted space of empirical existence in this world, has been a perennial feature of humanity. [...] It would require something close to a mutation of the species to extinguish this impulse for good (Berger, 1999: 13).

Indeed, I can accept that a quest for meaning is typical of humanity, however, all meaning systems do not need to be religious, a-religious and non-religious meaning systems do exist and function for particular groups (cf. Part I, pp. 148-152).

The qualitative change of religion, to wit, individual secularization, manifests itself in individual beliefs and practices. Research data confirm that religious authorities are increasingly losing their ability to control what people believe and how they practice their religion. People no longer uncritically rely on the beliefs, norms and practices that are magisterially imposed, they actively construct their own religious faith. By introducing the term "bricolage" into the sociology of religion, Luckmann (1979: 134-136) drew attention both to this process of combining, supposedly arbitrarily, heterogeneous religious beliefs and practices, as well as to the fact that choices were being broadened, *e.g.* selections made from "secular" ideologies (Luckmann, 1967: 113). Voyé (1995: 201), using the term "mixing of the codes" introduced by post-modernity, pointed out that this was reflected "in the religious field in a threefold manner: references and practices blending the institutional and the popular; occasional borrowings from scientific discourses as well as from religious ones; and inspiration sought in diverse religions, notably oriental religions". They and other researchers, registering the same facts, have used the terms "religion *à la carte*"; "patchwork", "kaleidoscopic" or "pick and chose" religion; or have referred to it by pointing out a process of re-composition (Hervieu-Léger, 1995: 159-161).

In a study of Religious Syncretism based on the RAMP-data (Dobbelaere, Tomasi and Voyé, in press), we came to the conclusion that combinations of beliefs and practices selected from institutional Christian religion, popular religion, superstitions, and beliefs from other religions were rather particularistic of individuals. No specific pattern of syncretistic beliefs and practices typical of countries, religions or people with certain social characteristics – such as men *versus* women; generations; or rural *versus* urban regions – was detected. The patterns were idiosyncratic: individuals made their own patchworks or bricolages. Indeed, as Hervieu-Léger has underscored, the "validation of faith remains [...] a truly individual discipline: to each his or her truth" (2001: 166), and the "groups and networks of the nebulous New Age movement constitute a fine instrument for analyzing contemporary religious reality because they bring to the fore [...] the tendencies generally present in renewal movements which shape historic religions" (*o.c.*: 165). Which are these general tendencies?

The people whom Van Hove studied expressed this general tendency very well (2000). First of all, they rejected dogmatic religion, which is imposed by church leaders and religious professionals. Taking responsibility for their religious faith, they were forced to compose it themselves, which required a constant individual reflexivity. They even preferred to speak of a *spiritual* rather than a *religious* quest. Secondly, in order to make their own *bricolage*, they engaged temporarily in different movements, or followed courses, weekends, and sessions organized by such movements as: Shamanism, Rajneeshism, Rosicruceanism, Tai Chi, Shiatsu, yoga, Theosophy, bio-energetics, psycho-energetics, meditation, psycho-dynamics, parapsychology, rebirthing-sessions and massage. They were looking for experiences of the Greater Whole, for holism, for religious feelings, for interesting ideas and parts of meaning systems that they could integrate in their own *bricolage*, which was never finished, and which had to be constantly re-invented. These sessions, courses, and experiences offered them *possible* interpretative schemes, *possible* strategies and *possible* answers that they had to try out. The organizers of these sessions or courses were not allowed to impose their views upon them, to proclaim the truth: their discipline was understood as one way, not *the* way: reproduction was unacceptable. It was expected that they would offer insights, experiences, and that they would be helpful: stimulating those taking courses to find their own way for themselves. What had to be found was inside, the way led inside (see also Hanegraaff, 1996).

American research also documents this trend towards spirituality, away from dogmatic religion (*e.g.* Roof, 1993 and 1999; McNamara, 1992). Such studies are not referred to in the writings of those criticizing the secularization paradigm (Yamane, 1997: 116), although, Bellah (1985: 235) and his colleagues identified such a trend already in the nineteen eighties and typified it as a religion that is "rooted in the effort to transform external authority into internal meaning". A religious attitude described as "a perfectly natural expression of current American religious life" (*o c.*: 221), was exemplified by a young American nurse: "I believe in God. I'm not a religious fanatic. I can't remember the last time I went to church. My faith has carried me a long way. It's Sheilaism. Just my own little voice" (*ibid.*). And Yamane (1997: 116) quotes a supermodel stating more succinctly her religious privatism: "I'm religious but in my own personal way. I always say that I have a Cindy Crawford religion – it's my own".

On the basis of a quantitative and qualitative study involving 565 non-heterosexual Christians in the United Kingdom, Yip (2002: 199) came to the conclusion that the "data suggested that the self, rather than religious authority structures, steers the respondents' journey of spirituality and sexuality". The respondents made a clear distinction between spirituality and religion. To them:

> [T]he term "religiosity" contains two integral elements: the adherence to doctrines and beliefs, propagated by religious authority structures; and the observance of rituals and practices, led by such structures, within a communal religious context. On the other hand, "spirituality" denotes an internal journey of exploration and discovery of the divine, steered by the self, with emphasis on personal lived experiences. It is about the relationship between the individual believer and his or her own faith, not necessarily mediated through the churches (*o.c.*: 206).

Although the majority of the non-heterosexual Christians continued to attend churches, the basis of their Christian faith was foremost "personal experience"; "the Bible" and "Human Reason" ranked second; "Church Authority" ranked last, which is a clear indication that pronouncements of religious authorities had not much of an influence on their spirituality (*o.c.*: 206-207). This study is another indication that individual secularization is not only about *decline* of religiosity, it is also about *changes, shifts, or transformations of the authority structure of the beliefs and practices* one holds: from church authorities to the self and his or her experiences, which is clearly indicated by the growing use of the term "spirituality" instead of "religiosity" or "religiousness" to label one's faith. This study confirms the trend established by the afore-mentioned studies. These analyses express the impact of another aspect of post-modernity: "the collapse of hierarchical distinction" (Featherstone, 1988: 203) between what emanates from church authorities and what arises from the people based on their own experience.

A third aspect of individual secularization is *compartmentalization* or "secularization-in- mind", which we discussed in a previous section. To the degree that compartmentalization is linked negatively to church commitment, we may expect that the differentiation of religion and the other societal sub-systems will continue because of the declining level of church commitment and the transformation of individual religiosity.

A last question about individual secularization should be asked: is individual secularization limited to the Western world? In a synthetic

study of Islamic societies, Pace (1998: 168) distinguishes two processes: "secularization from above, and [secularization from below] that
[...] stems from a drive towards modernization especially on the part of
the younger generation", which produces a change in attitudes towards
the Islamic tradition that has been fossilized since the 15th century. The
process of modernization as regards this fossilization of mentality and
customs is being promoted by conflicts, which have produced the secularization of customs especially among the younger generation (*o.c.*:
170-173). Important for individual secularization are: the conflict between country and city – the latter having created new classes, who
have a different attitude to religious traditions and who are more willing
to accept new choices and values – and emigration that has affected the
religion of emigrants, but also of those who stayed behind, who compare themselves with their emigrated children, relatives or friends (*o.c.*:
171-172).

Finally, Demerath's study reports what he calls "cultural religion" in
the Judeo-Christian orbit and outside it – in the Muslim world, which
confirms Pace's "secularization from below", and also in the Hindu,
Shinto, Confucian and Taoist world. According to Demerath (2001b:
227-228):

> In all these cases, cultural religion is pervasive. Indeed, it is perhaps the
> world's most common form of religious affiliation and one that is hardly
> uncommon in the United States. Cultural religion is less a matter of present
> conviction or commitment than of continuity with generations past and con-
> trast with rival groups and identities. [...] It involves a label that is self-
> applied [...] It is a way of being religiously connected without being relig-
> iously involved. It is a recognition of a religious community but a lapsed in-
> difference to the core practices around which the community originally
> formed. It is a tribute to the religious past that offers little confidence for the
> religious future. [...] Within any religion's long-term historical trajectory –
> or any individual's experience of waning faith – cultural religion represents
> the penultimate stage of religious decline, the last loose bond of religious at-
> tachment before the ties are let go altogether.

In other words, it is a world-wide form of individual secularization that
is described by both authors.

# CHAPTER 3

# Bringing the Actors Back In

Throughout this book, I have insisted that secularization is not a mechanical, evolutionary process, which implies that we have to study the impact of actors – among others, religious and lay social movements, groups, and quasi-groups; and also professionals and politicians – on latent and manifest attempts to secularize or to sacralize organizations and society.

The laicization process of society in France and the USSR are good examples of the effect of a manifest policy by governments. Is this process limited to the Western world? In his study of the Muslim world, Pace distinguishes between "secularization from below" (cf. *supra*) and "secularization from above", the process of laicization. This latter process, the unyoking of politics from religious factors, started at the end of last century and gained momentum from the 1950s on, after the end of colonial domination. There was either a complete and traumatic break with the religious tradition – *e.g.* as caused by Kemal Atatürk in Turkey and the Ba'th party in Syria and Iraq, which provoked the development of strong fundamentalist movements – or, a transfer of functions of religion to the field of politics – *e.g.* in North African and the Indian sub-continent.

> A variety of political solutions were adopted. ... But they all boil down to the same basic problem of modernity: how to build a modern state with an economy capable of competing in the international market, an independent administrative apparatus (public offices, schools, social services, hospitals etc.), a power basis for the leaderships founded on what is traditionally regarded as "political". [...] The ultimate goal is to turn the religious unity of the *Umma* (the community of the believers) into a resource for establishing political consensus, by secularizing, so to speak, the religious capital accumulated over time and which forms an integral part of the collective consciousness (Pace, 1998: 168-169).

Such processes initiated by politicians provoke reactions, *e.g.* the development of strong fundamentalist movements in the Muslim world. Similar reactions, although not fundamentalist in nature, also occurred in the Western world. In the second half of the 19th century, anti-religious radical liberal and socialist politicians also wanted to laicize Belgian society by creating "schools without God", which was enacted

181

by a parliamentary majority. The church hierarchy and leading Catholics mobilized the population to boycott the state schools and to build a Catholic school system. This was the start of the development of a Catholic pillarized system: a Catholic "island" to protect Catholics from a- and anti-religious influences. In the Netherlands, a Catholic and a Protestant pillar emerged, and Catholic pillars were gradually established in Austria, Germany, Italy and Switzerland (Righart, 1986). It is a form of segmental differentiation in a functionally differentiated society, which promoted exclusiveness and an in-group mentality. It is not only the institutionalized churches that erected pillars: sects and NRMs have also done so[1].

Another example is the New Christian Right (NCR) that tried to preserve the "American Christian tradition", as they saw it, opposing "secular humanism". This value and life-style clash manifested itself in issues related to television (because secular humanism was being implanted in modern consciousness by TV); the public school (*e.g.* the NCR firmly supported Bible reading and prayer in public schools, and opposed evolutionism seeking to have creationism taught); and the family (*e.g.* it sternly opposed abortion, homosexuality and pornography). The success of such social movements depends, to a large extent, upon the number of people they are able to motivate and eventually to mobilize, their location in society, their unanimity about the issues and means, and strong leadership. This is not the place to make a thorough evaluation of the achievements of NCR. I want to make two points: a methodological one, and, secondly, to underscore the importance of the ability to mobilize the population. Studies of the sacralizing or secularizing potency of social movements could teach us a great deal about the process of secularization and sacralization. However, certain methodological rules should be observed in these studies. To evaluate the effect of social movements on matters concerning *e.g.* the family, education, and ethics, we should measure their impact on the enactment and enforcement of laws and on court decisions in preserving traditional mores, and not concentrate on the presence of a vocal minority or their self-proclaimed victories (Dobbelaere, 1989: 35-38). For that reason in-depth studies of the mobilizing force of such movements, and an analysis of their constituency and its social location are very important in evaluating their success. Several studies question the mobilizing force of the NCR. Shupe and Stacey (1983: 114) concluded: "Our analysis suggests that the constituency of the New Religious Right is much more limited and much less unified than the Reverend Falwell and others

---

[1]  Good examples are The Seventh-Day Adventist Church for the sectarian movements, and Scientology and Soka Gakkai (a non-Western New Religious Movement) for the New Religious Movements (Dobbelaere, 2000a and Dobbelaere, 2000b: 233-256).

would lead us to believe" (see also Bromley and Shupe, 1984). They (*ibid.*: 103 and 114) further point out that, even if evangelicals are a large part of the constituency of the NCR, according to a study on the buckle of the Southern Bible Belt, "[w]here support should logically be strongest and where the electronic church is most heavily syndicated", the constituency of the NCR is much more limited and much less unified than its leaders proclaim.

Demerath and Williams did a methodologically sound study in a New England city (1992). It allows us to point towards the actors, the composition of the movement and the tactics used, in a sacralizing counter-thrust in a city where secularization was however the dominant tendency. Homelessness, black neighborhood development, abortion and sex education, were the three instances in which religion played a critical role. The sacralizing counterweight within the community's political arena was provided by minority movements, which were "more likely to share a basic ecumenism rather than a zealous religious particularism". They "took up specific issues in a kind of single-interest politics", and were rather "*ad hoc* movements" and, consequently, "smaller, more flexible" but also "less enduring" than the "established church structures", which served "as staunch bulwarks of the mainstream and the status quo". In fact, none of the conventional churches, synagogues, or other religious organizations were involved as major protagonists in the different issues. The Catholic religious and clergy of various faiths "were acting more on their own initiative than as formal representatives of their basic communities", and in one of the issues "several of these clergy found themselves at odds with home congregations over their tactics and belligerent behavior". Indeed, they "are far more likely than their secular opponents to take on the shrill tone and extreme tactics of the true believer". The "resources mobilized" for effective action in taking the issues to the public, were "cultural" rather than "structural", to wit "sacred cultural images and arguments which had retained some currency even in a secularizing religious economy" and "moral fundamentals" (*o.c.*: 201-205).

We should note, however, that changes, if they happen in one or the other direction, are not always the result of manifest actions; they may also come about as the result of certain actions which latently produce a secularizing effect. In the first part, I referred to the role of the professionals (medical doctors and teachers) who secularized the Belgian Catholic pillar, without intending to do so. In the Muslim world, Pace points to "secularization from below" resulting from conflicts (Pace, 1998: 171-172) – conflict over the patriarchal model contested by sons and daughters, especially in North-Africa. The access of women to professions, which has weakened "ancient bonds which limited women's social activity to the confined space of the home or the *hammam* (the public baths)", however, without liberating them from their ancient submission, "in many cases, the 'double presence' has resulted in a double burden and a duplication of subservient roles at home and at work" (*o.c.*: 171). Finally, emigration has affected the Islamic models of family, reproduction, education, society and religion of both the emigrants and of those who stayed behind who compare themselves with their emigrated children, relatives or friends

Another example of latent secularization is given in a study done by Voyé on Christmas decorations in a Walloon village in Belgium (1998: 299-303). Two decades ago, Isambert (1982:196) had already underscored the increasing slide from "the scriptural and liturgical basis of the Nativity, which is altogether oriented towards the Incarnation and Redemption, which it precedes" toward "the Christ child". Indeed, the Christ child is placed at the centre of the familial Christmas-celebrations and also in the decorations displayed by city authorities. In this Walloon village, however, the decorations evoke a further sliding away: signboards, many meters square, erected on the lawns in front of the houses and illuminated in the evening, represented Walt Disney cartoon characters. "It is for the children", said the couple that started it all, "December is the children's month, with (the feast) of St-Nicolas (early December) and Christmas" (Voyé, 1998: 299). At the time of Voyé's interviews, when she asked why they did not set up a manger scene, the couple who initiated the display of signboards and who tried to co-ordinate it, answered: "some neighbours are thinking about it [...] but, we told them 'If we put a manger scene, we've got to find among the Disney characters a couple of animals who have a little one. Because we, well we want to stick with the Walt Disney characters. Or at least with characters of the same type [...] we don't want to do like in X, the first village in which this type of thing was done: they put up Walt Disney characters too; but last year, they changed the theme, they took film characters [...]'" (*o.c.*: 300). Here Christmas is not only child oriented, but as Voyé rightfully underscores: "With the Disney characters, we are no longer in History, but in the fairytale and the domain of the marvelous. (Fairytales) peopled with fictive beings" (*o.c.*: 302). These decorations convey implicitly the idea that Christmas is a marvelous fairytale, a nice story (in the village that uses film characters), far removed from the original Incarnation-Redemption idea that the religious message of Christmas carries. By putting up these decorations, people latently secularize the Christian message.

And this process of latent secularization goes on, and, at the same time, points towards the level of individual secularization reached by parts of the population who promote organizational secularization.

Hiernaux and Voyé directed a study of Catholics in French speaking Belgium who want to have a religious burial when deceased. About one hundred in-depth interviews were conducted with men and women, ranging from 25 to 65 years of age. Some parts of the interviews centered around the religious ritual, and these interviews were further supplemented by participant observation (*o.c.*: 288-296). According to these observations and interviews, "the priest is no longer the grand commander of the rite faced with a passive congregation", he "is now very often relegated to the role of performer". "Either he just carries out the orders of the funeral director[2], or when the families have a relatively high socio-cultural status, the priest performs in a scenario designed by the closest relatives of the deceased" (*o.c.*: 291). According to Voyé, this shows that the deceased is first and foremost a member of a close emotional network and not of the Christian community, which is confirmed by the fact that the overwhelming majority of persons present at the ritual were family, friends and colleagues of the deceased and of his or her close family members, and no longer, as was the case in the past, members of the parish community.

It is also very interesting to note that, as far as the traditional Catholic rite has changed, this was partly favored by the recourse to the vernacular introduced by the hierarchy. When Latin was used in ritual and hymns, the priest had the central role. He used standardized formulae, which he knew and understood, creating a distance between daily life and after life: the ritual was centered upon the life to come and the mystery surrounding it. Now the ritual is centered upon the deceased: his life, his loves and friendships, his accomplishments. The texts read, the songs and the music played, are chosen by the family with reference to the deceased. If religious texts and hymns are used, they are chosen to express the qualities of the deceased and not because they refer to God. Quite often, "God is never brought up – except in the rare sacramental words pronounced by the priest" (*o.c.*: 292-293). The change here was favored by the use of the vernacular, but the authors of the changes that are occurring, are not the professionals of the religious institution, but the funeral directors or the close family, who de-sacralize the ritual and bring about organizational secularization.

All these studies reveal to us the different types of actors involved in processes of secularization and sacralization, and the methods they are using. Politicians, because of their position, can laicize society. They can differentiate polity and religion, erect a laicized educational system; differentiate culture from the churches, and change laws on *e.g.* divorce,

---

[2]   The funeral director "'tells me what to do and say [...] and he's the one who pays me', said a priest in Brussels" (Voyé, 1998: 291).

abortion and euthanasia (cf. *supra*). If the majority of the population is not secularized, churches and leading opponents of such policies may mobilize sufficient people to block them or to create alternative organizations from which a pillar may ultimately emerge. However, if the major part of the population is secularized, politicians can laicize the laws without noticeable opposition, except from church leaders and small quasi-groups that want to preserve a Christian civilization. Secularized individuals do not oppose changing the laws on divorce and abortion. This became manifest in the results of referenda about proposed legislation on the liberalization of such laws in *e.g.* Ireland and Italy, and more recently in Switzerland. The argument for such legislation is that these laws do not impose but rather permit particular behavior: thus the legislator only adapts the laws of the country to a growing religious pluralism in the population. This legitimation implicitly refers to the process of individual secularization, to wit, a decline in religiosity and transformations in the religious outlook of more and more people who, in such matters, no longer refer to religious authorities.

Lobbying is another strategy religious groups may use, for lack of popular support. Yamane (1997: 117) refers to an interesting study by Hertzke (1988) about religious lobbies in Washington (DC), the number of which augmented from 16 major religious lobbies in 1955 to at least 80 by 1985. However, the major question, according to Yamane (*o.c.*: 118), is "the extent to which their religious legitimations are authoritative in the political sphere". Indeed, sheer numbers of religious lobbies reveal only that they are trying to influence legislation, not that they actually do so. Hertzke noted "one major case in which religious lobbies were effective in realizing their goal: the Equal Access Act of 1984" (Yamane, 1997: 118). However,

> In lobbying for this act, fundamentalist groups came to "embrace the language of rights", which "is more appealing than the language of moral imperatives" in the congressional context. As a Moral Majority lobbyist told Hertzke: We can't afford to say "God settled it, that's it". The Moral Majority learned from the success of 'rights talk' over "God talk" in the Equal Access Act, and would attempt to apply it to other issues in which they were involved. Speaking of the abortion issue in particular, Jerry Falwell has said, "We are reframing the debate. This is no longer a religious issue, but a civil rights issue" (*o.c.*, citing Hertzke, 1988: 196).

From this Yamane rightfully concludes:

> The congressional milieu shapes and constrains religious groups which seek to influence Congress. [... I]n a secularized society, religious groups have no power to set the norms of political institutions which operate according to their own rationality because of institutional differentiation (*ibid.*).

Voyé (1997: 169-173) has underscored the fact that the influential Cardinal Danneels, who is close to the Pope, and the Pope himself also refer to "human rights" to establish their "moral" authority when publicly addressing evil in the world. Indeed, neither would "God talk" nor the Christian notion of "sin" function in addressing the general population because of individual secularization.

It is this individual secularization that, in the study of religious burials by Hiernaux and Voyé, produced a latent process of organizational secularization, and that recently forced the *Parti Social Chrétien* (the Belgian French speaking "Social *Christian* Party") to change its name. The party was losing more and more votes in each successive election, reaching fewer and fewer of the younger generations. Analyzing this situation, the party came to the conclusion that they had to drop such reference since the Christian principles and values no longer motivated the younger generations to join the party and to vote for it. The secularization of the younger generations – made up by persons who overwhelmingly think in a compartmentalized way and who are for more than fifty per cent unchurched – made the party change its name by dropping the term Christian and referring instead to humanism. In 2002, the Social Christian Party became the Democratic and Humanist Centre Party.

# Chapter 4

# Epilogue

## Societal and Individual Secularization: A Relationship

Societal secularization is a consequence of the process of functional differentiation on the societal level and the autonomization of the societal sub-systems. Diagnosing the loss of religion's influence in the so-called secular world, the members of the religious sub-system were the first to talk about secularization. If secularization is only the particularization of the general processes of functional differentiation in the religious sub-system, should we then retain the term? Since the term points towards a specific social conflict, *i.e.* a religiously based resistance to functional differentiation, we may keep it as a purely *descriptive* concept (see also Chaves, 1997: 443). Furthermore, modern, functionally highly differentiated societies may have very different levels of secularization, *i.e.* different levels of differentiation between religion and the other sub-systems. Indeed, traditional structures may survive like churches functioning as civil religion, *e.g.* Lutheranism in some Scandinavian countries; or the state may continue to pay directly the salaries of church personnel (in Belgium for example); or, in a laicized country like France continue to have an extensive Catholic school system.

With Wilson (1982: 150), I state forcefully that the first meaning of secularization refers to "no more than that religion ceases to be significant in the working of the social system". This says nothing about the religious consciousness of individuals, although it may affect it. We may then define societal secularization as "a process by which the overarching and transcendent religious system of old is being reduced in modern functionally differentiated societies to a sub-system alongside other sub-systems, losing in this process its overarching claims over the other sub-systems". As a result, the *societal* significance of religion is greatly diminished. This conception of the process of secularization allowed Chaves (1994: 750) to state that it refers to the "declining scope of religious authority" on the societal level, or "Secularization at the societal level may be understood as the declining capacity of religious elites to exercise authority over the other institutional spheres" (*o.c.*: 575).

We have discussed the impact of societal secularization on individuals: referring to their *compartmentalized* views, *i.e.* the secularization-in-mind. Many people think in terms of a secularized world refusing to give religious elites authority over the other spheres, and they act accordingly, for example, voting and establishing a family without reference to religion. Research also indicates that church affiliation and church commitment *decline*, but that does not mean that secularization theory suggests the "extinction" of religion. Finally, we have pointed out the *transformation* of religion on the individual level: the rejection of dogmatic religion imposed by church authorities and the rising use of the term spirituality to express that. This concept suggests that the individual composes his or her own faith, and selects or creates rites that fit their beliefs. These changes we have called individual secularization. This indicates that individuals have liberated themselves from religious authorities and that their experiences are the basis of their faith. It is the expression of their spiritual journey. The decline of religious authority that undermined the credibility of the "Christian collective consciousness" has also opened up the religious sub-system for competing religious, a-religious and non-religious meaning systems (Dobbelaere, 1999: 235-236): a pluralistic religious "market" has developed.

## Organizational Secularization and Sacralization

Opening up the "religious market" for New Religious Movements (NRMs) is also related to the process of globalization and intercontinental mobility. Some NRMs, such as the Unification Church, the Family, and ISCON, want to re-sacralize the world and its institutions by bringing God (Krishna) back in the different groups operating in different sub-systems like the family, the economy, and even the polity. Wallis (1984) has called these "world rejecting new religions". However, the vast majority of NRMs are of another type, they are "world affirming". They offer their members esoteric means for attaining immediate and automatic assertiveness, heightened spirituality, recovery, success and a clear mind. Mahikari provides an "omitama" or amulet; Transcendental Meditation (TM) a personal mantra for meditation; Scientology auditing with an e-meter; Human Potential movements offer therapies, encounter groups or alternative health and spiritual centres; Soka Gakkai promotes chanting of an invocation before a mandala, the Gohonzon; while Elan Vital offers the Knowledge revealed by Maharaji or one of his appointed instructors.

Luckmann (1990) has rightly argued that in many NRMs the level of transcendence was lowered, they had become *"this worldly"* or *mundane*. The historical religions, to the contrary, are examples of "great transcendences", referring to something other than everyday reality, notwithstanding the fact that they were also involved in mundane or "this-worldly" affairs. However, the reference was always transcendental, *e.g.* the incantations to the Holy Mother, Jesus or saints for healing, for success in examinations or work, or for "*une âme soeur*". Most world-affirming NRMs appear to reach *only* the level of "intermediate transcendences". They bridge time and space, promote intersubjective communication, but remain at the immanent level of everyday reality. Consequently, some, like TM, claim to be spiritual rather than religious movements. Calling NRMs spiritual or religious, is not important for our argument, what matters is that we register a change: the ultimate has become "this-worldly".

Referring to my baseline definition of religion (Part I), the registered change should be conceived as a form of organizational secularization: in these religious organizations, the sacred is no longer a "great transcendence". Even when we take a functional definition of religion, we may come to the same conclusion. Luhmann, stated that "the problem of simultaneity of indefiniteness and certainty" is the typical function of religion (1977: 46). Indeed, most of these world-affirming new religions are not concerned with the problems of *simultaneity* of transcendence and immanence since they focus on the immanent, on everyday life, on the secular. They are adapted to the secular world. Mundane orientations of religion are not new. Berger and Luckmann have suggested that the "higher" church attendance in America compared to Europe might be explained by the mundane orientation of religion in America. Luckmann (1967: 36-37) called it "internal secularization": "a radical inner change in American church religion [...] today the secular ideas of the American Dream pervade church religion". In asserting that American churches were "becoming highly secularized themselves" (Berger 1967: 108) these authors sought to reconcile empirical findings at the individual level, *i.e.* church attendance, which appeared to conflict with secularization theories, by pointing out changes at the organizational level, *i.e.* within the churches. The point of interest for our argument is that the idea of organizational secularization is not new: the concept of "internal" secularization was its predecessor.

Another process of organizational secularization occurred in the Catholic pillars. In the early second half of the 20th century, the Dutch Catholic pillar started to totter, partly because of the internal crisis in the Dutch Catholic Church, which started with the "nuclear" Catholics (Thurlings, 1978: 170-181; and Laeyendecker, 1987 and 1989), but, also under external pressures, among others financial needs, which stimulated mergers; legal regulations; and the professionalization of services (Thurlings, 1978: 224-225; and Coleman, 1979). In Belgium, in response to the same internal and external causes, the Catholic pillar had to adapt to the changing situation. Research has documented that the core philosophy no longer consists of the strict religious rules of the Catholic Church, but rather refers to so-called typical values of the gospel such as social justice; a humane approach toward clients and patients; well-being; solidarity between social classes with special attention to marginal people; and *Gemeinschaftlichkeit*. These are values that have a universal appeal, and which are not specifically Christian. However, by backing them up with a religious source, the gospels, and occasionally solemnizing them with religious rituals, they acquired a sacred aura. This new collective consciousness is still symbolized by a "C", referring to Christian, that is evangelical, instead of to Catholic, the latter being considered to have a more restricted appeal and to be more confining. This "Socio-Cultural Christianity" functions now as the sacred canopy for the segmented Catholic world of olden days (Dobbelaere and Voyé, 1990: 6-8; Laermans, 1992: 204-214). The process of *organizational* secularization on the meso level is a good example of an adaptation to individual secularization in the Catholic world.

However, the Catholic Church does not give up its fight against secularization. In recent years, it has called for a second evangelization of Europe, and Opus Dei, an organization that endeavors to de-secularize the different sub-systems, became a personal prelature. This special status relates Opus Dei directly to the Vatican, and where it operates, confers on it independence of local bishops. Other "new religious movements" exist within the Catholic Church and are examples of movements trying to re-sacralize the world, *e.g.* Communione e Liberazione. The same is true in other Christian Churches: the rise of Evangelicalism in the United States is a good example. But the Evangelical success is not limited to the States, the most remarkable growth occurred in Latin America, where Pentecostalism is the most successful component (Martin, 1990 and 1996). Berger (1999: 6-9) also gives examples in the Islamic world. This again indicates that secularization and sacralization are the result of actions by collective actors and not mechanical evolutionary processes.

Berger (*o.c.*: 6) refers also to the "remarkable revival of the Orthodox Church in Russia". It seems to me that this is linked to the need of rebuilding the nation after the collapse of the Communist regime. If the new leaders want to connect the nation with historic Russia, they cannot overlook a central part of it: the Orthodox Church.

Here, of course, we touch upon the function of *civil religion* that was discussed in the first part. Suffice it to mention here the interesting instrument that Fenn has developed, to wit a "hypothetical spectrum": "a range along which we may describe societies with regard to how they institutionalize the sacred" (2001: 122). To the left of the spectrum he puts "societies that do indeed merge their political with their religious institutions and who subscribe to a theistic notion of the universe" (*o.c.*: 122), *e.g.* Eastern Orthodoxy. Further to the right, countries like Japan and "Marxism and Nazism", "where religion[1] remains central to their political systems but has been somewhat transformed into less traditional forms of display and ceremony" (*ibid.*). Still further to the right, according to Fenn, are "societies that merely have the vestiges of a civil religion that once was "established", in the sense of being closely tied to dominant political institutions. At this point civil religion decomposes into a species of public religiosity: Norway, for instance, may belong about here" (*o.c.*: 122-123). And, finally, to the far right "countries that are in agreement only on basic procedures rather than principles" (*o.c.*: 123), here integration is based on cognitive rather than normative mechanisms. This hypothetical spectrum allows us to compare societies, and also to see how a single society moves along the spectrum. As far as Russia is concerned, Russian Orthodoxy now replaces Marxism as a sacred canopy, which is a clear move to the left of the spectrum.

## Pluralism: Secularization and Rational Choice Theories

The consequences of pluralism are differently integrated in Secularization Theory and Rational Choice Theory (RCT). In his earlier work on secularization, Berger has taken the position that pluralism led to (individual) secularization, which he now retracts on the basis of the American case (2001: 194):

> What pluralism does (and there I was right) is to undermine all taken-for-granted certainties, in religion as in all other spheres of life. But it is possible to hold beliefs and to live by them even if they no longer hold the status of taken-for-granted verities.

However, I have already pointed out that Berger neither takes the transformation of religion on the individual level into account, nor the corrections that should be applied to American survey data on church practice. Bruce also refutes Berger's present position and confirms the traditional position in secularization theory that pluralism undermines the plausibility of religion, which in turn promotes "liberal" religion, which is nothing less than a transformation of religion or a form of individual secularization. About liberal religion Bruce (2001: 98-99)

---

[1] According to my substantive definition, Marxism is a meaning system and not a religion; neither is Nazism, although it used religious symbols like "Gott mit uns". Instead of religion, one may use here the term "sacred canopy"

states: Berger "believes that it is possible for people to sustain a loose and amorphous faith that accepts uncertainty. I disagree", and he then argues his point (*o.c.*: 99-100), which is not important for our argument here. It is clear from Bruce's arguments and mine that secularization theory holds that pluralism undermines the taken-for-granted certainties of religion, which in turn promotes individual secularization.

To the contrary, RCT holds that a religious pluralistic situation may promote church commitment. This theory makes three important points. RCT postulates a *latent religiosity* on the demand side (Stark 1997: 8), that should become manifest by *active competition* between religious firms on the supply side (Stark 1997: 17). However, this is only possible in *a pluralistic religious situation* where religious firms compete for customers and to the extent that the supply-side is not limited by state regulations, suppressing or subsidizing religions (Iannaccone 1997: 40-41, and Finke: 1997: 50-51).

Stated this way, RCT only works in states that are secularized on the societal level. State and religion should be de-regulated to allow competition between religious firms, in the opposite case, religious firms are "lazy" (Stark and Iannaccone, 1994) since there is no need for competition. Consequently, there is no opposition between secularization theory and RCT. To check if RCT works in Europe, we have analyzed the effect of religious pluralism on church commitment with the Ramp-data (Billiet *et al.*). The effect of religious pluralism disappeared completely in our multilevel regression model for church commitment when denominational membership is introduced. It seems that the important issue is not so much religious monopoly or pluralism as such but rather which church is the dominant one. The Roman Catholic Church seems to handle a monopolistic situation far better than the mainline Protestant churches. A simple market model can therefore hardly explain our findings.

It could of course be argued that in all European countries under study[2] state and church are not completely de-regulated, which could mean that in some countries even pluralism does not mean competition. However, comparing countries as units, also contradicts RCT. In the European countries we are studying, there are eight countries with an almost monopolistic religious situation – Catholicism in Belgium, Italy, Poland and Portugal; Lutheranism in Denmark, Finland, Norway and Sweden – and three religiously mixed countries – Great Britain, Hungary and the Netherlands. According to RCT, church practice should be lowest in the monopolistic religious situation and highest in the religious mixed countries. However, in the Catholic countries

---

[2]     See footnote 2, *supra* p. 167.

Belgium, Italy, Poland, and Portugal, they are higher (resp. 25,7; 50,4; 74,1 and 38,31 per cent going minimum monthly to church at the weekend) than in the religious mixed countries Hungary, the Netherlands and United Kingdom (resp. 19,8; 20,1 and 17,7 per cent). It is clear that RCT cannot explain these data.

The problem with RCT is that it measures religious pluralism and equates that with competition. If we take the idea of competition seriously, then RCT should be extended. In many European countries there is a competition between churches and religious movements, on the one hand, and social movements with a- and anti-religious meaning systems, on the other. But, then we are back on the level of the struggle for the laicization of society: bringing actors back in in the process of societal secularization. On the level of the individual, one could use ideas of the RCT to analyze the effect of these societal conflicts on individual secularization. But more important, instead of measuring only *religious* pluralism, one should measure the impact of competing *meaning systems* – religious, a-religious and anti-religious – on the behavior, the opinions and attitudes of the individuals. By so doing, sociologists of religion might combine both theoretical approaches and, maybe, integrate them. This should bring us further in understanding human behavior than the sterile discussion about which part of the world – Europe or the USA – is the exception and the apodictic self-affirmation that one's approach is the only valid one disregarding the results of the other approaches. At the moment, some sociologists of religion behave like "priests" of a scientific "church" promoting their own "truth".

# References

Acquaviva, S. (1979), *The Decline of the Sacred in Industrial Society*, Oxford, Basil Blackwell.

Archer, M. and M. Vaughan (1970), "Education, Secularization, Desecularization and Resecularization", in D. Martin and M. Hill (eds.), *A Sociological Yearbook of Religion in Britain*, 3, London, S. C. M. Press.

Bahtijarevic, S. (1971), "Some Characteristics of the Religiosity of Secondary School Attendants", in *Actes de la 11e Conférence Internationale de la CISR. Opatija – Yougoslavie 20-24 septembre 1971*, Lille, CISR.

Bainbridge, W. and R. Stark (1980), "Scientology: To Be Perfectly Clear", *Sociological Analysis*, 41(2).

Balandier, G. (1997), *Conjugaisons*, Paris, Fayard.

Baubérot, J. (1997), *La morale laïque contre l'ordre moral*, Paris, Éd. Du Seuil.

Bauberot, J. (1998), "La laïcité française et ses mutations", *Social Compass*, 45 (1).

Becker, H. (1957), "Current Sacred-Secular Theory and its Development", in H. Becker and A. Boskoff (eds.), *Modern Sociological Theory in Continuity and Change*, New York, The Dryden Press.

Bell, D. (1977), "The Return of the Sacred? The Argument on the Future of Religion", *British Journal of Sociology*, 28(4).

Bellah, R. (1964), "Religious Evolution", *American Sociological Review*, 29(3).

Bellah, R. (1967), "Civil Religion in America", *Daedalus*, 96(1).

Bellah, R. (1970), *Beyond Belief. Essays on Religion in a Post-Traditional World*, New York, Harper and Row.

Bellah, R. (1971), "The Historical Background of Unbelief", in R. Caporale and A. Grumelli (eds.), *The Culture of Unbelief: Studies and Proceedings from the First International Symposium on Belief Held at Rome, March 22-27, 1969*, Berkeley, The University of California Press.

Bellah, R. (1975), *The Broken Covenant: American Civil Religion in Time of Trial*, New York, The Seabury Press.

Bellah, R. (1976), "Response to the Panel on Civil Religion", *Sociological Analysis*, 37(2).

Bellah, R. et al. (1985), *Habits of the Hart: Individualism and Commitment in American Life*, Berkeley/Los Angeles/London, University of California Press.

Berger, P. (1961), *The Noise of Solemn Assemblies: Christian Commitment and the Religious Establishment in America,* Garden City NY, Doubleday and Company.

Berger, P. (1963), "A Market Model for the Analysis of Ecumenicity", *Social Research,* 30(1).

Berger, P. (1967), *The Sacred Canopy: Elements of a Sociological Theory of Religion,* Garden City NY, Doubleday and Company.

Berger, P. (1974), "Second Thoughts on Defining Religion", *Journal for the Scientific Study of Religion,* 13(2).

Berger, P. (1999), "The Desecularization of the World: A Global Overview", in P. Berger (ed.), *The Desecularization of the World: Resurgent Religon and World Politics,* Washington, Ethics and Policy Center.

Berger, P. (2001), "Postscript", in L. Woodhead, P. Heelas and D. Martin (eds.), *Peter Berger and the Study of Religion,* London/New York, Routledge.

Berger, P. and T. Luckmann (1967), *The Social Construction of Reality: A Treatise in the Sociology of Knowledge,* Garden City N Y, Doubleday, (Anchor Books Edition).

Beyer, P. (1990), "Privatization and the Global Influence of Religion in Global Society", in M. Featerstone (ed.), *Global Culture: Nationalism, Globalization, and Modernity,* London, Sage.

Bibby, R. (1979), "Religion and Modernity: The Canadian Case", *Journal for the Scientific Study of Religion,* 18(1).

Billiet, J. (1973), "Secularization and Compartmentalization in the Belgian Educational System", *Social Compass,* 20(4).

Billiet, J. (1976), "Beschouwingen over het samengaan van secularisatie en verzuiling", *De Nieuwe Maand,* 19(7).

Billiet, J. (1977), *Secularisering en verzuiling in het onderwijs. Een sociologisch onderzoek naar de vrije schoolkeuze als legitimatieschema en als sociaal process,* Leuven, Universitaire Pers Leuven.

Billiet, J. and K. Dobbelaere, (1976), *Godsdienst in Vlaanderen: Van kerks katholicisme naar sociaal-kulturele kristenheid?,* Leuven, Davidsfonds.

Billiet, J. et al. (2002), "Church Commitment in Western and Central Europe", paper presented by K. Dobbelaere at the *Annual Society for the Scientific Study of Religion (SSSR) Conference,* in Salt Lake City, Utah October 31-November 3, 2002.

Blumer, H. (1954), "What is Wrong with Social Theory?", *American Sociological Review,* 19(1).

Blumer, H. (1969), *Symbolic Interactionism: Perspective and Method.* Englewood Cliffs NJ, Prentice Hall.

Bourg, C. (1976), "A Symposium on Civil Religion: Precis on R. Fenn, W. Garrett, R. Stauffer, R. Wimberley", *Sociological Analysis,* 37(2).

Bromley, D. and A. Shupe (eds.) (1984), *New Christian Politics*, Macon GA, Mercer University Press.

Bruce, S. "The Curious Case of the Unnecessary Recantation: Berger and Secularization", in L. Woodhead, P. Heelas and D. Martin (eds.), *Peter Berger and the Study of Religion*, London/New York: Routledge.

Calvez, J. (1969), *La pensé de Karl Marx*, Paris, Editions du Seuil.

Caporale, R. and A. Grumelli (eds.) (1971), *The Culture of Unbelief: Studies and Proceedings from the First International Symposium on Belief Held at Rome, March 22-27, 1969*, Berkeley, The University of California Press.

Castelli, E. (ed.) (1976), *Herméneutique de la sécularisation. Actes du colloque organisé par le Centre International d'Études Humanistes et par l'Institut d'Études Philosophiques de Rome, 3-8 janvier 1976*, Paris/Aubier, Editions Montaigne.

Champion, F. (1993), "Les rapports Eglise-Etat dans les pays européens de tradition protestante et de tradition catholique: essai d'analyse", *Social Compass*, 40(4).

Chaves, M. (1994), "Secularization as Declining Religious Authority", *Social Forces*, 72(3).

Chaves, M. (1997), "Secularization: A Luhmanian Reflection", *Soziale Systeme*, 3(2).

Chaves, M. and D. E. Cann (1992), "Regulation, Puralism, and Religious Market Structure: Explaining Religion's Vitality", *Rationality and Society*, (4)3.

Christenson, J. and R. Wimberley (1978), "Who is Civil Religious?", *Sociological Analysis*, 39(1).

Cimic, E. (1971), "Structure de la conscience religieuse dans les milieux ruraux et urbains", in *Actes de la 11e Conférence Internationale de la CISR, Opatija – Yougoslavie 20-24 septembre 1971*, Lille, CISR.

Cole, W. and P. Hammond (1974), "Religious Pluralism, Legal Development, and Societal Complexity: Rudimentary Forms of Civil Religion", *Journal for the Scientific Study of Religion*, 13(2).

Coleman, J. (1978), *The Evolution of Dutch Catholicism: 1958-1974*, Berkeley, University of California Press.

Dahm, K. and V. Hoerner (1975), "Religiöse Sinndeutung und gesellschaftliche Komplexität: Religionssoziologische Beobachtungen zur evolutionären Differenzierung der Religionen", in R. Volp (ed.), *Chancen der Religion*, Gütersloh, Gerd Mohn.

Davie, G. (1999), "Europe: The Exception That Proves the Rule?", in P. Berger (ed.), *The Desecularization of the World: Resurgent Religon and World Politics*, Washington, Ethics and Policy Center.

Davie, G. (2001), "Patterns of Religion in Western Europe: An Exceptional Case", in R. Fenn (ed.), *The Blackwell Companion to Sociology of Religion*, Oxford/Malden MA, Blackwell.

Davie, G. (2002), *Europe: The Exceptional Case. Parameters of Faith in the Modern World*, London, Darton, Longman and Todd Ltd.

Deliège, D. and X. Leroy (1978), *Humanisons les hôpitaux*, Paris, Malaine.

Delumeau, J. (1975), "Déchristianisation ou nouveau modèle de christianisme?", *Archives de sciences sociales des religions*, 20(40).

Demerath III, N. J (1968), "Trends and Anti-Trends in Religious Change", in E. Sheldon and W. Moore (eds.), *Indicators of Social Change: Concepts and Measurements*, New York, Russell Sage Foundation.

Demerath III, N. J (2001a), "Secularization Extended: From Religious Myth to Cultural Commonplace", in R. K. Fenn (ed.), *The Blackwell Companion to Sociology of Religion*, London, Blackwell.

Demerath III, N. J. (2001b), *Crossing the Gods: World Religions and Worldly Politics*, New Brunswick/New Jersey/London, Rutgers University Press.

Demerath III, N. J. and R. Williams (1992), "Secularization in a Community Context: Tensions of Religion and Politics in a New England City", *Journal for the Scientific Study of Religion*, 31(2).

De Neve, A. (1973), "Secularization in Russian Sociology of Religion", *Social Compass*, 20(4).

Dobbelaere, K. (1974), "Une critique sociologique des définitions de la religion en sociologie des religions", *Cahiers des religions africaines*, 8(15).

Dobbelaere, K. (1979a), "Professionalization and Secularization in the Belgian Catholic Pillar", *Japanese Journal of Religious Studies*, 6(1-2).

Dobbelaere, K. (1979b), "Religious Situation of Catholics in Belgium. The Secularization of Flanders", in *Acts of the 15th International Conference on Sociology of Religion, Venice 1979*, Lille, CISR.

Dobbelaere, K. (1981), "Secularization: A Multi-Dimensional Concept", *Current Sociology*, (29)2.

Dobbelaere, K. (1989), "The Secularization of Society? Some Methodological Suggestions", in J. Hadden and A. Shupe (eds.), *Religion and the Political Order III: Secularization and Fundamentalism Reconsidered*, New York, Paragon House.

Dobbelaere, K. (1999), "Towards an Integrated Perspective of the Process Related to the Descriptive Concept of Secularization", *Sociology of Religion*, (60)3.

Dobbelaere, K. (2000a), "The Rationale of Pillarization: The Case of Minority Movements", *Journal of Contemporary Religion*, 15(2).

Dobbelaere, K. (2000b), "Toward a Pillar Organization?", in D. Machacek and B. Wilson (eds.), *Global Citizens: The Soka Gakkai Buddhist Movement in the World*, Oxford, Oxford University Press.

Dobbelaere, K. (in press), "Assessing Secularization Theory", in P. Antes, A. W. Geertz and R. R. Warne (eds.), *New Approaches to the Study of Religion*, Berlin/New York, Verlag de Gruyter.

Dobbelaere, K. and J. Lauwers (1969), "Involvement in Church Religion: A Sociological Critique", in *Actes de la 10e Conférence de la Conférence Internationale de Sociologie Religieuse, Rome*, Lille, CISR.

Dobbelaere, K. and J. Lauwers (1973), "Definitions of Religion. A Sociological Critique", *Social Compass*, 20(4).

Dobbelaere, K. and L. Voyé (1990), "From Pillar to Postmodernity: The Changing Situation of Religion in Belgium", *Sociological Analysis*, 51(S).

Dobbelaere, K. and L. Voyé (2000), "Religie en kerkbetrokkenheid: ambivalentie en vervreemding", in K. Dobbelaere, *et al.* (eds.), *Verloren zekerheid: De Belgen en hun waarden, overtuigingen en houdingen*, Tielt, Lannoo.

Dobbelaere, K., J. Billiet and R. Creyf (1978), "Secularization and Pillarization. A Social Problem Approach", *The Annual Review of the Social Sciences of Religion*, 2.

Dobbelaere, K., J. Gevers and L. Halman (1999), "Religion and the Family", in Halman, L. and O. Riis (eds.), *Religion in Secularizing Society: The European's Religion at the End of the 20th Century*, Tilburg, Tilburg University Press.

Dobbelaere, K., M. Ghesquiere-Waelkens and J. Lauwers (1975), *La dimension chrétienne d'une institution hospitalière*. Vol. 3: *Une analyse sociologique de sa légitimation: humanisation, sécularisation et cloisonnement*, Brussels, Editions 'Hospitalia'.

Dobbelaere, K., L. Tomasi and L. Voyé (in press), "Religious Syncretism", in R. Piedmont, and D. Moberg (eds.), *Research in the Social Scientific Study of Religion*, Leiden, Brill, Volume 13.

Döbert, R. (1973), *Systemtheorie und die Entwicklung religiöser Deutungssysteme: Zur Logik des sozialwissenschaftlichen Funktionalismus*, Frankfurt am Main, Suhrkamp.

Douglas, M. (1973), *Natural Symbols: Explorations in Cosmology*, London, Barrie and Jenkins.

Drehsen, V. and G. Kehrer (1975), "Religion – ein gesellschaftlicher Agent für Stabilität oder Wandel? J. Milton Yinger, Robert N. Bellah und Thomas F. O'Dea", in K.-W. Dahm, V. Drehsen and G. Kehrer (eds.), *Das Jenseits der Gesellschaft: Religion im Prozess sozialwissenschaftlicher Kritik*, München, Claudius Verlag.

Dumon, W. (1977), *Het gezin in Vlaanderen*, Leuven, Davidsfonds.

Dunn, E. and S. Dunn, (1975), "Religious Behaviour and Sociocultural Change in the Soviet Union", in B. Bociurkiw and J. Strong (eds.), *Religion and Atheism in the USSR and Eastern Europe*, London, Macmillan.

Durkheim, E. (1964), *The Divison of Labor in Society*, New York, The Free Press.

Durkheim, E. (1965), *The Elementary Forms of the Religious Life*, New York, The Free Press.

Eisenstadt, S. (ed.) (1968), *The Protestant Ethic and Modernization: A Comparative View*, New York, Basic Books.

Farber, B. (1973), *Family and Kinship in Modern Society*, Glenview IL, Scott, Foresman and Company.

Featherstone, M. (1988), "In pursuit of the Postmodern: An Introduction", *Theory, Culture and Society*, (5)2-3.

Fenn, R. (1972), "Toward a New Sociology of Religion", *Journal for the Scientific Study of Religion*, 11(1).

Fenn, R. (1974), "Religion and the Legitimation of Social Systems", in A. Eister (ed.), *Changing Perspectives in the Scientific Study of Religion*, New York, J. Wiley.

Fenn, R. (1978), *Toward a Theory of Secularization*, Storrs CO, Society for the Scientific Study of Religion.

Fenn, R. (1979), "The Rules for Secular Discourse: An Inquiry into Politics and Religion in Modern Societies", in *Acts of the 15th International Conference on Sociology of Religion, Venice 1979*, Lille, CISR.

Fenn, R. (2001), *Beyond Idols: The Shape of a Secular Society*, Oxford, Oxford University Press.

Flere, S. (1978), "Religiousness and Irreligiousness in Vojvodina", *Sociolovski Pregled*, 12.

Finke, R. (1997), "The Consequences of Religious Competition: Supply-Side Explanations for Religious Change", in L. Young (ed.), *Rational Choice Theory and Religion: Summary and Assessment*, New York/London, Routledge.

Fürstenberg, F. (ed.) (1970), *Religionssoziologie*, Neuwied am Rhein, H. Luchterhand Verlag.

Geertz, C. (1968), "Religion as a Cultural System", in: M. Banton (ed.), *Anthropological Approach to the Study of Religion*, London, Tavistock.

Germani, G. (1968), "Secularization, Modernization, and Economic Development", in S. Eisenstadt (ed.), *The Protestant Ethic and Modernization: A Comparative View*, New York, Basic Books.

Gerth, H. and C. Wright Mills (eds.) (1958), *From Max Weber: Essays in Sociology*, New York, Oxford University Press.

Glasner, P. (1977), *The Sociology of Secularization: A Critique of a Concept*, London, Routledge and Kegan Paul.

Glock, C. (1965), "On the Origin and Evolution of Religious Groups", in C. Glock and R. Stark, *Religion and Society in Tension*, Chicago, Rand McNally & Co.

Glock, C. and R. Bellah (eds.) (1976), *The New Religious Consciousness*, Berkeley, University of California Press.

Glock, C. and T. Piazza, (1978), "Exploring Reality Structures", *Society*, 15(4).

Glock, C., B. Ringer and E. Babbie (1967), *To Comfort and to Challenge: A Dilemma of the Contemporary Church*, Berkeley, University of California Press.

Gouldner, A. (1971), *The Coming Crisis of Western Sociology*, London, Heinemann.

Greeley, A. (1974), *Unsecular Man: The Persistence of Religion*, New York, Dell Publishing.

Greeley, A., W. McCready and K. McCourt (1976), *Catholic Schools in a Declining Church*, Kansas City MO, Sheed and Ward.

Hadaway, C., P. Marler, and M. Chaves (1993), "What the Polls Don't Show: A Closer Look at U.S. Church Attendance", *American Sociological Review*, (58)6.

Halman, L. (1991), *Waarden in de westerse wereld*, Tilburg, Tilburg University Press.

Halman, L. (2001), *The European Values Study: A Third Wave. Source Book of the 1999/2000 European Values Study Surveys*, Tilburg, WORC.

Halman, L. and T. Pettersson (1999), "Globalization and Patterns of Religious Beliefs", in L. Halman and O. Riis (eds.), *Religion in Secularising Society: The European's Religion at the End of the 20th Century*, Tilburg, Tilburg University Press.

Hammond, P. (1976), "The Sociology of American Civil Religion: A Bibliographic Essay", *Sociological Analysis*, 37(2).

Hanegraaff, W. (1996), *New Age Religion and Western Culture: Esoterism in the Mirror of Secular Thought*, Leiden/New York/Köln, Brill.

Helle, H. (1975), "Tendenzen zu einer Religiosität der Erfahrbarkeit: Eine soziologische Analyse", in R. Volp (ed.), *Chancen der Religion*, Gütersloh, Gerd Mohn.

Hellemans, S. (1998), "Secularization in a Reliogeneous Modernity", in R. Laermans, B. Wilson and J. Billiet (eds.), *Secularization and Social Integration: Papers in honor of Karel Dobbelaere*, Leuven, Leuven University Press.

Herberg, W. (1967a), "Religion in a Secularized Society: The New Shape of Religion in America", in R. Knudten (ed.), *The Sociology of Religion: An Anthology*, New York, Appleton-Century Crofts.

Herberg, W. (1967b), "Religion in a Secularized Society: Some Aspects of America's Three Religion Pluralism", in: R. Knudten (ed.), *The Sociology of Religion: An Anthology*, New York, Appleton-Century Crofts.

Hertzke, A. (1988), *Representing God in Washington: The Role of Religious Lobbies in the American Polity*, Knoxville TN, University of Tennessee Press.

Hervieu-Léger, D. (1995), "The Case of French Catholicism", in W. Roof, J. Caroll and D. Roozen (eds.), *The Post-War Generation and Establishment Religion: Cross-Cultural Perspectives*, Boulder/San Francisco/Oxford, Westview Press.

Hervieu-Léger, D. (2001), "Individualism, the Validation of Faith, and the Social Nature of Religion in Modernity", in R. Fenn (ed.), *The Blackwell Companion to Sociology of Religion*, Oxford/Malden MA, Blackwell.

Hild, H. (1974), *Wie stabil ist die Kirche? Bestand und Erneuerung*, Geinhauser/Berlin, Burckhardthaus-Verlag.

Hobart, C. (1974), "Church Involvement and The Comfort Thesis in Alberta", *Journal for the Scientific Study of Religion*, 13(4).

Hoge, D. (1979a), "A Test of Theories of Denominational Growth and Decline", in D. Hoge and D. Roozen (eds.), *Understanding Church Growth and Decline 1950-1978*, New York, The Piligrim Press.

Hoge, D. (1979b), "National Contextual Factors Influencing Church Trends" in D. Hoge and D. Roozen (eds.), *Understanding Church Growth and Decline 1950-1978*, New York, The Piligrim Press.

Hoge, D. and J. Carroll (1978), "Determinants of Commitment and Participation in Suburban Protestant Churches", *Journal for the Scientific Study of Religion*, 17(2).

Hoge, D. and D. Roozen (eds.) (1979a), *Understanding Church Growth and Decline 1950-1978*, New York, The Piligrim Press.

Hoge, D. and D. Roozen (1979b), "Some Sociological Conclusions About Church Trends", in Hoge, D. and D. Roozen (eds.), *Understanding Church Growth and Decline 1950-1978*, New York, The Piligrim Press.

Hoge, D. and D. Roozen (1979c), "Research on Factors Influencing Church Commitment" in Hoge, D. and D. Roozen (eds.), *Understanding Church Growth and Decline 1950-1978*, New York, The Piligrim Press.

Howard, J. and A. Strauss (eds.) (1975), *Humanizing Health Care*, New York, John Wiley & Sons.

Huyse, L. (1969), *De niet aanwezige staatsburger: De politieke apathie sociologisch in kaart gebracht*, Antwerp, Standaard Wetenschappelijke Uitgeverij.

Iannaccone, L. (1997), "Rational Choice: Framework for the Scientific Study of Religion", L. Young (ed.), *Rational Choice Theory and Religion: Summary and Assessment*, New York/London, Routledge.

Isambert, F.-A. (1976) "La sécularisation interne du christianisme", *Revue française de sociologie*, 17(4).

Isambert, F.-A. (1982), *Le sens du sacré: Fête et religion populaire*, Paris, Alcan.

Isambert, F.-A. and J. Terrenoire (1980), *Atlas de la pratique religieuse des catholiques en France*, Paris, Editions du CNRS.

Jagodzinski, W. and K. Dobbelaere (1995), "Secularization and Church Religiosity", in J. W. van Deth and E. Scarbrough (eds.), *Beliefs in Government, Volume 4: The Impact of Values*, Oxford, Oxford University Press.

Janowitz, M. (1976), *Social Control of the Welfare State*, New York, Elsevier.

Klohr, O. (1966), "Ursachen des Sakularisierungsprozesses im Sozialismus", *Religionssoziologie*, 2.

Klohr, O. (1967), "Marxistischer Atheismus – Sozialismus und Säkularisierungsprozess", *Religionssoziologie*, 4.

Kluegel, J. (1980), "Denominational Mobility: Current Patterns and Recent Trends", *Journal for the Scientific Study of Religion*, 19(1).

Knowles, M. and D. Obolensky (1968), *Nouvelle histoire de l'Eglise: 2. Le Moyen Age*, Paris, Editions du Seuil.

Laermans, R (1992), *In de greep van de "Moderne Tijd": Modernisering en verzuiling. individualisering en het naoorlogs publiek discours van de ACW-vormingsorganisaties: een proeve tot cultuursociologische duiding*, Leuven, Garant.

Laeyendecker, L. (1967), *Religie en conflict: De zogenaamde sekten in sociologisch perspectief*, Meppel, Boom.

Laeyendecker, L. (1987), "Du Cardinal Alfrink au Cardinal Simonis: Vingt ans de catholicisme hollandais", in P. Ladrière and R. Luneau (eds.), *Le retour des certitudes*, Paris, Le Centurion.

Laeyendecker, L. (1989), "Beweging binnen de R. K. Kerk in Nerderland", in L. W. Huberts and J. W. van Noort (eds.), *Sociale bewegingen in de jaren negentig*, Leiden, DSWO Press.

Landecker, W. (1951), "Types of Integration and Their Measurement", *American Journal of Sociology*, 56(4).

Lane, C. (1978), *Christian Religion in the Soviet Union: A Sociological Study*. London, George Allen and Unwin.

Lauwers, J. (1974), *Secularisatietheorieën: Een studie over de toekomstskansen van de godsdienstsociologie.* Leuven, Universitaire Pers Leuven.

Lazarsfeld, P. (1959), "Problems in Methodology", in R. Merton, L. Broom and L. Cottrell (eds.), *Sociology Today: Problems and Prospects,* New York, Basic Books.

Le Bras, G. (1963), "Déchristianisation: mot fallacieux", *Social Compass,* 10(2).

Lemmen, M. (1977), "Rationaliteit en seculariteit bij Max Weber", *Politica,* 27(1).

Lenin, W. (1959), "Sozialismus und Religion", in W. Lenin, *Werke,* Vol. 10, Berlin, Dietz Verlag.

Lenski, G. (1966), *Power and Privilege: A Theory of Social Stratification,* New York, McGraw Hill.

Lidz, V. (1979), "Secularization, Ethical Life, and Religion in Modern Societies", *Sociological Inquiry,* 49(2-3).

Lübbe, H. (1975), *Säkularisierung: Geschichte eines ideenpolitischen Begriffs,* Freiburg, Verlag Karl Alber.

Luckmann, T. (1967), *The Invisible Religion: The Problem of Religion in Modern Society,* New York, Macmillan.

Luckmann, T. (1976), "A Critical Rejoinder", *Japanese Journal of Religious Studies,* 3(3/4).

Luckmann, T. (1977), "Theories of Religion and Social Change", *The Annual Review of the Social Sciences of Religion,* 1.

Luckmann, T. (1979), "The Structural Conditions of Religious Consciousness in Modern Societies", *Japanese Journal of Religious Studies,* (6) 1-2.

Luckmann, T. (1980), *Lebenswelt und Gesellschaft: Grundstrukturen und geschichtliche Wandlungen,* Paderborn, Ferdinand Schoningh.

Luckmann, T. (1990), "Shrinking Transcendence, Expanding Religion", *Sociological Analysis,* (51)2.

Luckmann, T. and P. Berger (1964), "Social Mobility and Personal Identity", *Archives Europénnes de Sociologie,* 5(2).

Luhmann, N. (1972), "Die Organisierbarkeit von Religionen und Kirchen", in J. Wössner (ed.), *Religion im Umbruch: Soziologische Beiträge zur Situation von Religion und Kirche in der gegenwärtigen Gesellschaf,* Stuttgart, Enke.

Luhmann, N. (1977), *Funktion der Religion,* Frankfurt, Suhrkamp.

Luhmann, N. (1982), *The Differentiation of Society,* New York, Columbia University Press.

Lukes, S. (1977), *Emile Durkheim. His Life and Work: A Historical and Critical Study,* Middlesex, Penguin Books.

Lutter, H. 1966), "Die Säkularisierung in der sozialistischen Grossstadt", *Religionssoziologie*, 2.

Machalek, R. and M. Martin (1976), "Invisible Religions: Some Preliminary Evidence", *Journal for the Scientific Study of Religion*, 15(4).

McCready, W. and A. Greeley, (1976), *The Ultimate Values of the American Population*, Beverly Hills, Sage.

McLaughlin, T. (ed.) (1957). *The Church and the Reconstruction of the Modern World: The Social Encyclicals of Pius XI*, Garden City NY, Doubleday.

McLeod H. (1980), "The Dechristianisation of the Working Class in Western Europe (1850-1900)", *Social Compass*, 27(2-3).

McNamara, P. (1992), *Conscience First, Tradition Second: A Study of Young American Catholics*, New York, State University of New York Press.

McNamara, P. and A. St. George, (1978), "Blessed are the Downtrodden? An Empirical Test", *Sociological Analysis*, 39(4).

Martin, D. (1969), *The Religious and the Secular. Studies in Secularization*, London, Routledge and Kegan Paul.

Martin, D. (1978), *A General Theory of Secularization*, Oxford, Blackwell.

Martin, D. (1990), *Tongues of Fire: The Explosion of Protestantism in Latin America*, Oxford/Cambridge MA, Blackwell.

Martin, D. (1996), *Forbidden Revolutions: Pentecostalism in Latin America and Catholicism in Eastern Europe*, London, SPCK.

Marty, M. (1964), *Varieties of Unbelief*, New York, Holt Rinehart.

Marx, K. and F. Engels (1959), "Manifest der Kommunistischen Partei", in K. Marx and F. Engels, *Werke*, Vol. 4, Berlin, Dietz Verlag.

Marx, K. (1961a), "Zur Judenfrage", in K. Marx and F. Engels, *Werke*, Vol. 1, Berlin, Dietz Verlag,

Marx, K. (1961b), "Zur Kritik der Hegelschen Rechtsphilosophie", in K. Marx and F. Engels, *Werke*, Vol. 1, Berlin, Dietz Verlag.

Matthes, J. (1967), *Religion und Gesellschaft: Einfahrung in die Religionssoziologie 1*, Reinbek bei Hamburg, Rowohlt Taschenbuch Verlag.

Merton, R. (1957), *Social Theory and Social Structure*, Glencoe IL, The Free Press, [Revised and enlarged edition].

Mol, J. (1970), "Secularization and Cohesion", *Review of Religious Research*, 11(3).

Mueller, S. and P. Sites (1977), "Calvinism, Lutheranism, and the American Civil Religion", in *Acts of the 14th International Conference on Sociology of Religion, Strasbourg 1977*, Lille, C.I.S.R.

Nash, D. (1968), "A Little Child Shall Lead Them: A Statistical Test of an Hypothesis that Children Were the Source of the American Religious Eevival", *Journal for the Scientific Study of Religion*, 7(2).

Nash, D. and P. Berger (1962), "The Child, the Family, and the 'Religious Revival' in Suburbia", *Journal for the Scientific Study of Religion*, 2(1).

Nelsen, H. *et al.* (1976), "A Test of Yinger's Measure of Non-doctrinal Religion: Implications for Invisible Religion as a Belief System", *Journal for the Scientific Study of Religion*, 15(3).

Newport, F. (1979), "The Religious Switcher in the United States", *American Sociological Review*, 44(4).

Nijk, A. (1968), *Secularisatie. Over het gebruik van een woord*, Rotterdam, Lemniscaat.

Nuyens, I. (1971), "Naar een humanisering van het ziekenhuis", *Het Ziekenhuis*, 1(8).

Ochavkov, J. (1966a), "Les résultats d'une étude sociologique de la religiosité en Bulgarie", *Revue française de sociologie*, 7(4).

Ochavkov, J. (1966b), "Problèmes méthodologiques d'une enquête sur la religiosité en Bulgarie", *Archives de Sociologie des Religions*, 21.

Ochavkov, J. (1978), "Sociological Problems of Religion", in N. Yakhiel (ed.), *Contemporary Sociology in Bulgaria*. Sofia, Publishing House of the Bulgarian Academy of Sciences.

Pace, E. (1998), "The Helmet and the Turban: Secularization in Islam", in R. Laermans, B. Wilson and J. Billiet (eds.), *Secularization and Social Integration: Papers in Honor of Karel Dobbelaere*, Leuven, Leuven University Press.

Parsons, T. (1966), *Societies: Evolutionary and Comparative Perspectives*, Englewood Cliffs NJ, Prentice Hall.

Parsons, T. (1967), "Christianity and Modern Industrial Society", in E. Tiryakian (ed.), *Sociological Theory, Values, and Sociocultural Change. Essays in honor of Pitirim A. Sorokin*, New York, Harper and Row.

Parsons, T. (1974), "Religion in Postindustrial America: The Problem of Secularization", *Social Research*, 41(2).

Pawieczynska, A. (1971), "Les attitudes de la population rurale envers la religion", in *Actes de la 11e Conférence Internationale de la CISR, Opatija – Yougoslavie 20-24 septembre 1971*, Lille, CISR.

Pfautz, H. (1955-56), "The Sociology of Secularization: Religious Groups", *The American Journal of Sociology*, 61(2).

Pfautz, H.(1956), "Christian Science: A Case Study of the Social Psychological Aspect of Secularization", *Social Forces*, 34(3).

Reid, D. (1979), "Summary of Discussion, Session 1", *Japanese Journal of Religious Studies*, 6(1-2).

Remy, J. (1970), "Désacralisation et insertion culturelle de l'église", *Economie et humanisme*, 196.

Righart, H. (1986), *De katholieke zuil in Europa: Een vergelijkend onderzoek naar het ontstaan van verzuiling onder katholieken in Oostenrijk, Zwitserland, België en Nederland*, Meppel, Boom.

Rigney, D., R. Machalek, and J. Goodman (1978), "Is Secularization a Discontinuous Process?", *Journal for the Scientific Study of Religion*, 17(4).

Robertson, R. (1970), *The Sociological Interpretation of Religion*, New York, Schocken Books.

Robertson, R. (1971), "Sociologists and Secularization", *Sociology*, 5(3).

Robertson, R. (1978), *Meaning and Change: Explorations in the Cultural Sociology of Modern Societies*, Oxford, Basil Blackwell.

Roof, W. (1976), "Traditional Religion in Contemporary Society: A Theory of Local-Cosmopolitan Plausibility", *American Sociological Review*, 41(2).

Roof, W. (1978a), *Community and Commitment: Religious Plausibility in a Liberal Protestant Church*, New York, Elsevier.

Roof, W. (1978b), "Social Correlates of Religious Involvement: Review of Recent Survey Research in the United States", *The Annual Review of the Social Sciences of Religion*, 2.

Roof, W. (1979), "Concepts and Indicators of Religious Commitment. A Critical Review", in R. Wuthnow (ed). *The Religious Dimension: New Directions in Quantitative Research*, New York, Academic Press.

Roof, W. (1993), *A Generation of Seekers: The Spiritual Journeys of the Baby Boom Generation*, New York, HarperCollins.

Roof, W. (1999), *Spiritual Marketplace: Baby Boomers and the Remaking of American Religion*, Princeton NJ, Princeton University Press.

Roof, W. and C. Hadaway (1977), "Shifts in Religious Preference – the Mid-Seventies", *Journal for the Scientific Study of Religion*, 16(4).

Roof, W. and C. Hadaway (1979), "Denominational Switching in the Seventies: Going Beyond Stark and Glock", *Journal for the Scientific Study of Religion*, 18(4).

Roof, W. and D. Hoge (1980), "Church Involvement in America: Social Factors Affecting Membership and Participation", *Review of Religious Research*, 21(4).

Roof, W. *et al.* (1977), "Yinger's Measure of Non-Doctrinal Religion: A Northeastern Test", *Journal for the Scientific Study of Religion*, 16(4).

Roozen, D. and J. Carroll (1979), "Recent Trends in Church Membership and Participation: An Introduction", in Hoge, D. and D. Roozen (eds.), *Understanding Church Growth and Decline 1950-1978*, New York, The Pilgrim Press.

Roter, Z. (1971), "Nature et structure de la religiosité en Slovénie", in *Actes de la 11e Conférence Internationale de la CISR, Opatija – Yougoslavie 20-24 septembre 1971*, Lille, CISR.

Rouleau, J.-P. (1972), *Present Situation and Future of Catholic Hospitals in Canada,* Québec, Université Laval, Centre de Recherches en Sociologie Religieuse.

Schelsky, H. (1965), "Ist die Dauerreflexion institutionalisierbar? Zum Thema einer modernen Religionssoziologie", in H. Schelsky, *Auf der Suche nach Wirklichkeit: Gesammelte Aufsätze,* Düsseldorf/Köln, Eugen Diedericks Verlag.

Schmidtchen, G. (1972), *Zwischen Kirche und Gesellschaft. Forschungsbericht über die Umfragen zur Gemeinsamen Synode der Bistümer in der Bundesrepublik Deutschland.* Freiburg, Herder.

Schmidtchen, G. (1973a), *Gottesdienst in einer rationalen Welt. Religionssoziologische Untersuchungen im Bereich der VELKD,* Freiburg, Herder.

Schmidtchen, G. (1973b), *Protestanten und Katholiken: Soziologische Analyse konfessioneller Kultur.* Bern, Francke Verlag.

Schreuder, O. (1962), *Kirche im Vorort. Soziologische Erkundung einer Pfarrei,* Freiburg im Breisgau, Herder Verlag.

Séguy, J. (1973), *Les conflits du dialogue,* Paris, Les Editions du Cerf.

Shiner, L. (1967), "The Concept of Secularization in Empirical Research", *Journal for the Scientific Study of Religion,* 6(2).

Shupe, A. and W. Stacey (1983), "The Moral Majority Constituency", in R. Liebman and R. Wuthnow (eds.), *The New Christian Right,* New York, Aldine.

Smidt, C. (1980), "Civil Religious Orientations Among Elementary School Children", *Sociological Analysis,* 41(1).

Sorokin, P. (1962), *Society, Culture and Personality: Their Structure and Dynamics. A System of General Sociology,* New York, Cooper Square Publishers.

Sorokin, P. (1966), "The Western Religion and Morality of Today", *International Yearbook of the Sociology of Religion,* 2, Köln, Westdeutscher Verlag.

Stark, R. (1972), "The Economics of Piety: Religious Commitment and Social Class", in G. Thielbar and A. Feldman (eds.), *Issues in Social Inequality,* Boston, Little Brown.

Stark, R. (1997), "Bringing Theory Back In", in L. Young (ed.), *Rational Choice Theory and Religion: Summary and Assessment,* New York/London, Routledge.

Stark, R. (1999), "Secularizarion, R.I.P.", *Sociology of Religion,* (60)3.

Stark, R. and L. Iannaccone (1994), "A Supply-Side Reinterpretation of the 'Secularization' of Europe", *Journal for the Scientific Study of Religion,* 36(3).

Stauffer, R. (1973), "Civil Religion, Technocracy, and the Private Sphere: Further Comments on Cultural Integration in Advanced Societies", *Journal for the Scientific Study of Religion*, 12(4).

Swiecicki, A. (1971), "La foi religieuse des jeunes en Pologne", in *Actes de la 11e Conférence Internationale de la CISR, Opatija – Yougoslavie 20-24 septembre 1971*, Lille, CISR.

Swiecicki, A. (1977), "Situation de la sociologie des religions en Pologne", in *Actes de la 14e Conférence Internationale de la CISR, Strasbourg 1977*, Lille, CISR.

Tamaru, N. (1979), "The Problem of Secularization: A Preliminary Analysis", *Japanese Journal of Religious Studies*, 6(1-2).

Thurlings, J. (1978), *De wankele zuil: Nederlandse katholieken tussen assimilatie en pluralisme*, Deventer, Van Lochum Slaterus, 2nd ed.

Timofeyev, V. (1974), *The Scientific and Technological Revolution and the Process of Overcoming Religious Beliefs*, Moscow, Soviet Sociological Association.

Tönnies, F. (1963), *Community and Society*, New York, Harper and Row.

Troeltsch, E. (1931), *The Social Teaching of the Christian Churches*, London, George Allen & Unwin, 2 vols.

Tschannen, O. (1992), *Les théories de la sécularisation*, Geneva, Librairie Droz.

Van Heek, F. (1973), *Van hoogkapitalisme naar verzorgingsstaat: Een halve eeuw sociale verandering, 1920-1970*, Meppel, Boom,

Van Hemert, M. (1979), *Kerkelijke gezindten: Een analyse op basis van de volkstelling 1971*, 's Gravenhage, Staatsuitgeverij.

Van Hemert, M. (1980), *En zij verontschuldigden zich... De ontwikkeling van het misbezoekcijfer 1966-1979*. Den Haag, KASKI.

Van Hove, H. (2000), *De weg naar binnen: spiritualiteit en zelfontplooiing*. Unpublished doctoral dissertation, Katholieke Universiteit Leuven, Leuven.

Van Outrive, L. (1969), *Sociologie en vakbond: Het onderzoek naar de vakbondsparticipatie binnen onderscheiden sociologische modellen*. Antwerpen, Standaard Wetenschappefijke Uitgeverij.

Vergote, A. (1976), "La sécularisation: de l'héliocentrisme à la culture d'ellipse", in E. Castelli (ed.), *Herméneutique de la sécularisation. Actes du colloque organisé par le Centre International d'Etudes Humanistes et par l'Institut d'Etudes Philosophiques de Rome, 3-8 janvier 1976*, Paris/Aubier, Editions Montaigne.

Voyé Liliane (1973), *Sociologie du geste religieux: De l'analyse de la pratique dominicale en Belgique à une interprétation théorique*, Bruxelles, Les Editions Vie Ouvrière.

Voyé Liliane (1979), "Situation religieuse des catholiques en Belgique. De l'adhésion ecclésiale au catholicisme socio-culturel en Wallonie", in *Acts of the 15th International Conference on Sociology of Religion, Venice 1979*, Lille, CISR.

Voyé, L. (1995), "From Institutional Catholicism to 'Christian Inspiration': Another Look at Belgium", in W. Roof, J. Caroll and D. Roozen (eds.), *The Post-War Generation and Establishment Religion: Cross-Cultural Perspectives*, Boulder/San Francisco/Oxford, Westview Press.

Voyé, L. (1997), "Religion in Modern Europe: Pertinence of the Globalization Theory", in N. Inoue (ed.), *Globalization and Indigenous Culture*, Tokyo, Institute for Japanese Culture and Classics, Kokugakuin University.

Voyé, L. (1998), "Death and Christmas revisited", in R. Laermans, B. Wilson and J. Billiet (eds.), *Secularization and Social Integration: Papers in Honor of Karel Dobbelaere*, Leuven, Leuven University Press.

Vrcan, S. (1977), "Working-Class Commitment to Religion and Church in Yugoslavia", in *Acts of the 14th International Conference on Sociology of Religion, Strasbourg 1977*, Lille, C.I.S.R.

Wallis, R. (1984), *The Elementary Forms of the New Religious Life*, London, Routledge and Kegan Paul.

Weber, M. (1920), *Gesammelte Aufsätze zur Religionssoziologie*, Tübingen, Mohr.

Weber, M. (1947), *The Theory of Social and Economic Organization*, New York, Macmillan.

Weber, M. (1958), *The Protestant Ethic and the Spirit of Capitalism*, New York, Charles Scribner's Sons.

Weber, M. (1964), *Wirtschaft und Gesellschaft: Grundriss der verstehenden Soziologie*, Köln/Berlin, Kiepenheueru Witsch.

Weber, M. (1973), *Soziologie. Universalgeschichtliche Analyse: Politik*, Stuttgart, Alfred Kröner Verlag.

Wils L. (1977), "De politieke ontwikkeling in België 1847-70", and "De politieke ontwikkeling in België 1870-94", in *Algemene geschiedenis van de Nederlanden*, part 12 and part 13, Haarlem, Fibula-Van Dishoek.

Wilson, B. (1958), "Apparition et persistance des sectes dans un milieu social en evolution", *Archives de sociologie des religions*, 3(5).

Wilson, B. (1969), *Religion in Secular Society: A Sociological Comment*, Baltimore MD, Penguin Books.

Wilson, B. (1970), *Religious Sects: A Sociological Study*, London, Weidenfeld and Nicolson.

Wilson, B. (1976a), "Aspects of Secularization in the West", *Japanese Journal of Religious Studies*, 3(3/4).

Wilson, B. R. (1976b), *Contemporary Transformations of Religion*, Oxford, Oxford University Press.

Wilson, B. (1979), "The Return of the Sacred", *Journal for the Scientific Study of Religion*, 18(3).

Wilson, B. (1982), *Religion in Sociological Perspective*, Oxford, Oxford University Press.

Wilson, B. (1985), "Secularization: The Inherited Model", In Ph. Hammond (ed.), *The Sacred in a Secular Age*, Berkeley, University of California Press.

Wilson, B. (1998), "The Secularization Thesis: Criticisms and Rebuttals", in R. Laermans, B. Wilson and J. Billiet (eds.), *Secularization and Social Integration: Papers in honor of Karel Dobbelaere*, Leuven, Leuven University Press.

Wimberley, R. (1976), "Testing the Civil Religion Hypothesis", *Sociological Analysis*, 37(4).

Wimberley, R. (1979), "Continuity in the Measurement of Civil Religion", *Sociological Analysis*, 40 (1).

Wimberley, R. *et al.* (1976), "The Civil Religious Dimension: Is It There?", *Social Forces*, 54(4).

Winckelmann, J. (1980), "Die Herkunft von Max Webers 'Entzauberungs' Konzeption. Zugleich ein Beitrag zu der Frage, wie gut wir das Werk *Max Webers* kennen können", *Kölner Zeitschrift für Soziologie und Sozialpsychologie*, 32(1).

Wuthnow, R. (1976), "Recent Patterns of Secularization: A Problem of Generations?", *American Sociological Review*, 41(5).

Wuthnow, R. (1976), *The Consciousness Reformation*, Berkeley, University of California Press.

Wuthnow, R. and K. Christiano (1979), "The Effects of Residential Migration on Church Attendance in the United States", in R. Wuthnow (ed.), *The Religious Dimension: New Directions in Quantitative Research*, New York, Academic Press.

Yamane, D. (1997), "Secularization on Trial: In Defence of a Neosecularization Paradigm", *Journal for the Scientific Study of Religion*, 36(1).

Yinger, J. (1962), *Sociology Looks at Religion*, New York, Macmillan.

Yinger, J. (1967). "Pluralism, Religion and Secularism", *Journal for the Scientific Study of Religion*, 6(1).

Yinger, J. (1969), "A Structural Examination of Religion", *Journal for the Scientific Study of Religion*, 8(1).

Yinger, J. (1970), *The Scientific Study of Religion*, New York, Macmillan.

Yinger, J. (1977), "A Comparative Study of the Substructures of Religion", *Journal for the Scientific Study of Religion*, 16(1).

Yip, A. (2002),"The Persistence of Faith among Nonheterosexual Christians: Evidence for the Neosecularization Thesis of Religious Transformations", *Journal for the Scientific Study of Religion*, 41(2).

Young, L. A. (ed.) (1997), *Rational Choice Theory and Religion: Summary and Assessment*, New York/London, Routledge.

Zaretsky, E. (1976), *Capitalism, the Family and Personal Life*, New York, Harper and Row.

Zijderveld, A. (1973), *De theorie van het symbolisch interactionisme*, Meppel, Boom.

# "Gods, Humans and Religions"

While most traditional world religions seem to face a fundamental identity and cultural crisis, signs are indicating that there is a universal need for new spiritual demands and revival, new awakenings of religious practices and feelings. What are the facts beyond these movements? Is there a new human religiosity in the making?

This series will try to bring together witnesses, thinkers, believers and non-believers, historians, scientists of religion, theologians, psychologists, sociologists, philosophers and general writers, from different cultures and languages, to offer a broader perspective on one of the key issues of our new world civilization in the making.

*Series Editor* : Gabriel FRAGNIÈRE,
*Former Rector of the College of Europe (Bruges) and
Professor at the Central European University (Warsaw)*

No. 1– Karel DOBBELAERE, *Secularization: An Analysis at Three Levels*, P.I.E.-Peter Lang, Brussels, 2002, ISBN 90-5201-985-1

No.2– Peter Chidi OKUMA, *Towards an African Theology. The Igbo Context in Nigeria*, P.I.E.-Peter Lang, Brussels, 2002, ISBN 90-5201-975-4

No. 3– John Bosco EKANEM, *Clashing Cultures. Annang Not(with)standing Christianity – An Ethnography*, P.I.E.-Peter Lang, Brussels, 2002, ISBN 90-5201-983-5

**Peter Lang – The website**

Discover the general website of the Peter Lang publishing group:

**www.peterlang.net**

You will find

- an online bookshop of currently about 15,000 titles from the entire publishing group, which allows quick and easy ordering
- all books published since 1993
- an overview of our journals and series
- contact forms for new authors and customers
- information about the activities of each publishing house

Come and browse! We look forward to your visit!